THE NEW MIDDLE AGES

BONNIE WHEELER, *Series Editor*

The New Middle Ages is a series dedicated to transdisciplinary studies of medieval cultures, with particular emphasis on recuperating women's history and on feminist and gender analyses. This peer-reviewed series includes both scholarly monographs and essay collections.

PUBLISHED BY PALGRAVE:

Women in the Medieval Islamic World: Power, Patronage, and Piety
  edited by Gavin R. G. Hambly

The Ethics of Nature in the Middle Ages: On Boccaccio's Poetaphysics
  by Gregory B. Stone

Presence and Presentation: Women in the Chinese Literati Tradition
  by Sherry J. Mou

The Lost Love Letters of Heloise and Abelard: Perceptions of Dialogue in Twelfth-Century France
  by Constant J. Mews

Understanding Scholastic Thought with Foucault
  by Philipp W. Rosemann

For Her Good Estate: The Life of Elizabeth de Burgh
  by Frances A. Underhill

Constructions of Widowhood and Virginity in the Middle Ages
  edited by Cindy L. Carlson and Angela Jane Weisl

Motherhood and Mothering in Anglo-Saxon England
  by Mary Dockray-Miller

Listening to Heloise: The Voice of a Twelfth-Century Woman
  edited by Bonnie Wheeler

The Postcolonial Middle Ages
  edited by Jeffrey Jerome Cohen

Chaucer's Pardoner and Gender Theory
  by Robert S. Sturges

Crossing the Bridge: Comparative Essays on Medieval European and Heian Japanese Women Writers
  edited by Barbara Stevenson and Cynthia Ho

Engaging Words: The Culture of Reading in the Later Middle Ages
  by Laurel Amtower

Robes and Honor: The Medieval World of Investiture
  edited by Stewart Gordon

Representing Rape in Medieval and Early Modern Literature
  edited by Elizabeth Robertson and Christine M. Rose

Same Sex Love and Desire Among Women in the Middle Ages
  edited by Francesca Canadé Sautman and Pamela Sheingorn

Sight and Embodiment in the Middle Ages: Ocular Desires
  by Suzannah Biernoff

Listen Daughter: The Speculum Virginum and the Formation of Religious Women in the Middle Ages
  edited by Constant J. Mews

Science, the Singular, and the Question of Theology
  by Richard A. Lee, Jr.

Gender in Debate from the Early Middle Ages to the Renaissance
  edited by Thelma S. Fenster and Clare A. Lees

Malory's Morte Darthur:
Remaking Arthurian Tradition
  by Catherine Batt

The Vernacular Spirit: Essays on Medieval Religious Literature
  edited by Renate Blumenfeld-Kosinski, Duncan Robertson, and Nancy Warren

Popular Piety and Art in the Late Middle Ages: Image Worship and Idolatry in England 1350–1500
  by Kathleen Kamerick

Absent Narratives, Manuscript Textuality, and Literary Structure in Late Medieval England
  by Elizabeth Scala

Creating Community with Food and Drink in Merovingian Gaul
  by Bonnie Effros

Representations of Early Byzantine Empresses: Image and Empire
  by Anne McClanan

Encountering Medieval Textiles and Dress
  edited by Désirée G. Koslin and Janet Snyder

Eleanor of Aquitaine: Lord and Lady
  edited by Bonnie Wheeler and John Carmi Parsons

Isabel La Católica, Queen of Castile
  edited by David A. Boruchoff

Homoeroticism and Chivalry: Discourses of Male Same-Sex Desire in the Fourteenth Century
  by Richard Zeikowitz

Portraits of Medieval Women: Family, Marriage, and Politics in England 1225–1350
  by Linda E. Mitchell

Eloquent Virgins: From Thecla to Joan of Arc
  by Maud Burnett McInerney

The Persistence of Medievalism: Narrative Adventures in Contemporary Culture
  by Angela Jane Weisl

Capetian Women
  edited by Kathleen Nolan

Joan of Arc and Spirituality
  edited by Ann W. Astell and Bonnie Wheeler

The Texture of Society: Medieval Women in the Southern Low Countries
  edited by Ellen E. Kittell and Mary A. Suydam

Charlemagne's Mustache: And Other Cultural Clusters of a Dark Age
  by Paul Edward Dutton

Troubled Vision: Gender, Sexuality, and Sight in Medieval Text and Image
  edited by Emma Campbell and Robert Mills

Queering Medieval Genres
  by Tison Pugh

QUEERING MEDIEVAL GENRES

Tison Pugh

QUEERING MEDIEVAL GENRES
© Tison Pugh, 2004

All rights reserved. No part of this book may be used or reproduced in any manner whatsoever without written permission except in the case of brief quotations embodied in critical articles or reviews.

First published 2004 by
PALGRAVE MACMILLAN™
175 Fifth Avenue, New York, N.Y. 10010 and
Houndmills, Basingstoke, Hampshire, England RG21 6XS
Companies and representatives throughout the world

PALGRAVE MACMILLAN is the global academic imprint of the Palgrave Macmillan division of St. Martin's Press, LLC and of Palgrave Macmillan Ltd. Macmillan® is a registered trademark in the United States, United Kingdom and other countries. Palgrave is a registered trademark in the European Union and other countries.

ISBN 1–4039–6432–7 hardback

Library of Congress Cataloging-in-Publication Data
Pugh, Tison
   Queering Medieval genres / Tison Pugh.
     p. cm. — (The new Middle Ages)
   Includes bibliographical references and index.
   ISBN 1–4039–6432–7
     1. English poetry—Middle English, 1100–1500—History and criticism. 2. Sex in literature. 3. Gawain (Legendary character)—Romances—History and criticism. 4. Homosexuality and literature—England—History—To 1500. 5. Chaucer, Geoffrey, d. 1400—Criticism and interpretation. 6. Homosexuality and literature—France—History—To 1500. 7. French poetry— To 1500—History and criticism. 8. Literary form—History— To 1500. 9. Sexual orientation in literature. 10. Homosexuality in literature. 11. Gawain and the Grene Knight. 12. Rhetoric, Medieval. I. Title. II. New Middle Ages (Palgrave Macmillan (Firm))

PR317.S48P84 2004
821'.109353—dc22   2004044456

A catalogue record for this book is available from the British Library.

Design by Newgen Imaging Systems (P) Ltd., Chennai, India.

First edition: September 2004
10 9 8 7 6 5 4 3 2 1

Printed in the United States of America.

To my parents

CONTENTS

Acknowledgments		ix
1.	Introduction: Queering Medieval Genres	1
2.	Queering the Lyric: Personae, Same-Sex Desire, and Salvation in the Poetry of Marbod of Rennes, Baudri of Bourgueil, and Hildebert of Lavardin	21
	The Queering Poets and Their Cultural Milieu	23
	The Queering Lyrics of Marbod of Rennes: The Rewards and Punishments of the Beautiful Male Body	27
	The Queering Lyrics of Baudri of Bourgueil: Amatory Lyrics of Same-Sex Desire	30
	The Queering Lyrics of Hildebert of Lavardin: The Delights of the Same-Sex Past and the Dangers of the Homoerotic Present	33
	Queer Salvation Through Same-Sex Sinfulness	35
	Speaking the Unspeakable: Identities and Personae in Queer Lyrics of Same-Sex Desire	40
3.	Chaucer's Queering Fabliaux	45
	Queer Anxiety, Homosocial Aggression, and Masculine Heteronormativity Under Duress in Chaucer's Fabliaux	46
	Queering Genres, Battering Males: The Wife of Bath's Narrative Violence	63
4.	Queering Tragedy: Queer Desires and Queering Genres in Chaucer's *Troilus and Criseyde*	81
	Queer Pandarus? Silence, Sexual Ambiguity, and the Pandering of Courtly Love	82
	Pandarus and the Queering of Tragic Teleology	96
5.	Queering Arthurian Romance: Genres, Godgames, and Sadomasochism in *Sir Gawain and the Green Knight*	107
	Gawain and the Godgames of Romance and Exemplum	108

	Reluctant Masochism, Saints' Lives, and the Sadistic Godgames of *Sir Gawain and the Green Knight*	130
6.	Conclusion: Queering Genres, Medieval Ideology, and Today's Readers	151

Notes 159
Works Cited 205
Index 223

ACKNOWLEDGMENTS

My debts of gratitude are large and long reaching. I give special thanks to the immensely dedicated medievalists at the University of Oregon, including Barbara Altmann, Martha Bayless, Louise Bishop, James Boren, Jim Earl, Anne Laskaya, Clare Lees, Mavis Mate, and Regina Psaki, who were unflagging in their encouragement and constant in their demands when, as a graduate student, I succumbed to the rhythms of Old English poetry and the vulgar excesses of Chaucer. I cannot think of a single moment when they were anything but encouraging, supportive, and challenging, both individually and collectively. Among the non-medievalists at the University of Oregon, I deeply appreciate the support of Smita Avasthi, Michael Ayhan, Hayden Bass, Erin Connors, Melanie Conroy-Goldman, Mark Ditton, Sandy Falby, Sarah Goss, Chris Hitt, Margaret Johnson, Alex Kent, Nicole Kristal, Brendan Mahaney, Mita Mahato, Ajuan Mance, Mark Merrit, Amy Novak, Kathleen O'Fallon, Susan Rich, David Sandner, Miles Taylor, Meredith Webb, Betsy Wheeler, Laurie Wilson, and Mary Wood. Within the wider community of medievalists, I have been most fortunate to share critical exchanges with Carolyn Bergquist, Holly Crocker, Glenn Davis, Ellen Friedrich, Steven Guy-Bray, Janet Knepper, Anne Latowsky, Erin Mullally, Masha Raskolnikov, Martin Shichtman, Barbara Stevenson, Bruce Venarde, and Angela Jane Weisl. At the University of California at Irvine, I benefited greatly from conversations with Clayton Bullock, Douglas Hodapp, Benjamin Lima, Sheila Murphy, and Rob Sanford; at the University of Central Florida, I have relied on Kathy Bell, John Carpenter, Keith Folse, José Fernandez, Tony Grajeda, Pam Hammons, Judith Hemschmeyer, Anna Jones, Mark Kamrath, Lisa Logan, Patrick Murphy, Rick Schell, Jerry Schiffhorst, Dawn Trouard, and David Wallace for their collegial support. I am also indebted to the University of Oregon Humanities Center and the University of Central Florida Office of Sponsored Research for material support along the way, as well as to the libraries and inter-library loan departments of the University of Oregon, the University of California at Irvine, and the University of Central Florida. Portions of various chapters have been previously published in *Christianity and Literature*, *Comitatus*, *Journal of Narrative Theory*, and *Philological Quarterly*,

I gratefully acknowledge the editors' permissions to include this material. Research conducted at the Huntington Library provided invaluable access to primary materials, and special thanks go to Clint Bowers, who twice greased the wheels of funding in times of desperate need. Final thanks go to Bonnie Wheeler, who has championed this project; to my grandmother, who modeled addictive reading practices; and to my parents, who consistently support me in all of my queer endeavors.

CHAPTER 1

INTRODUCTION: QUEERING MEDIEVAL GENRES

Human sexuality is an ideological genre. As works of literature are classified according to their tropes and codes of discourse, so too are individuals constructed ideologically according to the discursive and somatic signs of sexuality. Sexual acts position one either inside or outside the realm of the heteronormative, and cultural assumptions about the meanings of various sexual acts thus lead to classifications of the people who engage in such acts. The two predominant and overarching classifications of modern sexuality—homosexuality and heterosexuality—are ideologically aligned with symbolic and material advantages and disadvantages. Through the classification of people on the basis of sexual acts, the ideological force of binary ordering bears significant consequences for those generically and sexually inscribed as the Other. As Michel Foucault trenchantly points out, "[Ideological] power is essentially what dictates its law to sex. Which means first of all that sex is placed by power in a binary system: licit and illicit, permitted and forbidden."[1] Genres of sexuality are one such tool of ideologies, by which they construct and conscript agents as normative and non-normative: the heterosexual is rewarded with cultural approbation while the queer is punished with societal opprobrium. Within this system, both rewards and punishments are based squarely upon the genitalia of one's sexual partners.[2]

If we see sexualities as cultural genres, it becomes apparent that a vexed relationship between artistic genres and the queer arises because the ideological force of genre, if unchecked, would tend to stifle the queer. Tzvetan Todorov's admirably succinct definition of genre—"the historically attested codification of discursive properties"—stresses the historical basis of genres;[3] as genres represent narrative patterns that solidify over time into a recognizable body of forms with shared features, they arise from historically specific cultural discourses and ideologies. For much of Western culture both in the past and in the present, these cultural discourses and ideologies entail the social pressures of heteronormativity. In part due to this tendency toward conservatism, a common view of genre is as a somewhat constrictive, if not altogether boring, system: writers and readers must know the rules of genre in order to play the game of literature, and heteronormative discourse thus stands as one of genre's chief rules. Benedetto Croce humorously captures the common critical frustration with genre as a restrictive and unenlightening hermeneutic tool: "All books dealing with classification and systems of the arts could be burned without any loss whatsoever."[4] Jacques Derrida agrees with this view of genre as pedantic and antiquated in his essay "The Law of Genre," which begins with his mocking and ironic declaration that "Genres are not to be mixed. I will not mix genres. I repeat: genres are not be mixed. I will not mix them."[5] This is the "law" of genre, but mercifully, as Derrida reveals, it is a law that is not necessarily heeded by authors and artists; deconstruction need only parody generic claims of authority to subvert and reduce them to ridiculousness. I mention this reductively conservative view of genre, not to establish the straw man of this argument, but to expose the conservative ideology inherent in a particular aspect of genre and generic criticism. Genre itself is not necessarily a conservative mode, but implicit heteronormativity, in genre or other cultural forms, is indeed a recalcitrant foe of the queer.

Because heteronormativity provides a latent (and sometimes blatant) backdrop to most genres, it is difficult to imagine a genre within literary history belonging specifically and wholly to the queer, a genre that voices the multiple sensibilities and desires of the queer to the exclusion of heteronormative discourse. If the focus of this inquiry were queer genres, that is, modes of discourse historically attuned to, if not privileging, queer desires, it would end immediately, as no specific genre is predicated upon the elevation of queer desires over heteronormative ones.[6] If queer genres appear a chimerical illusion of gay self-empowerment, do *queered* and/or *queering* genres exist? Most certainly. All genres face the possibility of an author's manipulation for the purpose of expressing, exposing, and confronting the queer. As a strategy of resistance to ideological heteronormativity, the act of queering genres allows the taboo to be present within the familiar structures of recognizable genres. As Glen Johnson observes, "Queering appears especially in how [gay] novelists take familiar genres and subvert their conventions."[7] The medieval genres I address in this book—lyric, fabliau, tragedy, and Arthurian romance—typically foreground heterosexual desire and heteronormativity, but all risk being high-jacked by queer and queering sensibilities. When backgrounds of generic heteronormativity are shattered, the queer emerges with a vengeance for auditors and readers anticipating the pleasures of a heteronormatively inscribed genre but discovering something altogether different.[8]

The authorial process of queering genres depends upon the shock of narrative, its ability to jolt audiences into positions unanticipated, unexpected, and perhaps undesired. Queering genres, as a matter of praxis, involves destabilizing the audience's typical expectations with the purpose of subverting subject positions.[9] Within the historical trajectory of many genres, heteronormativity privileges certain actors, while others are denied the full force of their agency due to their perceived failures to act within the range of the sexually normative. The knight of a medieval romance, for example, typically assumes a privileged position through his participation in heteronormative social codes. If a knight is perceived to fail in his heteronormativity, as famously occurs in Marie de France's "Lanval," his overarching male privilege is threatened. When the queen admonishes Lanval for refusing her sexual advances, the threat of homosexuality, with its concomitant fracturing of heroic identity, serves as her rhetorical weapon:

> "Lanval," fet ele, "bien le quit,
> Vuz n'amez gueres cel delit;
> Asez le m'ad hum dit sovent
> Que des femmez n'avez talent.
> Vallez avez bien afeitiez,
> Ensemble od eus vus deduiez.
> Vileins cuarz, mauveis failliz,
> Mut est mi sires maubailliz
> Que pres de lui vus ad suffert;
> Mun escïent que Deus en pert!"
>
> ("Lanval," she said, "I am sure
> You don't care for such pleasure;
> people have often told me
> that you have no interest in women.
> You have fine-looking boys
> with whom you enjoy yourself.
> Base coward, lousy cripple,
> my lord made a bad mistake
> when he let you stay with him.
> For all I know, he'll lose God because of it.")[10]

This passage brings together disparate but related elements of medieval homophobia, including disgust, insults, and a fear of the corruptive nature of same-sex sexuality. Although in many ways the prescriptive force of genre encourages the reproduction of earlier bias, queering agents need neither accept nor replicate the historic and homophobic bent of a given genre; rather, by overturning the heteronormative bias of a genre through the introduction of the queer, previously marginalized agents radically reconfigure the parameters of subject and object inside and outside the narrative, both for the textual world created within the genre and for the audience of that genre.

As scholarly debates of medieval sexualities have well established, discussing homosexuality, heterosexuality, and heteronormativity, as they were experienced in the Middle Ages, is fraught with the possibility of anachronism.[11] From Foucault's perspective, the birth of the homosexual in nineteenth-century medical discourse argues against a transhistorical construction of homosexuality predicated upon an essential uniformity of same-sex desire, as embodied in individuals who see their sexuality as a crucial part of their personal and cultural identity. Furthermore, if a transhistorical construction of homosexuality reductively creates a unified vision of nonnormative sexualities, neither can heteronormativity be constructed as a monolithic and transhistorical "truth." In regard to the construction of medieval heteronormativity as a straw man against which queer theorists repeatedly take aim, Karma Lochrie judiciously observes that "queer medieval scholarship might begin to question the whole grid of 'heteronormativity' that we have so consistently used to delineate the queer."[12] As important a point as Lochrie establishes, however, recognizing that medieval constructions of heteronormativity would appear dissimilar to their current constructions does not preclude an overlap in their policing of desires that are socially constructed as acceptable or unacceptable. Likewise, recognizing that medieval constructions of queerness would appear dissimilar to current constructions does not preclude an overlap in its marginalized position vis-à-vis heteronormativity. It is through this perspective that I formulate the ensuing analysis: homosexuality, queerness, and heteronormativity historically shift in relation to one another, but dynamic interactions in reference to ideological power and marginalization nonetheless characterize their relationship in medieval literature, as they do today.

As the culturally shifting relationship between homosexuality and heteronormativity demands that we pay close attention to the ways in which ideologies act in specific historical moments to privilege those who engage in some sexual acts while marginalizing those who engage in others, so too does the relationship between homosexuality and queerness demand an equally observant eye. The critical distinction between homosexuality and queerness arises in their relationship to heteronormativity. The queer can never be heteronormative; homosexuality, on the other hand, can in fact be a part of cultural normativity. If a given ideological system permits or encourages homosexuality, if homosexual sex does not preclude one from full participation in cultural privilege, there need be nothing queer or resistant to normativity about homosexuality per se. The queer, on the other hand, disrupts heteronormativity and resists societal and ideological sexual regimes. Looking to classical Greece for an example, the revolutionary feminism of *Lysistrata* likely appeared queerer (in terms of resisting normative codes of behavior) to its intended Greek audience than it does to readers today. In contrast, the original audiences of *The Iliad* likely perceived nothing particularly queer in the romanticized friendship of Achilles and Patroclos; since the relationship bears elements of homosexuality, however, it often appears queer to today's reader ignorant of classical Greek sexual practices.[13] Homosexuality is only queer if ideology constructs it as such. Thus, homosexuality might correlate with queerness, but the two terms are not blanket synonyms for each other on any level, either semantically or culturally. Likewise, although the queer might comprise homosexual acts and actors, homosexuality is not the only sexual force resistant to cultural heteronormativity. Phrases such as "homosexually queer" and "heterosexually queer" are respectively neither redundant nor oxymoronic, as they both point to the ways in which myriad sexual acts and actors frustrate conceptions of normativity.

Because many queer theoretical interpretations of literature address sexual issues almost exclusively, some readers may expect this study similarly to focus predominantly on sex. In this book, however, I follow Allen Frantzen's lead in foregoing a move to establish sexual identities for medieval people in preference of describing " 'same-sex love' and 'same-sex relations' that range from sexual intercourse to expression of non-sexual affection."[14] The term "queer" need not be limited to the sexual, as it also describes relations of power predicated upon relations of sexuality. Current scholarly debates over medieval homosexuality highlight the difficulties of discussing sexuality and queerness in all of their multiple historical permutations.[15] For this book, "to queer" means to disrupt a character's and/or the reader's sense of self by undermining his or her sense of heteronormatively inscribed sexuality, whereas "homosexual" and "homosexuality" are used to describe sexual relationships between members of the same sex (of whatever degree, from kissing to intercourse).[16] Thus, heteronormative identity stands at stake in the queer as much as any specific sexual act. By using "queer" beyond its immediate sexual connotations, my goal is to expose the wider applicability of sexual hermeneutics to medieval literature.[17] My hope is that this monograph will contribute to a widened view of the implications of medieval queerness beyond the somewhat limited arena of sexual contact.

Such a move, however, bears considerable hermeneutic risk to queer theory: if "queer" were to denote all nonnormative behaviors, how queer would "queer" be? From Richard Zeikowitz's perspective, " 'Queer' can thus signify any nonnormative behavior, relationship, or identity occurring at a specific moment. It may also describe an alternative form of desire that threatens the stability of the dominant norm."[18] Despite the risk of expanding the terrain of the queer to include a myriad of power as well as sexual dynamics, the benefits of interrogating the intersections of power and sexual desire outweigh the liabilities of an expansive definition of "queer." Exploring the intersections of genre, sexuality, and ideological power as inscribed in a given text enlightens the ways in which medieval writers negotiate taboo terrains. Thus, in using the word "queer," my primary concern is to deconstruct heteronormative bias and patriarchal privilege within genres rather than pointing to a latent homosexuality within the narratives. Uncovering same-sex desires and actions lurking beneath the surface of the text often serves as an important step in the process, but the presence of homosexuality then allows us to see the ways in which variant sexual identities transgress readerly expectations and confront the audience with the limits of ideological power to rein in illicit sexualities.

The necessity of a queer theory approach for this interpretive task arises because the vexed relationships with sexuality expressed in these narratives lie not merely in their constructions of gender but in the ideological pressures of heteronormativity. Eve Sedgwick charts the various ways in which homosexuality disturbs the heteronormative matrix and, thus, the ways in which the historic and social valence of homosexuality shifts:

> among the things that have changed radically in Western culture over the centuries, and vary across cultures, about men's genital activity with men are its frequency, its exclusivity, its class associations, its relation to the dominant culture, its ethical status, the degree to which it is seen as defining nongenital aspects of the lives of those who practice it, and, perhaps most radically, its association with femininity or masculinity in societies where gender is a profound determinant of power.[19]

By questioning, if not subverting, the heteronormative male's privileged position as sexual agent and thereby revisioning the paradigms of heteronormativity, queering authors compel the heteronormative audiences of these genres to be interpellated into the very positions of powerlessness where ideology would relegate queer men and women. In the wake of recent anti-gay violence ("fag-bashing") in several urban centers, homosexuals adopted a slogan of resistance: "Fags bash back." In this reconfiguration of the semantic powerlessness embedded in the phrase "fag-bashing," homosexuals warn potential attackers that violence is not only the tool of their oppressors; violence can be used by the "victims" whom vicious homophobes attempt to create. So too do queering authors and genres function with a similar rhetorical, if not physically violent, fashion: they undermine the forces of heteronormativity surrounding them with the very rhetorical and narrative tools that would silence them.

Before continuing to outline the hermeneutic model of queering genres and its relationship to queer theory, I must acknowledge the debts of this study to feminist analyses of gender and genre. As is well known, the nexus of gender and genre creates a critical space for interrogating literary meaning and ideology, and feminist criticism on gender and genre offers many examples and critiques of the interplay of gender codes and literary forms.[20] Crucial to this line of inquiry are the realizations that genres are inextricably connected to the social world in which they are created and that generic choices can expose the ideological underpinnings of cultures and of the authors who inhabit them. Due to this confluence of generic structure and ideological expression, it is no surprise that gender and genre are intertwined. As Susan Crane observes in her landmark study of Chaucer's deployment of gender and genre,

> Gender and genre have phonic and etymological but also more substantial bonds. Both are systems of distinction that are susceptible to hierarchization; both have an informing relation to specific persons and works. They can be conceived as the inspiring potential that generates intelligible identities and texts; they can also become measures that constrain and evaluate. Gender and genre can make claims to transhistorical permanence, when they ground their claims in nature in the former case and art in the latter, but both categories prove to be subject to negotiation as they are mobilized in particular identities and works. Finally the historicity of both categories must be accepted: both are persistent over time but also reperformed and reinterpreted in their every instantiation.[21]

In this overview of the relationship between genre and gender, Crane connects the pair as transhistorical hermeneutics that reify certain meanings and interpretations through their "informing relation to specific persons and works." Likewise, Simon Gaunt argues in regard to gender and genre in medieval French and Occitan literature "that genres…inscribe competing ideologies, that the construction of gender is a crucial element in an ideology, and that the distinct ideologies of medieval genres are predicated in part at least upon distinct constructions of gender."[22] Both Crane and Gaunt reveal the ways in which ideology underpins the relationship between gender and genre in medieval literature.[23] Genres communicate cultural meaning by their very presence, and a central focus of feminist criticism has been to investigate the ways in which genres inform—and misinform—readers about the ideological position of women.[24]

Given the success of feminist criticism in exploring gender and genre, why is a queer theoretical approach necessary? Feminist critics have amply exposed the interplay of gender and genre in which gender resists what genre might confine. Throughout this monograph, I ask some of the same questions that feminist inquiry examines, but queer genre theory allows us to see different, if at times complementary, answers. Eve Sedgwick suggests that "gay/lesbian and antihomophobic inquiry still has a lot to learn from asking questions that feminist inquiry has learned to ask—but only so long as we don't demand to receive the same answers in both interlocutions."[25] Building on feminist theory's interest in gender, queer theory examines the ways in which sexuality is likewise constructed in relation to access to ideological power. Judith Butler distinguishes between feminist and queer analyses of sexuality thusly:

> If the "sex" which feminism is said to study constitutes one dimension of the multidimensional "sex" that lesbian and gay research is said to study, then the implicit argument is that lesbian and gay studies does precisely what feminism is said to do but does it in a more expansive and complex way. This distinction between "sex" as anatomical identity and "sex" as regime or practice will become quite crucial to the formulation of lesbian/gay studies as the analysis of sex and sexuality, for the ambiguity of sex as act and identity will be split into univocal dimensions in order to make the claim that the kind of sex that one *is* and the kind of sex that one *does* belong to two separate kinds of analysis: feminist and lesbian/gay, respectively.[26]

Butler's distinction between what sex "is" and what sex "does" locates the need for queer theoretical analyses within the functionality of sex to do, to act, to perform. From this perspective, the ensuing analysis explores the effects of queer sex and queering agents on medieval texts and audiences.

The distinction between gender and sexuality—the former comprising the social roles determined by cultural constructions of biological sex, the latter comprising sexual acts that reflect upon an individual's position within given cultural and ideological regimes—blurs both in real life and in fiction: gender and sexuality are often inextricably intertwined, and they are so enmeshed for the authors analyzed in this study. My focus lies primarily in the authors' interest in sex as a destabilizing force of genre and the ways in which queerness resists heteronormative ideology; this objective demands a queer theory approach so that we may appreciate the nuanced distinctions between gender and sexuality inscribed throughout the texts. These writings address both gender and sexuality, and thus it is necessary to see the ways in which these two core constituents of a person's identity function both separately and in unison. Sue-Ellen Case states that "queer theory...works not at the site of gender, but at the site of ontology, to shift the ground of being itself, thus challenging the Platonic parameters of Being—the borders of life and death."[27] A feminist approach to the generic issues raised by these authors reveals the gender dynamics at play, and a queer theory approach allows us to examine the ways in which the authors both destabilize the heteronormative aspects of medieval Christian sexuality and expand the ontological claims of Christian ideology in relation to human sexuality. Male/female gender roles crumble throughout these narratives, but so too do male/female sexual roles.

In addition to their complementary perspectives on gender and sexuality, another overlap between feminist and queer analyses of genre lies in the space between the feminine and the homosexual. Although masculinist and heteronormative ideologies place both the feminine and the queer on the margins of society, it does so in different manners with different purposes at different times. Beyond the focus on queer issues as an extension of the concerns raised by feminist criticism, the concept of queering genres allows us to examine the ways in which the queer is figured not merely as the presence of the homosexual within a traditional genre but also as a strategy of destabilizing the audience's own sense of heteronormative privilege. A queering genre represents an active, volitional tactic that alludes to the queer as a means of resisting, if not subverting, both generic form and the audience's heteronormatively inscribed identity. It disrupts the heteronormativity of a historical genre through the intrusion of queer characters, acts, or plots into the standard paradigm of Western ideological discourse, and it also disrupts the heteronormativity of the text's intended audience by forcing the auditors and readers to re-conceive their relationship to heteronormative privilege. When heteronormative audiences read or hear the text of a queered genre, they must feel its subversive impact on their own invested sense of heteronormativity.

A final complementary overlap between feminist and queer theory arises in the ways in which they address communal and individual desires, as feminism tends to focus on the community, whereas queer theory focuses on the multiplicity of individual desires.[28] As Lee Edelman demonstrates, the strength of queer theory lies in its resistance of the communal to voice the disenfranchised desires of the individual: "We would do well to construct queer theory, then, less as the site of what we communally want than as the want of any communal site."[29] The utility of queer theory for analyzing generic play lies in its refusal to represent communal desire and its insistence on the polymorphous incarnations and destabilizing tendencies of multiple yet individual desires. Edelman then concludes that queer theory

> can only function as another mode of experiencing, and allegorizing, the persistent displacement that constitutes desire and enables it to function as both spur and resistance to every totalization that would claim to know its "state." Utopic in its negativity, queer theory curves endlessly toward a realization that its realization remains impossible, that only as a force of derealization, of dissolution into the fluxions of a subjectless desire, can it ever be itself.[30]

This description of queer theory accords well with the ways in which genres disruptively function, as they too can readily be viewed as "the persistent displacement that constitutes desire and enables it to function as both spur and resistance to every totalization that would claim to know its 'state.'" Genre represents a desire to tell a story in a specific mode, but the resulting narrative must also resist the parameters of its own genre if it is to be a text worth reading and to escape such dismissive labels as "a piece of genre fiction." The parallels between queer theory and genre, then, allow us to see queered genres as the narratival embodiment of queer theory, with the purpose of deconstructing totalizing social codes. The practice of queering genres can accomplish the objective of queer theory to be "utopic in its negativity," as it forces the utopic realization of fracturing heteronormative social codes, but it can only do so through the negativistic process of subverting previously constructed social identities.

Key to the concept of queering genres are the connections among author, narrative voice, and audience response in which genre is performed discursively to participate in and simultaneously to resist the ideological agendas of Western culture. Queering genres incarnate the subversive performances of historical forms. As Judith Butler demonstrates the performativity of gender, so too must both sexuality and genre be understood within such a performative hermeneutic. Gender, as a performative yet prescribed regulatory system, offers potential freedoms to the acting human agent. As Butler declares, "acts, gestures and desire produce the effect of an internal core or substance...[and] are *performative* in the sense that the essence or identity that they otherwise purport to express are *fabrications* manufactured and sustained through corporeal signs and other discursive means."[31] The freedoms of such gender performativity, however, are curtailed within the ideological systems in which they operate, and Butler stresses that "gender performance cannot be theorized apart from the forcible and reiterative practice of regulatory sexual regimes; [and] the account of agency conditioned by those very regimes of discourse/power cannot be conflated with voluntarism or individualism...and in no way presupposes a choosing subject."[32] Gender constricts, yet play bubbles up in the performative self. In this borderland between ideological conscription into gender and the freedoms of unbounded gender play, gender offers possibilities of disruptive agency through the very parameters that would curtail such freedom. The same paradigm is true for sexuality and genre: they share with gender similar imposed ideological limits of tradition and conservatism, as well as similar possibilities of queering play through the subversion of form.

As Butler's conception of the performativity of gender allows some hope of resistance to ideological constraints, the strategy of queering genres likewise provides a space for questioning the ideological construction of sexual agency within a stifling cultural milieu. Within the cultural homophobia of the West and the overarching homophobia of the Middle Ages, expressing queer desires openly and vocally risks censure, if not condemnation, punishment, and possibly execution. Elizabeth Keiser describes medieval homophobia as

> a peculiarly intense hostility to same-sex love and what it represents; this intensity is evident when hatred and abject horror combine with fear of the Other and comes to literary expression in the rankling attacks of the 'nature as sexual norm' tradition, where such authors as Peter Damian, Alain de Lille, and the [*Gawain*]-poet (as well as their modern successors) vilify what they consider to be the uniquely defiling corruption of men making love with men.[33]

Certainly, such authors as Peter Damian, Alain de Lille, and the *Gawain*-poet vilify homosexuality unequivocally. Peter Damian, for example, compares sodomites to the mentally insane: "When a male rushes to a male to commit impurity, this is not the natural impulse of the flesh, but only the goad of diabolical impulse. This is why the holy fathers carefully established that sodomists pray together with the deranged since they did not doubt that the sodomists were possessed by the same diabolical spirit."[34] In *The Plaint of Nature*, Alain de Lille condemns homosexuality due to its non-procreative pleasures, charging that "For if the masculine gender, by a certain violence of unreasonable reason, should call for a gender entirely similar to itself, this bond and union will not be able to defend the flaw as any kind of graceful figure but will bear the stain of an outlandish and unpardonable solecism."[35] The *Gawain*-poet stridently vocalizes God's disgust with homosexuality in *Cleanness*: "Thay han lerned a lyst that lykez me ille, / That thay han founden in her flesch of fautez the werst: / Vch male matz his mach a man has hymseluen, / And fylter folyly in fere on femmalez wyse."[36] With due deference to the cultural, historical, and geographical specificity of these men, their opinions, backed by their appeals to the hegemonic authority of the Catholic Church, construct a social and artistic milieu antithetical to the sympathetic treatment of queerness.

Within this homophobic cultural milieu, that the queer appears at all is surprising; that it at times appears brazenly and boldly, if not impudently, is truly amazing (especially in the *Gawain*-poet's own writings). That the queer refuses to be hidden points to its narratival necessity, as some stories cannot be told without it, whether written by homosexual or heterosexual authors. And certainly, queering genres is not an exclusive tactic of homosexual authors: queering writers realize the potential of the queer to play with, subvert, or undermine the precarious limits of heteronormative identity, regardless of their own sexual orientation. Deciphering the sexuality of medieval authors represents a vexing critical conundrum, one that I find, for the most part, a distracting rather than enlightening line of inquiry since the sexual acts of these authors' private lives is not my concern. The question "How and why do homosexual authors queer texts?" is less interesting than the question "How and why do authors queer texts?" I prefer the more inclusive question, not in deference to a utopian view of sexuality in which heterosexuality and homosexuality are respected equally by law and society, but because it expands the meaning of the queer beyond the sexual into a true strategy of liberation from ideological normativity and conformity, a liberation that many (if not all) heterosexuals need as urgently as homosexuals. Heteronormative discourse grounds genre, and every queering text fights a legacy of heteronormative form. Against this backdrop of an ideological hegemony of heteronormativity, straight authors in search of innovation, shock, and surprise might well turn to the queer.

As previously mentioned, the critical fracases over the words "queer," "homosexual," "heterosexual," and "heteronormative" stress that these conceptions of sexual difference represent modern rather than medieval constructions of personal identity. They are indeed anachronistic hermeneutics, but then so too are, for example, Marxist, feminist, and new historicist analyses of medieval literature. Despite the awkwardness of anachronism, these words allow us to see medieval literature in terms true to its complexity, in which sexual identities could be constructed as normative or nonnormative depending upon a given person's sexual partner. As is well known, all sexual sins were considered a subset of *concupiscence* in the Middle Ages, but despite this ostensible egalitarianism among sexual sinners, homosexual acts and actors were often the target of greater contempt and contumely than heterosexual acts and actors, as the words of Peter Damian, Alain de Lille, and the *Gawain*-poet attest. In light both of this expansive and somewhat contradictory queer lexicon and of the ways in which homosexuality has been ideologically constructed throughout history, the very fact that these terms are so hotly debated today points to the continuing attempts to understand how crucial aspects of an individual's existence conflict with social constructions of that individual. This tension between the self and the social structures contemporary analyses of sexuality, and these debates frequently focus on the dialectic between essentialist and social constructionist theories, in which the two viewpoints are described as organically at odds, if not altogether contradictory.

Essentialist theories refer to homosexuality as an innate, internal, and core characteristic of human life and propose that gay people have always been a part of human society; social constructionism, on the other hand, emphasizes that all sexualities are cultural formations articulated through ideological networks and that no intrinsic homosexuality exists.[37] As with many polarized debates, a more reasonable position may be found somewhere between these two viewpoints: cultures certainly construct sexualities, but these constructions could well take place upon individually irrefutable biological realities.[38] Regardless of where the truth lies on the binary continuum between essentialism and constructionism, both camps run the risk of what Claude Summers terms the "anxiety of anachronism, the fear of inappropriately imposing contemporary culture-bound conceptions of homosexuality on earlier ages."[39] Choosing a middle ground between essentialism and constructionism and acknowledging my own anxiety of anachronism, I contend that queerness existed in the Middle Ages in the disjuncture between sexual self and societal stricture, even if that queerness differs from the ways that we perceive homosexuality today. Given such a chasm between private desire and public discourse, queerness would inevitably bleed into the narrative record, at times with a vengeance. As Jonathan Dollimore argues, "the paradoxical dynamics of perversion in its pre-sexological senses enable an account of dissidence within sexuality which is not—hopefully can never again be—confined *to* sexuality."[40] Disruption of generic uniformity is one such powerful way in which ostensibly perverse sexualities refuse their confinement.

From this queering perspective, genres provide a structure of support to address queer issues despite the likelihood of their predominant heteronormativity. If the conservatively heteronormative aspects of genres would tend to mute the queer, genres also create a safe space and escape from cultural reprobation because they provide a measure of legitimacy to a piece of literature. Authors writing within genres, whether they write well or poorly, participate in a tradition. They reify, play with, or subvert tropes that signal to their readers their relationship to past authors and texts. Frederic Jameson notes that this authorial deployment of genre creates a quasi-contractual relationship between author and reader, emphasizing that "Genres are *institutions,* or social contracts between a writer and a specific public, whose function it is to specify the proper use of a particular cultural artifact."[41] These "genre contracts" establish a basis of authorial meaning and readerly interpretation, but they also construct a basis of trickery and deception in which the queer may appear. Authors participate in generic traditions, but they do so with their own unique agendas. By presenting the genre contract to the reader, medieval authors all but promise heteronormativity due to the ideological and religious biases of medieval genres; when the queer arises in the text, the genre has been reconceptualized to accommodate it, whether the reader sees this possibility in the genre contract or not.

A critical authorial strategy in queering genres (and thus in obfuscating the promises of the genre contract) surfaces in the play between and among different genres. Such a vibrant vision of generic multiplicity clashes with the previously mentioned conservative view of genres, which presumes that literary norms subsume authorial volition as monolithic participation in the rules of a predetermined game; such a conscriptive view of genre fails to account for the great varieties of genres within a single piece of literature. The playful aspect of genre underscores that the conservative view should not be mistaken for its true nature, as it would radically cripple any generic proclivity for innovation. In fact, authors often reveal genre to be a façade designed to entice the reader into deeper levels of meaning. As Thomas Beebee concludes, "the truly vital meanings of a text are often contained not in any specific generic category into which the text may be placed, but rather in the play of differences between its genres";[42] the terms "intergenres" and "intertextuality" highlight such a conception of generic and textual interplay.[43] The playful possibilities of generic openness create manifold opportunities for authors to raise, dash, fulfill, or frustrate readerly expectations.

Such modern hermeneutic conceptions of generic play accord well with medieval creative practice. With the breakdown of the classical generic system and the rise of vernacular languages, medieval literature embraced a plenitude of generic forms in which few clearly marked boundaries cordoned one genre from another. From the classical models of genre, which presented deep distinctions among narrative forms, medieval authors inherited a triadic schema of rhetorical creations dating back to Cicero's *De inventione*. Cicero's paradigm of *fabula, argumentum,* and *historia*—in which *fabula* represents fantastic fictions, *argumentum* represents realistic fictions, and *historia* represents historical events—demarcates narratives along lines of fact and fiction.[44] In regard to the interrelations of this generic schema, Päivi Mehtonen argues that "A basic criterion in this triad is then relationality: it defines three degrees of truthfulness according to their distance from reality."[45] But the classical models of genre were no longer operating in full force by the latter half of the Middle Ages.[46] Ernst Curtius and Eric Auerbach address the hybridization of generic forms in their classic studies, both using Dante as a touchstone for their observations. Curtius notes that "the antique system of genres had, in the millennium before Dante, disintegrated until it was unrecognizable and incomprehensible,"[47] while Auerbach declares that "the problem of levels of style is not consciously conceived in the vernacular until...the time of Dante."[48] Kathryn Gravdal likewise concludes that "the tendency of intergeneric composition is characteristic of medieval texts."[49] Within this generic playground, the mixing of generic tropes allows authors to experiment with literary form and queerness, creating a space for homosexual desires within the very narrative forms potentially hostile to their presence.

And when same-sex desires appear in medieval genres, they often do so with a rhetorical force disproportional to their marginalized status. Such a moment can be termed the vengeance of the queer: when a cultural outcast appears, with whatever intention, society often views its presence as bearing an element of aggression. Ostracized and marginalized, queers are forced to the borders of society. When homosexuality nonetheless reappears despite its ostensible ejection, the mere presence of the queer takes on the valence of a refusal to be ignored; an insistence on queer presence is often read by heteronormative culture as an attack on ideological and cultural purity due to the queer's disruptive valence. Where queerness should not even exist, its presence becomes in itself a powerful tool of aggressive resistance. Here we see the power of queering genres for a medieval audience: genre provides an expectation of heteronormativity but allows the queer in through the back door to play with, resist, and ridicule cultural insistence on purity.

The individual chapters of this monograph address the ways in which genre fosters a vengeance of the queer that nonetheless affirms medieval Christianity. If queering genres resist heteronormativity and scuffle with ideological constructions of homosexuality, this practice need not be used in an effort to subvert wholly the ideological structure of medieval Christianity itself. While medieval Christianity is, for the most part, upheld without question, these texts simultaneously showcase the agency of the individual within an overarching and conscripting ideological regime. The writers I analyze in this monograph share a common commitment to their religion, and, on the whole, I see little evidence to indicate their interest in subverting Christianity through their literature. Rather, though their queering authorial play, they resist, expand, and subvert Christian constructions of queerness while affirming a commitment to salvation and to Christ.

Chapter 2, "Queering the Lyric: Personae, Same-Sex Desire, and Salvation in the Poetry of Marbod of Rennes, Baudri of Bourgueil, and Hildebert of Lavardin" explores the vibrant tension between a resistant queerness and an enthusiastic Christianity. The lyric genre offers a queering author perhaps the greatest dangers, as the "I" of the lyric may be understood to offer unfettered access into the emotional life of the author (a decidedly problematic assumption, but queering authors must always face the possibility of unsophisticated and prejudicial readings). Within an unsympathetic cultural milieu, to speak of the queer in the lyric necessitates subtle shifts of voice and desire. These twelfth-century Franco-Latin poets queer the lyric both blatantly and latently, and this almost cacophonous plurality of desires exposes the contradictory impulse of the queered lyric to speak and to conceal simultaneously. Reading these lyrics with an eye both to their earthly and spiritual desires, it becomes apparent that Marbod, Baudri, and Hildebert straddle the boundaries of the licit and the illicit as they create poems praising male beauty and affection in some lyrics while simultaneously damning sodomites in others. More than mere play with poetic personae, however, the poets exploit the voice of the lyric genre to explore the contradictory position of queer desires within medieval Christianity and to locate salvation in the very locus of sin. Crucial to this authorial mission is the tacit invitation of the lyrics for the reader to inhabit the speaker's subject position, which results in the sharing of the author's queer desires.

Chapter 3, "Chaucer's Queering Fabliaux," addresses Chaucer's queer play with the fabliaux of *The Canterbury Tales*. For Chaucer's tale-tellers on their Canterbury pilgrimage, queering the fabliau arms the speaker with a rhetorical weapon in their overarching narrative contest. The Miller and the Reeve model the vicious play of queering genres to attack their enemies, a paradigm then reenacted by the Friar and the Summoner. The Cook's, Shipman's, and Merchant's fabliaux offer a contrast to the aforementioned fabliaux in their relative lack of aggression predicated upon homosexual insults, which suggests that Chaucer deploys the fabliau's queering pressures when Canterbury pilgrims are directly engaged in acrimonious rivalry with their fellow pilgrims. These three tales also showcase the ways in which female fabliau protagonists queer masculine characters from their heteronormative privilege through humorous female power rather than through violent male attacks. The chapter concludes with an analysis of Alison of Bath, the fabliau speaker of an Arthurian romance, and the queering strategies that provoke a bawdy woman to tell an ostensibly soothing tale contradictory to her own delightfully bawdy excesses. Of particular interest in *The Canterbury Tales* in terms of its queer play is that we witness the effects of queering on its intended audience and the ways in which this queering affects the other tellers of fabliaux. For Chaucer, the sexual politics of the fabliau metamorphose throughout the pilgrimage depending upon whose queering vision dominates a particular rhetorical moment.

The subject chapter 4, "Queering Tragedy: Queer Desires and Queering Genres in Chaucer's *Troilus and Criseyde*," is Chaucer's adventurous exploitation of genre as a means to address the slipperiness of sexual identity.[50] Reading Pandarus as a queer destabilizer of gender norms, it becomes apparent that the dissolution of gendered sexuality serves as one of Chaucer's chief narrative goals: through Troilus's sexual relationship with Criseyde, through his queer friendship with Pandarus, and, due to these relationships, through the fracturing of Troilus's sexual and spiritual identity, Chaucer lays the groundwork for his protagonist's realization of the futility of all earthly relationships. In a similar manner, the reader is seduced by the queering genres of the text. The vast array of generic possibilities available for *Troilus and Criseyde*—tragedy, epic, romance, history, Boethian comedy—provides the reader with no firm hermeneutic paradigm to make meaning. The final answer of the text—the moral lesson of the rejection of earthly pursuits—comes to a reader seduced by generic pleasures, as much as Troilus is seduced by amatory ones. Pandarus queers genre as much as he queers gender, and the result is a protagonist and a reader subverted into a higher moral purpose through the dissolution of heteronormative pleasures and the subtle questioning of Christian teleology.

In chapter 5, "Queering Arthurian Romance: Genres, Godgames, and Sado-Masochism in *Sir Gawain and the Green Knight*," Arthurian romance receives a queering critical eye from a generic perspective. The chapter begins, however, with a normative analysis because *Sir Gawain and the Green Knight* must be read both normatively and queerly. As every symbol of the text cloaks its true meaning in deceptive haziness, all signs in the semiotic system of the romance must be interpreted for their literal meanings and their figurative sense. By reading *Sir Gawain and the Green Knight* as an Arthurian romance with a moral purpose, the normative reading coincides with numerous interpretations of the text that highlight Gawain's spiritual journey as the heart of the narrative. The queer reading, however, looks at the dark side of the game Gawain must play, as it ponders the meaning of its cruelty and the ways in which this cruelty subtly questions Christianity. Criticism has been shy to tackle this question, but it is essential that we grapple with the implications of a text that demands Gawain to flirt with queerness—through his kisses with both the lady and the host—for his ultimate spiritual benefit. The textual game of the beheading contest mirrors the *Gawain*-poet's meta-textual genre game in which the conventions of romance, exemplum, and saint's life circulate contradictorily throughout the plot and confound Gawain's and the reader's attempts to determine both the meaning of the game and the ways in which it constructs their respective sexual and spiritual identities. Through the hermeneutics of sadomasochism, Gawain's reluctance to accede to a position of saintly masochism demands that he be queered into this position. By queering Arthurian romance, the *Gawain*-poet shocks and subverts both Gawain and the reader into a deeper awareness of their spiritual limitations.

If the focus on the queering individual against an overarching Christian background provides unity of interpretation for the chapters of this monograph, each chapter also makes its own unique contribution to the overall argument. In contrast to the subsequent three chapters that analyze fourteenth-century English literature, "Queering the Lyric" examines Latin poetry of twelfth-century France. Although the monograph's disparate congregation of authors admittedly results in a somewhat lopsided analysis, in which fourteenth-century English authors receive the lion's share of critical attention in a three-to-one chapter ratio, Marbod, Baudri, and Hildebert provide necessary ballast to the argument in their blatantly homoerotic praise of male beauty and sexuality. In contrast to the somewhat occluded queerness of Chaucer's fabliaux and *Troilus and Criseyde* and of the *Gawain*-poet's *Sir Gawain and the Green Knight*, Marbod, Baudri, and Hildebert, in varying degrees, articulate most passionately the joys, wonders, and blisses of male–male desire. And although it is essential to investigate the ways in which all authors, regardless of their personal sexuality, employ the queer, the ways in which authors who appear to have been sexually queer build a redemptive aspect into same-sex desires, and thus frustrate efforts to label it simply a sin, provides the cornerstone of the ensuing argument.[51] Thus, what this analysis loses in terms of historical and cultural specificity by moving between countries and centuries, it gains in turn by analyzing the literature of men with vastly different perceptions of male–male desire, who paradoxically agree on its utility as a means to disrupt audience expectations and to privilege individual desires over the prevailing social order.[52]

Whereas the chapters on lyric, tragedy, and Arthurian romance address in detail the intersection of the Christian and the queer, "Chaucer's Queering Fabliaux" does not specifically engage with the muted Christian elements of these tales.[53] Again, the monograph loses some cohesion in this move, but, on the other hand, the chapter allows us to see the effects of queering on the text's intended fictional audience, as we witness the pilgrims' reactions to one another's tales. Despite the fact that the tales are told during a spiritual journey, the aggression expressed in the Canterbury fabliaux do little to increase any awareness of Christian teachings and rather focus on the ways the individual tale-tellers pursue their own objectives by deploying the queer. Whereas I must hypothesize about the effect of queering genres upon their audiences in the other three chapters, we can directly witness the effects of queering genres on the textually inscribed intended audience of Canterbury pilgrims with Chaucer's fabliaux. As an example of the ways in which a queer rhetoric structures discourse and interaction, *The Canterbury Tales* is thus virtually unsurpassable as a subject for analysis.

On the whole, the various authors analyzed in *Queering Medieval Genres* show little interest in questioning Christianity's fundamental truths, but "Queering Tragedy: Queer Desires and Queering Genres in Chaucer's *Troilus and Criseyde*" engages with the question of how medieval Christianity attempts to make meaning of a pagan love story and demonstrates the ways in which queerness ultimately questions Christian teleology. Such a focus would likely be considered blasphemous to Marbod, Baudri, Hildebert, and the

Gawain-poet, but this perspective establishes a key distinction in the ways in which disparate medieval authors construct the queer in terms of its relationship to the hegemonic ideology of medieval Christianity. By investigating the tensions inherent in the triangulated game of courtly love, in which contradictory circulating desires work queerly to privilege the individual in a group game of love, this chapter addresses the ways in which the queer scuffles with Christian ideology and resists the very cultural system that places it on the margins. That Troilus "wins" through his ascension to the eighth sphere, however, asserts a Christian meaning that the poem itself cannot support. I do not argue for Chaucer's ultimate distrust or distaste for Christianity, but rather that he explores the ways in which, through its insistently destabilizing tendencies, the queer erodes the foundations of Christian teleology, if only mildly.

While the bulk of the analytical work offered in *Queering Medieval Genres* concentrates exclusively on queering interpretations of medieval texts, "Queering Arthurian Romance: Genres, Godgames, and Sado-Masochism in *Sir Gawain and the Green Knight*" (chapter 5) models a practice of queer reading that demonstrates the manner in which normative and queer analyses are mutually implicated. Often normative and nonnormative readings are coordinated through complex and vibrant tensions, and this chapter exposes how normativity and the queer interact in the construction of literary meaning. As such, I hope it to be equally illuminating both as a study of queer theory and methodology and as an examination of the *Gawain*-poet's unique play with queering genres.

The goal of *Queering Medieval Genres*, then, is not as much to create a unified vision of the ways in which medieval authors deployed the queer within a tightly circumscribed geographical space and chronological period as to create a kaleidoscopic view of points of congruency and incongruency among the chapters' various topics and points of analysis. The common thread of this argument arises not primarily from historical cohesion, if defined in terms of a given culture in a given century, but in the ways that queerness functions generically, rhetorically, and discursively to champion the queering individual over the heteronormative society.[54] The various chapters interlock and conjoin, despite differences in their respective focuses, to highlight unique truths of the queer in individual and culturally specific texts rather than to define its meaning with an overarching generality. Much work remains to be done on the ways in which medieval authors queer genres, in relation to such genres as hagiography, personification allegory, dream vision, and mystical writings, among others. *Queering Medieval Genres* lays the groundwork for a wide variety of such analyses by showcasing the disparate deployments of the queer within medieval literature.

The recent publication of two books on queerness and fourteenth-century literature—Glenn Burger's *Chaucer's Queer Nation* and Richard

Zeikowitz's *Homoeroticism and Chivalry: Discourses of Male Same-Sex Desire in the Fourteenth Century*—provide an additional means to contextualize and to distinguish the contributions of this study. Burger's readings of Chaucer are united in the thesis that "under the pressures of producing a poetic vision for a new vernacular English audience in the *Canterbury Tales*, Chaucer reimagines late medieval relations between the body and the community";[55] Zeikowitz examines affirmations and denigrations of male same-sex desire in chivalric texts of the fourteenth century. Burger's and Zeikowitz's books—Burger by focusing exclusively on Chaucer, Zeikowitz by concentrating on a specific historical and cultural period—explore queerness with cohesive visions that this analysis consciously lacks as it moves between centuries and cultures. *Queering Medieval Genres* shares critical perspectives with these books—most specifically, its attention to Chaucer's fabliaux and the Wife of Bath with Burger, to *Troilus and Criseyde* and *Sir Gawain and the Green Knight* with Zeikowitz—and the arguments complement one another well. In contrast to the focus of *Chaucer's Queer Nation* on a particular author and of *Homoeroticism and Chivalry* on social and literary practice in a specific century, *Queering Medieval Genres* focuses on the hermeneutic possibilities of queer genre theory and the ways in which it illuminates the tensions between the self and the social over a larger swath of the medieval world, with possible implications for queering genre studies beyond the Middle Ages.[56]

Queering genres allows us to see the forbidden expressed, but more than this, it allows us to see texts expand in directions unexpected and unexplored. As the conservative view of genre suggests, genres offer some constrictions, but, as the playfully queer view of genre highlights, they offer vast freedoms, subversions, and surprises as well. As Heather Dubrow concisely observes, "a concern for generic traditions, far from precluding originality, often helps to produce it."[57] From this perspective, queering genres allows readers to locate disjunctures between texts and sexualities and, in this space, they may find the queer that has for so long been hidden. Discovering the queer dynamics at play in these genres allows readers—both medieval and modern—to be queered themselves through the unexpected pleasures of the text.

CHAPTER 2

QUEERING THE LYRIC: PERSONAE, SAME-SEX DESIRE, AND SALVATION IN THE POETRY OF MARBOD OF RENNES, BAUDRI OF BOURGUEIL, AND HILDEBERT OF LAVARDIN

> *Luxuriae vitio castissimus en ego fio*
> *quod duros mollit, hoc molitiem mihi tollit.*
>
> (Lo, I am made completely chaste by the sin of lechery
> [The vice] which makes hard men soft takes away my softness.)
>
> Marbod of Rennes

The many lyric genres of the Middle Ages—troubadour lyrics, religious lyrics, secular lyrics, cantigas de amigo, dance songs, albas—offer opportunities for queering authorial play through the contradictory conflation of private desires expressed in public discourse.[1] The lyricists investigated in this chapter—Marbod of Rennes, Baudri of Bourgueil, and Hildebert of Lavardin—participate in the lyric genre labeled by Peter Dronke as "lyrics of realism," which comprises "lyrics that show the poet's response to specific historical circumstances, to people and events in the real world, and lyrics in which the poet disregards the expectations of his audience (in the way of genre and conventions) and writes primarily for himself."[2] For queering writers, the dual focus of realistic lyrics—on the external world and on the inner self—allows a destabilizing dynamic to enter the poet's work in which ostensibly taboo desires are expressed. What is celebrated in one lyric, however, is often disavowed in another, leaving a conflicted view both of the writers and of their writings.

In the Christian milieu of the western European medieval world, poets adopted a wide range of stances—from the laudatory to the condemnatory—toward same-sex relations. Marbod, Baudri, and Hildebert appear to conflate these two oppositional views, both praising male beauty in highly eroticized terms and damning men who fall to the pleasures of homoerotic desire. How is one to understand this apparent contradiction in which the right hand of the poet seems to praise what the left hand proscribes, in which the writer anathematizes what appear to be his own sexual predilections?[3] Through the paradox of holy men expressing unholy desires in queering lyrics, the poets unsettle both the lyric genre and the expected stability of the lyric speaker. Playing at the boundaries between licit and illicit identities, these men speak taboo desires by creating a safe space for themselves through the alternative performances of sinful and of saved personae. The performance of same-sex desire serves as yet another sign of the fallen world order, yet this authorial stance permits the forbidden to be expressed in a manner that paradoxically aligns it with salvation and postlapsarian hope. Thus, the lyric persona—by distancing the author from the desire—becomes the means by which nonnormative desire is simultaneously depicted and rejected. The assumed voice can praise the male form because the sin of desire paradoxically allows both the speaker and the reader to envision themselves as chaste through the redemptive possibilities located in the subsequent rejection of the sin.

Such a performance of same-sex desire embodies the speaker's desire and asserts personal objectives and goals antithetical to social and ideological conditioning.[4] The twelfth century, which is often discussed in terms of a renaissance, offered poets new opportunities of expression, a new "poetics of authorship," to use Burt Kimmelman's term, in which the "medieval poet strives to establish a ground for his or her own singular identity—even though to do so, to assert one's individuality, will mean having to set aside the authority of the collective, Christian community."[5] The articulation of same-sex desire delineates a queer conception of the self that is located both inside and outside of Western medieval Christianity due to the conflict between sexual desires and theological dictates. Within literary genres, the lyric suits a sensibility of queering and unqueering, of self-confession and external condemnation, as the malleable "I" of the poems evades interpretive efforts and leaves the reader with no firm theological grounds to disparage the queer. In this chapter, I first outline the contours of the poets' lives and their cultural and theological milieus; I then address each author's queering lyrics individually and conclude by analyzing the salvific aspects of queerness and queer personae within the lyric genres of the Middle Ages.

The Queering Poets and Their Cultural Milieu

Marbod of Rennes, Baudri of Bourgueil, and Hildebert of Lavardin were contemporaries of one another who lived much of their lives within a one-hundred mile radius of France as they followed similar religious and vocational pursuits. Marbod (ca. 1035–1123) studied at Angers; in 1069 he became the chancellor there and then served as bishop of Rennes, beginning in 1096. Marbod's writings include *De ornamentis verborum* (a rhetorical handbook), saints' lives, a lapidary poem, the moral *Decem capitula*, and personal letters in verse. Baudri (1046–1130) served as abbot of Bourgueil from 1089 until his appointment as archbishop of Dol in 1107; his literary corpus consists of 225 surviving poems, including a work of 1,367 lines to Adela, Countess of Blois. Hildebert (1056–1134) acted successively as archdeacon and bishop of Mans and subsequently as archbishop of Tours. Hildebert's writings concentrate on Rome, his exile, and the Mass, and his biblical epigrams were quite well known throughout the Middle Ages. Although to ascertain definitively the extent to which these three men knew one another is difficult, we do know that Baudri was a student of Marbod's. Also, the fact that Baudri dedicated poems to both Hildebert and Marbod suggests some sort of acquaintanceship. Certainly, the three poets share a literary theme in their alternate praise and condemnation of same-sex relationships between men, but whether the similarities of same-sex thematics in their poetry are a reflection of their mutual acquaintanceship or a coincidence derived from a common cultural context is difficult to determine.

Marbod, Baudri, and Hildebert wrote poetry in a wider cultural context than their same-sex lyrics might imply.[6] The three poets also wrote amatory verse addressed to women, and these poems to and about women appear part of a "new cult of love and beauty," which was directed toward the female sex and which "corresponded to a marked change of social taste and convention."[7] This chapter addresses exclusively the same-sex lyrics of Marbod, Baudri, and Hildebert, but I do not wish to eclipse the fact that they were also participating in the transmission of amorous epistolary verse to women during a time of complex cultural change. As V.A. Kolve points out, however, the allures of sexuality in any of its incarnations were a threat to the sanctity of the monastery: "the erotic choice presented in a monastery was not between what we call heterosexuality and homosexuality, but between maintaining and not maintaining chastity, between spiritual and carnal love."[8] My goal is to explicate the poets' conflicting attitudes toward same-sex desire, but such an understanding will also enlighten interpretations of their writings addressed to women, as sexual feelings devoted to either males or females were forbidden in the monastic milieu.

How are we to understand the conflation of praising boys in eroticized terms and of damning homoerotic acts, of presenting same-sex desire both as morally acceptable and as morally reprehensible? Ernst Robert Curtius, in his classic *European Literature and the Latin Middle Ages*, wonders if the sentiments expressed by such poets as Marbod and Baudri are genuine or if they are modeled upon classical sources: "when poets of the twelfth century choose male homosexuality as material, it is often difficult to decide whether we have to do with the imitation of literary models (*imitatio*) or whether actual feeling is speaking."[9] Given the wide range of classical sources with which medieval monks might practice their grammar and rhetoric, however, why would these poets employ the sinful tropes of male same-sex desire if they were not expressing experienced emotions? As Arno Karlen has pointed out in another context, "homosexuality is not an infectious disease, and people who do not practice it are unlikely to borrow it from military invaders, like children presented with an irresistible sweet."[10] Although the classic models of antiquity did not enter the cultural milieu in the manner of military invaders, Karlen's point that same-sex acts are likely to be lauded and engaged in by those predisposed to such activities is well taken. The mere presence of classical models offers insufficient explanatory force for these poets' contradictory stances on same-sex sexuality.

In considering Hildebert's poems that condemn same-sex affection, John Boswell follows Curtius's lead and alternately and contradictorily suggests both that Hildebert's attacks on homoerotic acts, with their many references to classical mythology, "were considered obligatory in declamations against the mores of the times and may have been entirely facetious" and that, in the poems expressing a more accepting view of such desire, "there is still ample reason to suspect his sincerity in such lines."[11] However, why are we to believe that Hildebert's polemics against same-sex acts are merely pedantic exercises while his homoerotic poetry represents his true feelings? The reverse of this interpretative paradigm is equally likely to be true, but neither hypothesis explains why the author would express such binary beliefs simultaneously. Further, the classical sources themselves often treat same-sex desire in a contradictory manner, and thus may reveal little about Hildebert's own feelings, if we see their influence as a determinate factor in the composition of his poetry.

Thomas Stehling likewise explains away the contradictions in the poets' works by hypothesizing that "[c]onflicting attitudes in Marbod's poems can suggest changes in his attitude as he grew older."[12] But Marbod's poems do not point to such a dramatic shift in opinion as he aged; rather, "Poenitudo lascivi amoris" ("Repentance for Lecherous Love") suggests that the two oppositional sentiments toward same-sex desire occurred quickly one after the other: "Strictus eram loris vesani nuper amoris, / Captus eram visco, sed nunc pudet, et resipisco" ("Recently I was bound by the whips of a mad love, / I was caught in birdlime, but now I'm ashamed, and I return to my senses").[13] This passage suggests that Marbod held diametrically opposed ideas about same-sex relations in rapid succession to each other rather than after a lengthy aging process.

Stephen Jaeger's investigation of the language of sex and love as an ennobling force in the Middle Ages provides a firmer foundation for analyzing male–male desire. In the many examples of homosocial eroticism he marshals to document his case, the somewhat excessive declarations of love and devotion are revealed to be eloquent displays of manners, etiquette, and, for the most part, nonsexual affections:

> Love as sexual discipline was a social form as important as courtesy, central to the social and political functioning of many European courts, cathedrals, and monastic communities. Of course, like any social form, it was also a mask, and behind it the whole spectrum of sexual practice could play itself out.[14]

Jaeger demonstrates that many medieval male–male relationships, although perhaps appearing highly sexualized to modern readers, enact a vision of love as an ennobling force through a chaste eroticism.[15] He construes the majority of the examples he cites as within the realm of the medieval normative, but judiciously concedes that, beneath the mask of the public performance of love, queer desires might nonetheless be in play. For Marbod, Baudri, and Hildebert, lyrics allow a poetic mask in which illicit erotics (if attached to personal homoerotic feelings) are licensed to appear publicly.

Along with the tension between a public display of chaste love and a masking of homoerotic desire, I propose that the authors could have believed that same-sex acts were both good and bad, both salvific and damning, without the cognitive dissonance such antithetical beliefs might imply to the modern mind. Christianity offers a paradigm of religious thought through which these contradictions can be explained. A significant strand of biblical teaching emphasizes that the mighty and powerful shall be lowered and the weak and helpless raised in the kingdom of heaven. This teaching can be found in such biblical quotations as "Multi autem erunt primi novissimi et novissimi primi" ("Many that are first shall be last; and the last shall be first" [Matthew 19:30, cf. Mark 10:31]) and "Deposuit potentes de sede et exaltavit humiles" ("He has put down the mighty from their seat, and exalted the humble" [Luke 1:52]).[16] These passages—and others that express similar themes—provide moral compass for such gender-switching medieval phenomena as Bernard of Clairvaux's assumption of a female persona in union with Christ in his *On the Song of Songs*,

Francis of Assisi's self-characterization as Lady Poverty, and Aelred of Rievaulx's description of the crucifix as inviting maternal union. Caroline Walker Bynum provides many similar examples of inversion, most notably medieval descriptions of Jesus as a maternal figure. She interprets this religious strategy as an attempt to ensure salvation for medieval men by degrading themselves as women before Christ:

> Indeed male appropriation of the notion of woman as weak sometimes became a claim to superior lowliness. . . . When male writers took femaleness as an image to describe their renunciation of the world, they sometimes said explicitly that women were too weak to be women. They sometimes implied that their own role reversal—that is, their appropriation of or choice for lowliness—was a superior "femaleness" to the femaleness of women, which was not chosen.[17]

Medieval men could claim great holiness by lowering themselves before Christ through the appropriation of female characteristics. Since they often served in stations of power and authority, they positioned themselves as weak and powerless in order to ensure their place in heaven. Bynum's argument analyzes the ways in which medieval men deployed gender for their salvific gain; I contend that medieval queers might similarly deploy performatively nonnormative constructions of sexuality for their ultimate spiritual benefit.

Marbod, Baudri, and Hildebert appear to be operating under a similar understanding of Christian thought in their contradictory attitudes toward same-sex desire. These queering lyricists employ inversionary tropes of Christian teaching in their performance of personae that express same-sex desire. Certainly, as Gerald Bond observes, poets often assume personae to escape suspicion while speaking about questionable topics, and the lyric is particularly suitable for this authorial obfuscation:

> First-person discourse becomes self-impersonation only when the referent for the word "I" is seen to vacillate between one who makes the text and one who speaks the text—and their respective intentions. . . . [Self-impersonation] seems to have been particularly handy to explain/excuse aberrant texts so that topic and voice could avoid censure.[18]

Although Marbod, Baudri, and Hildebert employ the voices of personae, their lyrics could well have been received in a theologically sanctioned interpretation. The poets assume personae that speak male–male desire—a desire inverted in terms of Christian morality—and infuse these poems with the very Christian morality with which same-sex desire would appear to be incongruous. Basing their poetry both in the security of lyric, fictive personae and within biblical teachings stressing inversions, the poets not only speak their illicit desires but also find redemptive possibilities through them. Lauding male beauty and same-sex sexuality and drawing attention to the inverted nature of the human world, the poets imbue their sinful lyrics with a salvific poetics.

The Queering Lyrics of Marbod of Rennes: The Rewards and Punishments of the Beautiful Male Body

Marbod of Rennes depicts same-sex desire in terms of enthusiastic acceptance and approval in some poems but with disgust and loathing in others, and his lyrics often highlight that he is writing to and among a community of like-minded men.[19] In his poetry, Marbod often concentrates on the sexual favors granted by boys to their lovers, and he presents these relationships openly and without embarrassment. In "Ad amicum absentem" ("To an Absent Friend"), the narrator admonishes a friend to hasten home so that his boy will not be tempted to leave him for another:

> Perdes in hac villa plusquam lucraris in illa:
> Namque quid tanti, quanti puer aequus amanti?
> Qui nunc est aequus, fiat mora, fiet iniquus.
> Blanditiis siquidem tentatur pluribus idem;
> Et qui tentatur, metus est ne decipiatur.[20]
>
> (You are losing more in this town than you are getting in that one. / For what is as precious as a boy who is fair with his lover? / Now he is even-tempered [but if] a delay is made, he will be made wicked. / Indeed, he is assailed with many flatteries, / And [if] he can be tempted, there is a fear that he could be beguiled.)

As the speaker offers advice to his friend, the poem addresses same-sex desire in a matter-of-fact tone. No hint of censure of same-sex relationships appears; the only fear expressed is that same-sex desire will be frustrated rather than realized. The poem also hints at a wide range of sexual partners for the boy through its reference to the "blanditiis...pluribis" (many enticements). This passage indicates that same-sex desire runs rampantly throughout the speaker and the boy's community.

Marbod's lyrics of same-sex love concentrate sexual attention on boys rather than men. In the poems, boys are depicted as the object of sexual attraction, but their prized status is threatened by the approach of age and maturity that will render them bereft of their beauty. Marbod thus admonishes the object of his affection in "Satyra in amatorem puelli sub assumpta persona" ("A Satire on the Lover of a Boy in an Assumed Persona") to take advantage of sexual opportunities now because they will disappear when age takes its toll upon his fair flesh:

> Haec caro tam levis, tam lactea, tam sine naevis,
> Tam bona, tam bella, tam lubrica, tamque tenella.
> Tempus adhuc veniet, cum turpis et hispida fiet:
> Cum fiet vilis caro chara caro puerilis.
> Ergo dum flores, maturos indue mores.
> Dum potes et peteris, cupido dare ne pigriteris.[21]
>
> (This flesh is so smooth, so milky, without moles, / So good, so pretty, so smooth, and so tender. / But the time will come when it will become base and coarse, / When [this] dear flesh, [this] boyish flesh will become vile. / Therefore, while you flourish, take up mature customs. / While you are able and you are sought, do not be slow to give [yourself] to a lover.)

The poem stresses the necessity of seizing earthly and sensual—rather than heavenly and spiritual—delights. As time will deprive the boy of his sexual attractiveness, he should enjoy these pleasures when they are so readily available. This poetic trope of *carpe diem* in youth appears frequently in premedieval homoerotic verse; as Norman Roth observes, "The theme of the adolescent whose approaching adulthood, signaled by the appearance of down on the cheek, brought an end to his desirability as an object of love was common in Greek, Arabic, and Hebrew poetry."[22] Also of note is the title of the poem, which highlights the fact that the lyric speaker's voice is an assumed one that ostensibly does not represent the poet's personal desires. (I return to this issue subsequently, in the section of this chapter entitled "Speaking the Unspeakable: Identity and Personae in the Queer Lyrics of Same-Sex Desire.")

In "Satyra in amatorem puelli sub assumpta persona," Marbod describes the boy's body in a highly sensualized and detailed manner. The words paint a vision of mortal beauty as the speaker's descriptions move from the top of the boy's head to his beautiful body below, ending with the poet's account of what anyone would want to do with such a boy with such a body:

> Undabant illi per eburnea colla capilli,
> Candida frons ut nix, et lumina nigra velut pix,
> Implumesque genae grata dulcedine plenae,
> Cum in candoris vernabant luce ruboris.
> Nasus erat justus, labra flammea, densque venustus.
> Effigies menti modulo formata decenti.
> Qui corpus quaeret quod tectum veste lateret,
> Tale coaptet ei quod conveniat faciei.[23]

(Over [his] ivory neck flowed his hair, / [His] forehead [was] white as snow, and [his] eyes black as pitch; / His hairless cheeks full of pleasing sweetness / When they bloomed in the light of the radiance of red. / His nose was straight, lips fiery, and teeth lovely, / The shape of [his] chin formed from a suitable model. / Anyone seeking the body which was hidden, covered by [his] clothes / Would find it comparable to that face it matches.)

This passage's luminous description of the boy's body is reminiscent of the imagery found in the Song of Songs' catalogue of features in which the colors of ivory, red, and black highlight the beloved's beauty; the biblical vision of unity between heterosexual lovers, which is commonly allegorized into the relationship between Christ and His Church in the medieval period, is here transformed into a paean to same-sex desire.[24] Also, the narrator's personal involvement with the boy is evident through the use of first-person narration; the lyric voice delineates his personal fascination with the male form. And although the speaker revels in his own appreciation of the boy's body, his declaration that others would find the boy equally attractive again suggests a community of men who would find such a boy sexually desirable.

Marbod's amatory and queering lyrics reveal that his sexual attentions have been directed to both men and women. In his "Dissuasio amoris venerei" ("Argument Against the Love of Venus"), the lyric speaker describes a love triangle in which he is pursued by a girl who is loved by the boy whom he desires. The girl's seductive maneuvers have no effect on the speaker, although he acknowledges that they might have succeeded in the past:

> Hanc puer insignis, cujus decor est meus ignis,
> Diligit hanc, captat, huic se placiturus adaptat;
> Quae, puero spreto, me vult, mihi mandat: Aveto:
> Et mihi blanditur, quia respuo, pene moritur.
> Si fecisset idem mihi turpis femina pridem,
> Ad Venerem motus fierem lascivia totus;
> Pectore nunc duro, nec verba, nec oscula curo.[25]

(This distinguished boy whose beauty is my fire, / Loves her, desires her, changes himself to please her; / She, disdaining the boy, wants me and commands me [to] desire [her]. / She coaxes me, [but] because I scorn [her], she almost dies. / Once if a base woman had done the same thing to me, / I would have been wholly lascivious, moved to Venus; / Now with a hard heart, I care neither for [her] words nor [her] kisses.)

Marbod's words highlight the fluidity of his sexual desires as he admits that both males and females have been the objects of his affections. Repudiating Venus in this lyric, Marbod acknowledges the love that he bears the boy.

The same-sex desires expressed in these poems represent a queering authorial tactic by inviting the reader to share illicit desire, but other poems by Marbod provide no such haven for queerness and queering.

In striking contrast to these works stands Marbod's "Dissuasio concubitus in uno tantum sexu" ("An Argument Against Copulation [Between People of] Only One Sex"); in this poem, the boy's body, which was the source of such beauty in "Satyra in amatorem puelli sub assumpta persona," has become the locus of damnation:

> Frons, oculi, nares, cervix, locus auricularis,
> Os, guttur, mammae fiunt ibi pabula flammae,
> Dorsa, latus, venter flagrant indeficienter,
> Nec frigent coxae, nec mentula conscia noxae.
> O quantum est tristis qui traditur ignibus istis!. . .
> Ergo concubitus, quem sexus perficit unus,
> Culpa minor nulla, punitur non minus ulla.[26]
>
> (Forehead, eyes, nostrils, neck, the place of the ear, / Mouth, throat, and breasts become nourishment of the flame. / Back, sides, belly burn continuously; / Nor do the thighs or guilty dick remain cool. / O, how sad the man who is given to these fires! /. . ./ Thus copulation which one sex performs, / A crime less serious than none, is punished not less than any other.)

In this lyric the male body is transformed from its sublimity in "Satyra in amatorem puelli sub assumpta persona" to the fulsome and loathsome incarnation of eternal suffering; the boy is now the foul source of corruption, decay, and damnation. Transforming the poetic device of tracing the beloved's body from head to toe in a catalogue of beauty, here Marbod employs the same technique to underscore the corruptive threats inherent in homoerotic practices. More than a damnation of physical beauty, the poem explicitly demarcates the chthonic end awaiting one who falls carnally to the pleasures offered from this boy with such a beautiful body. It appears that, if a non-heteronormative male reader enjoyed the depiction of queer desires in the homoerotic lyrics, he would be stripped of such enjoyment by the stridently homophobic "Dissuasio concubitus in uno tantum sexu."

The Queering Lyrics of Baudri of Bourgueil: Amatory Lyrics of Same-Sex Desire

Baudri of Bourgueil's lyrics evince a similar thematic dichotomy in his considerations of same-sex desire. In "Ad juvenem nimis elatum" ("To a Youth Too Proud"), the lyric voice portrays the rapturous effects of the boy's body upon him and his own tactile responses to it. No traces of remonstration mar the encomium to same-sex desire:

> Forma placet, quia forma decet, quia forma venusta est:
> Mala tenella placet, flavum caput osque modestum. . .
> His bene respondet caro lactea, pectus eburnum.
> Alludit manibus niveo de corpore tactus.
> Haec sunt quae debent aliisque mihique placere,
> Praesertim cum te nec agat lasciva juventus
> Nec reprobet divam membrorum composituram.
> Haec mihi cuncta placent, haec et mihi singula mando.[27]
>
> ([Your] appearance is pleasing because it is a proper appearance, because it is a beautiful appearance; / [Your] tender cheek is pleasing, [as are your] golden head and modest mouth. /. . ./ Your milky flesh and ivory chest agree with these features; / The touch of your snow-white body plays with my hands. / These are the things which ought to please others and me, / Especially since licentious youth does not control you / Or condemn the divine composition of your limbs. / All these are pleasing to me: I commend each one to myself.)

The lyric voice of the speaker claims the pleasures of the boy's body for himself. The passion for the male body, expressed in terms of fleshly fascination rather than spiritual salvation, is a key theme to Baudri's poetry, and, as Gerald Bond notes, "one cannot escape the conclusion that Baudri intentionally evoked homosexual relationships in many of his poems by discussing *amor* between males in a context devoid of explicit Christian values."[28] Focusing on fleshly and earthly delights, Baudri concentrates on tactile pleasures rather than fraternal chastity. Indeed, fraternal chastity appears outside of Baudri's worldview, as he underscores the fact that the boy's body should not only please himself, but others as well.

In his amatory verses, Baudri often stresses that his lyrics are epistolary, and these poems celebrate the literary erotics of reading and writing among a male community.[29] The lyric speaker of "Ad amicum cui cartam mittebat" ("To a Friend to Whom He Sent a Letter") declares his desire to be the epistle that carries his words of love so that his friend will touch him:

> O utinam legatus ego meus iste fuissem,
>   Vel quam palparet cartula vestra manus. . .
> Tunc explorarem vultumque animumque legentis,
>   Si tamen et possem me cohibere diu.
> Caetera propitiis diis fortunaeque daremus
>   Nam Deus ad veniam promptior est homine.[30]
>
> (O, would that I had been my own legate, / Or that I had been the card which your hand touched /. . ./ Then I would have searched [your] face and

spirit as you read, / If still I was able to restrain myself for a while. / We would give other things to favorable gods and to fortune / For God is more ready to pardon than man.)

The lover imagines the fulfillment of seeing the man's face as the friend touches and reads the letter. Pondering deeper satisfactions, the lyric voice trusts himself to God's pardon, a pardon more readily available than that from his fellow man. Baudri envisions a god willing and ready to forgive humanity's sinfulness, and the sins of same-sex desire thus lose their damning force.

Although "Ad amicum cui cartam mittebat" depicts wariness about possible censure from others, Baudri hints at an audience sympathetic to such desire in other queering lyrics, and his letters appear to be at least partially available to a reading public. For example, in "Ad juvenem nimis elatum" ("To a Youth Too Proud"), the speaker beseeches the letter's readers—who cannot solely be the eponymous "juvenem elatum"—to determine if the boy deserves the criticism that he levels:

> En dixi quicquid mihi displicet aut placet in te.
> *Censeat en lector an sit mea justa querela,*
> Justa querela quidem, vere querimonia justa,
> Tuque satisfacies si te correxeris ipse.[31]
>
> (O, I have told [you] whatever displeases or pleases me in you. / *O, let the reader determine if my lament is just,* / Indeed, [it is] a just lament, a truly just complaint, / And you will satisfy [me] if you correct yourself.)

The letter is written both to the beloved boy and to other readers who may determine the appropriateness of the youth's actions. These lines point to a readership beyond the addressee of the letter, a readership appreciative of such tactics of amatory pursuit involving literature, letters, and male same-sex desire. The queering dynamics of Baudri's poetry invite the sharing of same-sex desire within a community of like-minded men.

Baudri's poetry is more concerned with celebrating same-sex desire between men than condemning it, but he underscores the ease with which boys seduce men in his "Ad Vitalem" ("To Vitalis") in a somewhat weary tone. Here the descriptions of the boy emphasize how he conquers the will of older men. The body is alternately depicted as the incarnation of innocence, which inspires Baudri's passion, and of willfulness, which leads him to sin:

> Quem mihi complexum viscera nostra fovent.
> Visceribus nostris prae cunctis solus inhaesit. . .
> Si vero quaeris quid in hoc speciale notatur. . .
> Callidus ut serpens, simplex ut rauca columba
> Aetatem superat propter utrumque suam.[32]

(This one, embraced by me, our flesh embraces. / Before all others, he alone has stayed in our inmost hearts. /. . ./ But if you seek what excellence is known in him /. . ./ He is as cunning as a snake, simple as a cooing dove, / And with both these qualities he conquers age.)

The description of the boy both as snake and as dove recalls Jesus's command to his followers that they should follow the example of both animals in spreading the gospel. In Matthew 10:16, Jesus declares, "Estote ergo prudentes sicut serpentes et simplices sicut columbae" ("Therefore be wise as serpents and simple as doves"). Jesus employs the snake as a symbol of wisdom, and the dove has a threefold salvific signification: it suggests the end of God's punishment of humanity after Noah's flood; it is found within the amorous imagery of the Song of Songs; and it represents the Holy Spirit. In Baudri's queering lyric the conflation of snake and dove conquers any resistance the speaker might offer to the beautiful boy, and the fact that he would like to resist the boy indicates a different attitude toward queer desire than in some of his other verses. Thus, depending upon which of Baudri's poems one reads, contrasting views of same-sex desire emerge, as the image of the conquered man certainly does not carry the same sense of eagerness as many of Baudri's other homoerotic epistles.

The Queering Lyrics of Hildebert of Lavardin: The Delights of the Same-Sex Past and the Dangers of the Homoerotic Present

As V.A. Kolve notes, "one of the ways in which it was possible to talk freely of the love between men and boys in the world of the medieval monastery, abbey, or cathedral was in the language of mythology."[33] Although Hildebert of Lavardin appears not to be greatly concerned with defending same-sex practices in the present, his "Cum peteret puerum" ("When He Sought the Boy") locates same-sex desire in the classical past and then depicts a sympathetic and compassionate view of such relationships:

Cum peteret puerum Saturnius, Iphis Iantha
Coetus ait superum: "scelus est." Illud voco culpam.
Quo prohibente nefas, ludum ridente virorum,
Altera fit juvenis, fit femina neuter eorum.
Si scelus esset idem, sententia coelicolarum
Alterutrum transformaret, neutramve duarum.[34]

(When Saturn's son sought a boy and when Iphis [sought] Ianthe, / The council of gods said, "It is a crime." I call that wrong. / Prohibiting a treachery in one, laughing at the game of men [in the other]: / One [of the girls] is made a young man; neither of the men is made a woman. / If the crime were the same, the opinion of the heaven-dwellers / Should have transformed one or the other [man], or neither of the two [women].)

Hildebert is less concerned with the same-sex acts themselves than with the arbitrary judgments of the gods: neither Jove's relationship with Ganymede nor Iphis's relationship with Ianthe is depicted as inherently sinful in this poem.[35] The problem, according to Hildebert, is that the gods, by preventing same-sex relationships between women while allowing such liaisons between men, are not consistent in their decisions. If the same acts do not merit the same reactions from divine authority, then that authority is arbitrary rather than just. In contrast, no damning judgment is rendered on the poem's same-sex erotics.

Another of Hildebert's lyrics that expresses an accepting attitude toward same-sex desire is set in the mythology of the classical past as well.[36] Similar to "Cum peteret puerum," "Phoebus de interitu Hyacinthi" ("Phoebus on the Death of Hyacinth") locates and circumscribes its depiction of same-sex love within Greek mythology. The poem describes Phoebus's despair at the death of his beloved Hyacinth:

> Et deus et medicus et amans, rescindere frustra
>   Tentans Aebalidae funera, Phoebus ait:
> "Parcite, di, puero, si non moriatur uterque;
>   Malo sequi puerum quam superesse deum.
> Si prohibetis et hoc, sit pars utriusque superstes,
>   Par cadit, ignoscam sic minor esse deo.
> Quisque feret laetus propriae dispendia partis,
>   Dum pars ad manes, pars eat ad superos."[37]

(God and doctor and lover, in vain trying to take back / The funeral of Oebalus's son, Phoebus says: / "Gods, spare the boy. If [we] both won't die, / I prefer to follow the boy than to survive as a god. / And if you prohibit this, may a part of each [of us] survive, / A part fall. Thus, I would pardon that I was less than a god. / Each [of us] would happily bear the cost of a near part, / While a part [of us] went to the shadows, a part [of us] would go to the heavens.")

Offering to share both suffering and pleasure, the underworld and the heavens, Phoebus pleads for his beloved at any cost. Hildebert's depiction of the doomed love stresses with eloquence and compassion the emotional pain experienced when male lovers are separated.

Hildebert waxes eloquently on same-sex love in a mythological past, but he does not condone such queer behavior among his contemporaries. His "De malitia saeculi" ("Of the Wickedness of the Age") stands in direct contrast both to the accepting tone of "Cum peteret puerum" and to the melancholic mourning of "Phoebus de interitu Hyacinthi." This strident screed celebrates the infernal punishment that awaits those who practice homoerotic acts:

> Omnibus incestis super est sodomitica pestis,
>   Dantque mares maribus debita conjugibus.
> Innumeras aedes colit innumerus Ganymedes,
>   Hocque, quod ipsa solet sumere, Juno dolet.
> Hoc sordent vitio puer et vir cum sene laeno,
>   Nullaque conditio cessat ab hoc vitio.
> Quisquis ad hunc morem naturae vertis honorem
>   Et Venerem licitam negligis ob vetitam,
> Nonne recordaris quod per Sodomam docearis
>   Hoc scelus ut caveas, sulphure ne pereas?[38]

(The sodomitical pestilence is above all others lewdnesses. / Men give what is owed to their wives to men. / Innumerable Ganymedes tend innumerable hearths, / And Juno laments those things which she was accustomed to manage. / Boy and man with old man [and] panderer pollute [themselves] with this sin, / And no creation refrains from this sin. / You who turn the honor of nature to this custom / And neglect licit love for forbidden, / Do you not remember what you were taught through Sodom, / That you should beware lest you perish in sulfur-fire?)

In no uncertain terms, Hildebert presents same-sex activity as a sin that will lead inexorably to the damnation of its practitioners: the fires of Hell await the sinners of Sodom, and the only escape from such a punishment is to repent immediately. Furthermore, Hildebert stresses that the sin of homoerotic activity is widespread and has many practitioners; as such, it is a sign of the world's inverted and sinful nature, in which some men have taken over women's positions.

Queer Salvation Through Same-Sex Sinfulness

Marbod's, Baudri's, and Hildebert's poetic excurses on same-sex desire and the paradoxical viewpoints expressed therein can be seen as attempts to establish a pathway to God's forgiveness and salvation when interpreted in the light of biblical teachings of reversal and inversion. Salvation through sexual sin, however, is a queer salvation that bases redemption upon the very fact of humanity's fallen sexual nature. The poets underscore the topsy-turvy nature of same-sex desire through their depictions of an inverted world order, as the poems that condemn same-sex relationships describe a world turned upside-down, inverted in regard to right and wrong. In his "De malitia saeculi," Hildebert bemoans the moral quagmire that surrounds him in which the public and the private, the proper and the improper, the religious and the irreligious have changed roles:

> Omne bonum marcet foedumque pudor nihil arcet;
>   Quod decet hoc fugitur, quod pudet hoc editur;
> Subdola laudatur mens, simplex stulta putatur,
>   Et sentit pietas quid queat impietas.[39]

(All good [things] wither; shame prevents nothing detestable. / That which is proper has fled; that which shames is proclaimed. / The crafty mind is praised, the simple is thought foolish, / And piety senses what impiety can do.)

Hildebert describes a world washed over with reversals in which nothing receives its proper due. The poem then ponders the future if such a topsy-turvy state continues and asks God either to punish the wicked or to restore the lost order of the universe. With their eschatological focus, biblical passages of inversion highlight the sinful nature of the world; this sinfulness is readily delineated in terms of an inverted world order in which same-sex desire signifies the fallen state both of individuals and of the wider Christian community.[40]

In the same poem, Hildebert characterizes the prevalence of homoeroticism as a sign of the world's inversion and beseeches God to overturn the inversions, to correct the wrongful state of his earthly society:

> Da, qui cuncta regis, per quem stat sanctio legis,
>   Cui placet ille jocussit sibi poena focus;
> Aut homini parcens, sed quod tibi displicet arcens,
>   Evacuata suis instrue corda tuis,
> Et, vice mutata, caro jam nimium dominata
>   Mentis ad imperium, det sibi servitium![41]

(You who rule all things and through Whom the rule of law stands firm, / Give to him who this sport pleases that [his] hearth may be a punishment to him. / Or, sparing the man but preventing what displeases You, / Empty these hearts of their own [affairs] and fill [them] with Yours. / Turn things around again, and let flesh, which has excessively dominated, / Give service to the command of the mind.)

Hildebert constructs same-sex relations as the dominance of the earthly flesh over the heavenly spirit. Same-sex desire is the sexual incarnation of the fallen world, and it can only be conquered by the flesh being ruled by the spirit. Hildebert's prayer that the world be turned around again suggests his belief that the inverted world is the home of same-sex desire and that this sin would disappear if God's salvific force appeared. Also, Hildebert imagines this cleansing in terms of ironic reversals: the man who feels homoerotic desire is to be burned not with the sulfurous fires of Sodom, but with the heat of his own hearth. The site of his domestic sexual pleasures becomes the rack of his eternal torments.

Baudri's epicediums for deceased youths mirror the reasoning that Hildebert expresses in his poetry. His prayers for God's forgiveness of dead boys detail a similar understanding of Christian thought in which the fallen earthly world is the scene of a sin that ensnares men in illicit sexual liaisons. Baudri beseeches God to grant indulgence to such a young man in "Super Alexandrum Turonensem" ("Upon Alexander of Tours") specifically because of the sin:

> Canonicus Turonensis erat, puer indolis altae.
> Flos olim roseus, nunc cinis est luteus.
> Sique sibi maculas species attraxit et aetas,
> Tu tamen indulge rex utriusque dator.[42]
>
> (He was a canon of Tours, a boy of great talent. / Once a rosy flower, now he is ash and clay. / If his appearance and age attracted stains to him, / Nevertheless forgive [him], You, King, Bestower of both.)

According to Baudri, a sin in the inverted physical world should not prohibit the boy's spiritual salvation; thus, the stains of sin are the means by which the poet establishes his prayer for mercy. And as God's gifts of beauty and youth to the boy are the source of his moral corruption, Baudri exhorts his Lord to forgive sins founded upon ephemeral and worldly traits, traits that God Himself gave the boy. The boy's sins are indicative of a fallen world, but not of a lost soul.

Another of Baudri's prayers for Alexander—"Item de eodem" ("For the Same Boy")—employs similar themes in its depiction of Alexander's fall into sin but worthiness of salvation:

> Contuleritque licet quaecumque decora putantur,
> Mortuus attamen est; ecce cinis jacet hic.
> Supra quindenos vix quattuor attigit annos,
> Illi cum pariter omnia mors rapuit.
> En foetet vilis speciosae gloria carnis
> At Deus indulge quod male promeruit.[43]
>
> (And though [Nature] brought [him] whatever is deemed beautiful, / Nevertheless he is dead; behold, here lie [his] ashes. / He had scarcely reached over nineteen years / When death snatched all things at once from him. / Lo, the vile glory of [his] attractive flesh stinks, / But God, forgive what he badly earned.)

Again, Baudri concentrates on the necessity of God's forgiveness for sins: the rotting flesh signifies the earthly sins Alexander committed as he fell to corruptive practices on earth, but the focus on the earthly gives way to the hope for God's mercy in the closing lines of the poem. Although Alexander's transgressions merit his punishment, Baudri's plea for salvation attempts to free the sinner from eternal punishment for sins committed in an inverted world. The beautiful flesh begins to stink, both marking its corruption and earthliness and stressing the transformation of the fair into the foul.

In a similar manner, Marbod describes an inverted world in his poems that express disapprobation of acts of same-sex love. "Dissuasio amoris Veneris" paints a picture of an inverted world order in which human appetites have lost their accustomed domains:

> Versa natura mutantur pristina jura,
> Si cibus impastum facit, et lascivia castum,
> Si metus audacem, si mens secura fugacem.[44]
>
> (Nature is reversed, and ancient laws changed / If food makes [man] hungry and lechery [makes him] chaste, / If fear [makes him] brave, if a steadfast mind [makes him] ready to flee.)

In this poem, human desires and conditions are reversed with their ordered goals; the bodily appetites have lost their natural ends. These thematics of the inverted world are also found in Marbod's "Poenitudo lascivi amoris" ("Repentance for Lecherous Love"), in which the narrator laments his loves of both sexes and describes himself as a victim to a world in which all order is overturned. The queer voice that delighted in the male body now describes such sexual play as loathsome:

> O bone Salvator! quam decipit omnis amator!
> Turpia pulchra putat, pro nigris candida mutat.
> Coeni fetorem pigmenti credit odorem;
> Dulcia sicut mel testatur amara velut fel;
> Dum comedit lapidem, se pane frui putat idem,
> Et serpentinum virus potat quasi vinum. . . .
> Sicut odor floris sic tunc odor illius oris
> Esse videbatur, qui nunc secus esse probatur,
> Ut rosa candorem miscens simul atque ruborem,
> Sic mihi tunc vultus qui nunc pallore sepultus;
> Non quia mutatus fit odor, vel vultus amatus,
> Sed mutatus ego, quondam mihi chara relego.[45]
>
> (O good Savior! How all lovers are deceived! / He considers the detestable beautiful and changes white for black, / He believes the stink of filth to be the aroma of spice; / He swears that things sweet as honey are as bitter as bile. / When he eats a stone he think he enjoys bread / And he drinks the venom of serpents as if [it were] wine. /. . ./ Then the smell of his mouth

[was] like the smell of a flower, / He appeared to be [one way], who now is proved to be otherwise. / A rose mixing at once white and red, / So then [his] face [was] to me, which now has the pallor of death. / It is not because the odor has changed, or the beloved face [has changed]; / But I have been changed; I reread things formerly dear to me.)

Marbod describes himself as awakening to the sinfulness of the world's inversion; whereas he previously delighted in his sinful relationships with both sexes, he now realizes that all such couplings are immoral. In a world in which nothing is what it appears to be, where everything is both itself and its complete opposite, how is a lover to know on whom he should focus his desires, especially if his desires—whether for men or for women—are sinful?

Significantly, Marbod distances himself more from same-sex practices than from heterosexual desire. The following lines of "Poenitudo lascivi amoris" condemn same-sex desire in stronger terms than they condemn male/female relationships:

> Displicet amplexus utriusque quidem mihi sexus,
> Sed plus me laedit qui plus a jure recedit.
> Omnia sunto foris vitae delicta prioris.[46]
>
> (Indeed the embrace of both sexes displeases me, / But he harms me more, he who departs more from the law. / All delights of my former life are cast out.)

Sex either with a woman or with a man is constructed as an iniquitous act, but Marbod delineates his belief that same-sex desire is his greater transgression against God's will and that, to ensure his salvation, all such sexual practices will be cast aside. The rejection of homoerotic affection is essential for a rejection of the inverted world in its entirety.

The queerly redemptive power of Christianity is found when, in his repudiation of sexuality, Marbod is able to cast himself in a holier light: through his former sinfulness, he envisions himself as closer to his own salvation. In "Dissuasio amoris Venerei" ("An Argument Against Sexual Love"), the poet finds salvific power through his sexual experiences: "Luxuriae vitio castissimus en ego fio, / Quod duros mollit, hoc mollitiem mihi tollit" ("Lo, I am made completely chaste by the sin of lechery. / [The vice] which makes hard men soft takes away my softness").[47] In these lines, the excessive sexuality of Marbod's past is resignified to suggest his redemption. In the inverted world order, the degradations inflicted upon himself through his sex acts are the means by which he may visualize himself as a better, stronger Christian, one who is completely chaste before God. The sinful joys of homoeroticism are resignified into the basis of a claim to holiness in this inverted world; the sin itself is resignified into the seed of salvation. This sense of salvation is indeed queer, as it reconceptualizes the pleasures of sin into the foundation of eternal bliss in heaven. As the Gospels promise, Heaven rejoices more for one redeemed sinner than for ninety-nine righteous people (Luke 15: 3–7), and these poets take full advantage of this promise.

Speaking the Unspeakable: Identities and Personae in Queer Lyrics of Same-Sex Desire

The poets' constructions of their sexual proclivities as salvific due to the very fact of their queer sinfulness may appear curious, yet other concurrent practices founded upon Christian inversion show the saliency of the concept to the medieval mind. Bernard of Clairvaux's assumption of a female persona so that he may view himself as the Bride of Christ may appear equally odd to the modern mind, but for him the adoption of feminine characteristics was a powerful method of expressing his holiness and devotion to Christ.[48] As Bernard constructed himself as a woman to find himself with Christ, these men could likewise find redemptive power in same-sex relations, whether real or imagined, through envisioning themselves as engaging in sinful behavior that would lead them closer to Christ through their subsequent rejection of the desire. By positioning themselves as sympathetic to homoerotic longings and then rejecting such desires, they attain a higher state of holiness than before. It is unlikely that scholarship will ever ascertain whether Marbod, Baudri, and Hildebert had sex with other men; regardless of whether they did or did not, such paradoxical identification with and rejection of same-sex desire allows them to see themselves as saved due to their final rejection of real or imagined homoerotic sex acts.

In the final section of this chapter, I would like to return to the title of Marbod's "Satyra in amatorem puelli *sub assumpta persona*." The narrative voice that waxes so eloquently about male beauty is an assumed one, and this use of a persona suggests that Marbod was consciously adopting an authorial position that frees himself of contamination from the sins so amorously described. Again, I would like to stress that we cannot know whether or not Marbod experienced same-sex desires, but that he specifically assumes a persona other than his own voice and that he clearly directs the reader's attention to this persona through the poem's title signifies that he was fully aware of the contradictions of a Christian monastic lauding beautiful boys. The poetics of a persona occlude the writer behind the mask: as Steven Shurtleff notes in regard to the contemporaneous Archpoet's Confession, "This identification of a type with a persona is highly literary, removed and impersonal, qualities not ordinarily associated with autobiography."[49] The assumption of a different voice—a voice expressing taboo desire—is key to Marbod's treatment of same-sex desire; by emphasizing that he is playing the part of a sexual sinner in a world turned upside-down, Marbod not only speaks his desire, not only creates a safe space for speaking it, but develops an authorial position in which the voicing of same-sex desire becomes the basis of his future salvation.[50]

The assumption of a different voice by which one distances himself from his own works is a literary technique that Baudri likewise employs: as he declares in a letter to his friend Godfrey, "Non est in triviis alicuius amor recitandus, / Quisquis amat, cautus celet amoris opus" (Love ought not be recited in the public spaces of another / Whoever loves, let the cautious one conceal the work of love). The importance of such posturing is that it allows the poet to address topics that would otherwise be forbidden. As F.J.E. Raby notes,

> There are, [Baudri] goes on to confess, love-dialogues among his poems, but his own life is pure, and he is using only for amusement the characters who speak their own words and not his. And, after all, as he says to Godfrey, is it wrong to write about love if it gives pleasure, and one's own life is above reproach? No clergyman, who was really in love, would publish the fact in verse.[51]

Baudri, by positioning himself as separate from the speaking voice of his poems, frees himself from the moral culpability implicit in such secular odes to love. Speaking as a monk who is speaking as a lover, the poet walks a literary tightrope in which expressed desire is avowed and disavowed concurrently and the inverted world is exposed.

Hildebert similarly constructs an assumed voice for himself by casting his laudatory same-sex poems safely in the mythological past, rather than in the present of his polemics against same-sex desire. Figuring homoerotic desire as contained in a fictional past allows the poet to praise same-sex desire but to save himself from its implications. In his "Lumina, colla, genae" ("Eyes, Neck, Cheeks"), Hildebert describes same-sex kisses but frees himself from aspersion:

> Iliacum tulit ad superos, ad sidera sidus,
>   Et se tunc tandem credidit esse deum.
> Utque puer pelex visu tactuque liceret,
>   Oscula nocte Jovi, pocula luce dabat.[52]

> ([Jove] raised the Trojan to the heavens, a star to the stars, / And then at last he believed that he was a god. / And so that the boy-mistress would be

available to sight and to touch, / He gave kisses to Jove by night, cups by daylight.)

Hildebert's views of homoerotic acts vary according to the authorial stance taken. He is able to vacillate between poles of acceptance and intolerance because he demarcates two separate worlds in which separate voices speak, even though the two voices belong to the same poet. As Hildebert presents Ganymede's kisses to Jove with no hint of disapproval, the poet also damns his contemporaries who participate in such expressions of desire.

Thus, in these queering lyrics the "I" that speaks plays with different personae, but who is the "I" who speaks? "I" represents the author, but this amorphous and shifting pronoun also represents the plurality of personal possibilities that the queering author embodies: as Eugene Vance declares, " 'I' is a specific signifier whose referent necessarily varies with the circumstances of its enunciation. . . . [It] modulates, then, with the conditions (speaker, code, audience) of its enunciation."[53] Even more than modulating among the various subject positions of one individual, the "I" also serves as a shorthand indicator of a collective "we." Judson Boyce Allen refers to this construction as the "easy medieval plagiarism of first person pronouns [which] loosen[s the poet] from autobiographical reference. . .and does therefore tend toward the achievement of a discourse which is that of generic rather than particular man."[54] In these queerings of the lyric genre, the poets create virtuoso performances of the self in which the "I" both speaks individual same-sex desire but encapsulates this desire within the Christian theology of their communities at large. The performance of the "I" is both the performance of an individual "I" and a collective "we," as the redemptive possibilities of sin are open to all.

The paradoxical performance of a sinful self offers explanatory force for other puzzling instances of monks publicizing their own sinfulness. For example, Abbot Guibert de Nogent details in his memoirs, completed ca. 1116, both the sinful pride from his writing and the writing itself; Martin Stevens observes, "There is, thus, in the very existence of the *Memoirs* a reminder of Guibert's self-confessed sin of 'frivolous writing,' as well as the vanity of authorship for which he berates himself repeatedly. The quest of identity and the power of self-revelation are simply too large to be contained with the prescribed pieties of the day."[55] Likewise, Leo Spitzer suggests that Juan Ruiz, Archpriest of Hita,

> wished to depict that potential sinner which existed in himself, as in all human beings: he reveals himself, not as having committed the sins he describes, but as capable, in his human weakness, of having committed them. . . . [H]is is still the poetic "I" of the medieval tradition, which speaks in the name of man in general.[56]

Medieval monks saw in the inverted nature of the world a direct path to salvation through the promotion of their very sinfulness; by exploiting the generic freedoms offered by the lyric form and its multiplicities of "I," the poet celebrates and condemns all earthly desires because these desires have the potential to lead one to God, even if via a queering path.

Thus, are Marbod of Rennes, Baudri of Bourgueil, and Hildebert of Lavardin speaking the truth of their desires for same-sex relationships in the guise of a lie? We can see the many masks worn by Marbod, Baudri, and Hildebert, but it is virtually impossible to see who exactly lives beneath the mask. Regardless of whether the poets are speaking about whom they do or do not desire, their poetry paradoxically revels in the damning joys of homoeroticism in order to sanctify the writers before their God. Writing with two voices in an inverted world, Marbod, Baudri, and Hildebert are able to embrace and to castigate, to love and to loathe, male same-sex desire simultaneously in their queering reformulations of the lyric genre.

And what is the reader to do? A heteronormative reader who condemns queerness must nonetheless realize the possibilities of a queer salvation through Jesus's beneficent mercy; a queer reader who embraces same-sex desire must nonetheless admit its sinful valence within medieval Christianity. Both heteronormative and queer readers are left struggling with the contradictory significations of these lyrics, because no reader can find in them a firm hermeneutic foothold. Same-sex desire—whether embraced or condemned—matters less to these lyricists than their manifold and contradictory queernesses, which lead all readers painfully, trippingly, falteringly to Christ.

CHAPTER 3

CHAUCER'S QUEERING FABLIAUX

The medieval fabliau, with its "anything goes" ethos and farcical sexual situations, provides a plethora of queering opportunities in terms of its sexual politics.[1] With a vast array of sexual and gender permutations portrayed, many of which subvert, invert, parody, and ridicule traditional sexual roles, fabliaux offer a particularly apt setting for queering sensibilities. Due to the fabliau's flagrant flouting of normativity, my foremost purpose in this chapter is not merely to adumbrate the presence of homosexuality in Chaucer's fabliaux, although I certainly pay attention to its somewhat occluded depiction.[2] Beyond establishing a generic setting suitable to queer sexual politics, the fabliaux of *The Canterbury Tales* provide a gender and sexual crucible in which to examine the effects of queering narratives on their intended audience. By reading Chaucer's fabliaux with an eye to their repercussions on the sexual and ostensibly heteronormative identities of the Canterbury pilgrims, we see that *The Canterbury Tales* showcases the tense sexual politics of a destabilizing and queer narrative structure. In this chapter's first section, "Queer Anxiety, Homosocial Aggression and Masculine Heteronormativity Under Duress in Chaucer's Fabliaux," I first address the queering power of fabliaux in "The Miller's Tale," "The Reeve's Tale," "The Friar's Tale," and "The Summoner's Tale" to establish the limits of heteronormative identity among the male pilgrims as they jockey amongst themselves to humiliate their narrative foes; I then explore the ways in which "The Cook's Tale," "The Merchant's Tale," and "The Shipman's Tale" celebrate a particularly feminine narrative power of queering males from their heteronormative privilege, when no such aggressive homosocial motivations spur the telling of such bawdy tales. In the chapter's second section, "Queering Genres, Battering Males: The Wife of Bath's Narrative Violence," I examine how the Wife of Bath shocks her primarily male audience into a heteronormatively rhetorical powerlessness by subverting the traditional Arthurian romance through the queering implications of the fabliau. Throughout *The Canterbury Tales*, fabliaux are frequently told to affect, if not effect, the sexual identity of other pilgrims through the insulting and transgressive force of queering narratives.

Queer Anxiety, Homosocial Aggression, and Masculine Heteronormativity Under Duress in Chaucer's Fabliaux

By structuring *The Canterbury Tales* as a storytelling competition, Chaucer establishes a latent aggression in his narrative structure that at times threatens to erupt into outright violence. This competition sparks blatant rhetorical attacks in the frames of some fabliaux but not in others. Certainly, all of Chaucer's fabliaux—"The Miller's Tale," "The Reeve's Tale," "The Cook's Tale," "The Friar's Tale," "The Summoner's Tale," "The Merchant's Tale," and "The Shipman's Tale"—depict a world heavy with the potential for aggression through their focus on sexual farce, cuckoldry, and/or insult humor.[3] This antagonism may be expressed both by the tellers of the fabliaux to other pilgrims and by the characters of the fabliaux to one another in their efforts to humiliate their foes; both in narration and in plot, Chaucer's fabliaux foreground a potentially agonistic embodiment of social relationships.

In the framing narratives of four of Chaucer's fabliaux—"The Miller's Tale," "The Reeve's Tale," "The Friar's Tale," and "The Summoner's Tale"—battling men deploy queer insults as a tactic to degrade their opponents. These four fabliaux contain queer allegations both from one tale-teller to another or from one character to another, and homosexual desires are ridiculed, denigrated, and attacked both to establish the supremacy of heteronormative sexuality and to establish the tale's speaker as an active participant in such heteronormative sexuality. In contrast, "The Cook's Tale," "The Merchant's Tale," and "The Shipman's Tale" evince much less interest in homosexually queer anxieties sparking such aggressions; rather, these three fabliaux, through their depiction of quick-witted, sexually motivated heroines, celebrate the humorous power of female characters to operate as their own sexual agents and to circumscribe masculine sexual privilege. In *The Canterbury Tales*, the fabliau is a queer genre, and it is often a queering genre as well: *queer*, because all of these fabliaux contain depictions of the frailty of masculine heteronormativity; *queering*, because many of these fabliaux are deployed as verbal weapons by men seeking to remove their enemies from heteronormative privilege. (For the sake of convenience, I refer to "The Miller's Tale," "The Reeve's Tale," "The Friar's Tale," and "The Summoner's Tale" as the male queer fabliaux to highlight the masculine battles both within the tales themselves and within the tales' frames; I refer to "The Cook's Tale," "The Merchant's Tale," and "The Shipman's Tale" as the female queer fabliaux to highlight the increased feminine agency within these tales that are not told by men fighting with one another. These gendered descriptions of the fabliaux stress the gender of the primary queering agents—the eponymous tale-tellers of "The Miller's Tale," "The Reeve's Tale," "The Friar's Tale," and "The Summoner's Tale," and the female protagonists and characters of "The Cook's Tale," "The Merchant's Tale," and "The Shipman's Tale.")[4]

In Chaucer's male queer fabliaux, evident anxieties center around questions of heteronormative male identity. Queer anxieties arise in and incite the persecutor to attack his foe, but the term "queer anxiety" also suggests the fears that medieval men express of losing heteronormative privilege and, thus, of exclusion from the arena of masculine authority.[5] Male privilege (the social and ideological advantages accorded to men due to their gender) and heteronormative privilege (the social and ideological advantages accorded to heterosexuals due to their sexuality) are inextricably intertwined, and deep anxieties arise when either set of prerogatives is threatened. The dual thrust of queer anxieties, which exposes the antagonisms of the aggressor and the vulnerabilities of the attacked, creates a powerful rhetorical weapon in the hostilities barely cloaked by the Canterbury game. During the Canterbury journey, in which seriousness is often masked behind a veneer of play, stinging attacks against their fellow pilgrims surface in the storytelling "game."

The men who constitute the pairs of queerly anxious tale-tellers—the Miller and the Reeve, the Friar and the Summoner—perceive each other as enemies and struggle to establish individual dominance by coloring their enemies with the taint of the queer. These queer allegations carry with them a tremendous threat to sexually normative manhood, and the characters attempt to capitalize on these tensions in their attacks on one another. Eve Sedgwick's words remain an invigorating formulation of this dynamic:

> [T]he continuum of male homosocial bonds has been brutally structured by a secularized and psychologized homophobia, which has excluded certain shiftingly and more or less arbitrarily defined segments of the continuum from participating in the overarching male entitlement. . . . I argue that the historically shifting, and precisely the arbitrary and self-contradictory, nature of the way *homosexuality* (along with its predecessor terms) has been defined in relation to the rest of the male homosocial spectrum has been an exceedingly potent and embattled locus of power over the entire range of male bonds, and perhaps especially those that defined themselves, not *as* homosexual, but *as against* the homosexual.[6]

Particularly within the world of Chaucer's four male queer fabliaux, heteronormative sexuality lies at stake and under duress from homosocial antagonism; attacking the queer, even when the target himself is presumably not queer, protects the aggressor male's heteronormative privileges. Reading Chaucer queerly, then, allows one to expose the anxieties ostensibly hidden by heteronormativity; as Glenn Burger observes, "Queering Chaucer provides another way...to resist the hegemonic forces of a presumptive heterosexuality that would fix what Chaucer means by fixing who he 'is' in order to enjoy (or resist) the material and symbolic privileges of maleness."[7] For Chaucer and for his fabliau characters, the lability of sexuality undermines totalizing views of masculinity and heteronormativity, putting these "material and symbolic privileges of maleness" in jeopardy.

Certainly, two blatant visions of the queer dominate the landscape of Chaucerian fabliaux. The parody of same-sex anal intercourse enacted by Nicholas and Absolon in "The Miller's Tale" and the graphic vision of a swarm of friars in Satan's anus in the Summoner's "Prologue" both establish the characters' lines of attack through allegations of queerness. These two images—and other words and visions similar to them—adumbrate the queer in order to showcase a masculine world where masculinity itself is always under duress and in need of defense. The irony, ever apparent, is that a pilgrim's defense against the queer lies in attacking another pilgrim with the very queer threats from which he must defend himself. From this perspective, we see the nexus between homosocial competition and queer anxiety.

The three female queer fabliaux, unconcerned with homosocial competition in the prologues of the tales, evince notably less concern with issues of hostility and aggression that might darken the humor of the tales. The Cook, the Merchant, and the Shipman, despite their many character faults as outlined in "The General Prologue," do not engage in the storytelling competition with the explicit purpose of humiliating or attacking another pilgrim. The crucial difference between the male queer and the female queer fabliaux, then, may be found in the typically Chaucerian fault line between seriousness and play: the male queer fabliaux reveal the aggressive pilgrims' serious motivations of hatred in the ostensible play of their tales, as these men have personal goals of attack and revenge at stake through this storytelling game. Alternatively, the female queer fabliaux highlight the outrageous play of the genre for its own sake. From a Freudian perspective, the male queer fabliaux inscribe the aggressions of tendency wit, while the female queer fabliaux inscribe the playful humor of harmless wit.[8]

Such a narrative tactic relies heavily on the aggression built into the fabliau as a genre. With a delightful synthesis of form and function, Chaucer deploys the fabliau as a particularly apt genre of hostility and hilarity to express homosocial antagonism between men. From its very inception, the fabliau is ideally suited to the expression of antagonism through its origin and performance in the French courts, where its valence as entertainment derived primarily from its mocking jabs at the bourgeoisie and the clergy.[9] Charles Muscatine locates the fabliau within the "bourgeois tradition," which he discerns as a "cluster of genres...appearing freshly in the twelfth and thirteenth centuries [that] attend the emergence of the new middle class."[10] The tales thus appear to be jokes that the aristocracy shared at the commoners' expense, as expressing class antagonism and ridiculing the bourgeoisie lie at the heart of the genre. D.S. Brewer characterizes the fabliau as having "a typical French brilliance and harshness. They are aristocratic burlesques, contemptuously holding up to amusement the coarse buffooneries of lower classes and some clergy,"[11] and Ross Arthur agrees that "[m]ockery of social climbers is precisely the kind of theme to appeal to the courtly audience."[12] Within the range of medieval genres, fabliau provides a virtually organic form for expressing hostility and derision.

For Chaucer and fourteenth-century English society, fabliau provides a particularly appropriate genre to explore nascent class tensions both between the bourgeoisie and gentility and among competing members of the bourgeoisie. David Wallace situates Chaucer's fabliaux within the tensions between city and country life, noting their connections with the rising merchant class and the ways in which bourgeois economies created geographical boundaries that cordoned off classes of people from one another.[13] Of Chaucer's fabliau-tellers, the Miller, Reeve, Cook, Shipman, and Merchant all participate to one degree or another within the mercantile economy of fourteenth-century England. The Friar and Summoner should not explicitly participate in such an economy, yet unapologetically do so anyway; as I explore, the Wife of Bath may tell a romance, but this does not preclude her from revealing her bourgeois fabliau sensibility. The fusion of fabliau narratives with bourgeois tale-tellers indicates Chaucer's concern with the ways in which the rising merchant class structures English culture and its very landscape. Glending Olson observes the ways in which Chaucer's use of the fabliau is innovative in terms of social class:

> It seems likely that Chaucer's literary problem was not how to introduce the "low-class tales" to a court audience but rather how best to fit a fairly frivolous genre known to his circle into the context of the pilgrimage. The result is that for the first time in a medieval collection of tales fabliaux are told by characters who are at the same social and moral level as the protagonists of the stories.[14]

In terms of queering generic innovation, Chaucer gives the bourgeois a voice through genre.[15] Prior to Chaucer, fabliaux exhibited queering sensibilities in their mockery of heteronormative privilege, but in his hands, the queerness is expanded to allow the class anxieties of fourteenth-century England to explode across the pages of his manuscripts. As ideological power is intrinsically connected to depictions of sexuality and normativity, as well as to social class, Chaucer's fabliau lay bare the tensions sparked by a rising economic caste.[16]

Within fabliaux, satire and mockery appear to be essential plot elements, and these characteristics make the genre ideal for expressing antagonism. Advancing the masculine and potentially hostile ethos of these tales, all of Chaucer's fabliaux are under masculine control by the simple fact that each is told by a male pilgrim; moreover, the male queer fabliaux—"The Miller's Tale," "The Reeve's Tale," "The Friar's Tale," and "The Summoner's Tale"—are told by male pilgrims belligerently engaged in male–male rivalries. This aggression in the tale-telling emerges immediately after "The Knight's Tale," when Harry Bailly unwittingly invites the masculine battling to begin with his observation that "unbokeled is the male" (3115).[17] This phrase, which idiomatically suggests that "the game is well begun" while metaphorically adumbrating that a particularly male force has been unleashed, provokes the Miller to respond with a show of his own masculine and verbal force.[18] The Miller tells his tale with the explicit purpose to "quite" the Knight and to insult the Reeve; after the Miller completes his tale, the Reeve's aggressive story serves as a rebuttal to the insults he perceives in the Miller's bawdy tale. Likewise, the Friar offers his fabliau as an open attack against the Summoner, and "The Summoner's Tale" serves as a lengthy rejoinder to the Friar for his enemy's deprecating story of a summoner summoned to hell. The fabliau, in the mouths of Chaucer's battling male characters, serves not merely as a structure or genre for a story, but as a means of attack, of establishing dominance and victory over a rival through the extended insults such tales sanction. In the male queer fabliaux in which pilgrims fight with their fellow pilgrims, the threat of the queer, of ostracism from the heteronormative order, emerges as a powerful rhetorical weapon in these pilgrims' verbal assaults.[19]

Chaucer's queer male fabliaux constitute a man's genre in which aggression motivates speech. Certainly, masculine hostility lies at the foundation of *The Canterbury Tales*, as Emily Jensen observes that male competition is a unifying motif of the tales in Fragment A: "whether we look at the central action within the tales, the emphasis on 'quiting' in the links, or striking patterns in the rhyme, it seems clear that the primary means through which the 'degenerative movement' in Fragment A occurs is male competition."[20] In and beyond the tales of Fragment A, telling ribald tales—and out-telling ribald tellers—allows men a playing field in which dominance can be established and one's own heteronormativity established by tainting the other through the threat of the queer. In the subsequent sections of this chapter, I first analyze the aggressive dynamics behind the Miller and the Reeve with their dueling tales and prologues before considering the similar queer anxieties expressed by the Friar and the Summoner; this half of the chapter concludes by pondering the increased sexual agency of female characters and the relative lack of homosocial aggression in "The Cook's Tale," "The Merchant's Tale," and "The Shipman's Tale," as well as the ways in which increased female sexual agency queers masculine heteronormative privilege. After the first half of the chapter concludes, I move to an analysis of Alison of Bath's queering genre play through the strange intersection of fabliau and romance.

The Queering Tales of the Miller and the Reeve

In the Miller's "Prologue," the reader immediately discerns that tale-telling offers men the opportunity to establish supremacy over one another rather than merely to entertain their fellow pilgrims. Although the telling of their tales supposedly represents an egalitarian entertainment in which all can participate, the Knight privileges a courtly and aristocratic audience through his choice of a romance. Chaucer reports that the pilgrims enjoy this romance (3110–11), yet he also underscores that the gentlefolk appreciate the story more than the commoners. Everyone agrees the story is worthy "to drawen to memorie" (3112), but "namely the gentils everichon" (3113) most admire it. The Miller's inebriated response highlights the aggressive nature of their pastime and his intention to outdo the Knight: "By armes, and by blood and bones, / I kan a noble tale for the nones, / With which I wol now quite the Knightes tale" (3125–27). The Miller's drunken words, through their imagery of weapons and of mutilated bodies, stress the aggression promised in his tale-telling. For him, the fabliau offers an ideal generic form to debase the knight's courtly tale by reconstructing and degrading the tale of Palamon's and Arcite's idealized love for Emily into the story of Nicholas's and Absolon's earthly love for Alison.[21] More than merely a reconstruction and a degradation, however, "The Miller's Tale" especially aims to queer the Knight's courtly romance by replacing its promise of heterosexual consummation in marriage with the fabliau depiction of parodic sodomy.[22] The Knight is not the only targeted victim of the Miller and his queering fabliau, as the Reeve also finds himself threatened by the forthcoming tale. Perceiving the contumely directed at him in the figure of the cuckolded carpenter John through the Miller's foreshadowing rhyme of the Reeve's name "Osewold" (3151) with "cokewold" (3152), the Reeve attempts to stave off his foe's attack with his sharp cry for the Miller to "Stynt thy clappe" (3144). The Miller aims to defeat and to queer two men with one tale—the Knight by parodying his tale, the Reeve by incorporating him into the tale in the role of the cuckold. Both attacks succeed in good measure.

The plot of "The Miller's Tale," centering on the illicit pleasures afforded by cuckoldry, highlights the masculine aggression central to the fabliau. As Karma Lochrie argues, cuckoldry is a homosocially aggressive economy in which men establish dominance vis-à-vis one another and women are the currency in trade:

> Cuckoldry is, first of all, not the same as a wife's adultery. It is primarily a transaction between two men, a lover and a husband, for sexual possession of the wife. The desire which inspires a potential cuckolder is the desire to dispossess and to possess at the same time: to dispossess the husband and to possess the wife. Cuckoldry is thus a transaction between men, as well as an activity in which the wife engages with a lover.[23]

Nicholas's goal in cuckolding John is not merely to deceive his rival and to win a night of passion with Alison; the defeat of another man and the conquest of his opponent's "possessions" in the marital contract are also at stake. The martial contests enacted by Palamon and Arcite in "The Knight's Tale," engaged in for a courtly and rarefied love, are degraded by the Miller into a contest in which the winner not only triumphs in obtaining an earthly and debased love, but in humiliating his rival as well. John does not die, as Arcite does, but Arcite never suffers the public humiliation that befalls John. Therein lies the crucial queering movement: John's humiliation arises from the failure of his masculinity to protect his heteronormative privilege.

Nicholas's plan to humiliate John also entails a strategic move to effeminize him and, thus, to queer him by removing him from the realm of heteronormative sexuality. In his description of their escape from the supposed flood that will overwhelm the world, Nicholas reveals that he plans to construct John as female in the post-deluvian world they will inhabit: "Thanne shaltow swymme as myrie, I undertake, / As dooth the white doke after hire drake" (3575–76). The sexes of John and Alison are reversed in Nicholas's simile, with John appearing as the female animal and Alison appearing as the male.[24] With these words, Nicholas promises to queer John, to strip him of his overarching masculinity, and to remove him from the heteronormative order of masculine sexual control. We see here further evidence of the "desexualized body" that Glenn Burger locates in the fabliau: "the tale queers the heteronormative sexual politics of the Knight's and Reeve's tales by desiring instead a 'desexualized body' operating within, yet not completely controlled by, the ideological structures of desire."[25] This dynamic, however, must be seen as working both within the tale (the intersecting love triangles of John-Nicholas-Alison, John-Absolon-Alison, and Nicholas-Absolon-Alison) and within the tale's frame (the Miller's attempt to queer both the Knight by parodying his heteronormative romance and the Reeve by positioning him as the desexualized carpenter of the tale). The Miller employs the queering touches of the fabliau within the humor of his tale, but its aggressive force is directed toward queering the Reeve.

That Nicholas conceives of his paramour Alison as masculine in the preceding passage hints obliquely at his own queer desires, but the queerness of "The Miller's Tale" is most blatant in its parody of sodomy when Absolon "with his iren hoot, /...Nicholas amydde the ers he smoot" (3809–810). Seeking revenge on Alison, Absolon finds himself enacting a parody of anal intercourse with her lover. With this hilarious stroke, the Miller not only "quites" "The Knight's Tale" with his ending, he queers it as well. The promise of sexual union between Palamon and Emilye, so central to the resolution of the Knight's romance, is transformed into the parodic sodomitical union between Nicholas and Absolon. Roy Peter Clark sees the humiliation of John arising from his "unbirthing," as his fall represents that the "fruit of Absolon's symbolic rape of Nicholas is the comic 'unbirth' (unberthing) of the old carpenter who cuts the umbilical cord that attaches his tub to the rafters 'and doun gooth al'";[26] in a similar fashion, Tracey Jordan notes that this "imaginary 'hole an heigh' is part of the birth imagery Nicholas uses to recreate the Noah story for the carpenter."[27] John has been thrice unmanned, thrice queered: he is the victim of Nicholas's cuckoldry, which denies him his heteronormative privilege, his fall casts him as the product of simulated sodomitical intercourse, and he becomes the laughingstock of the town. His masculinity has been stripped from him, leaving only an unmanned joke behind. The genius of "The Miller's Tale" arises in its dual deployment of the fabliau both to defeat "The Knight's Tale" through its queer degradation of the elevated romance and to insult the Reeve. Through the ignominious defeat of the masculine carpenter John at the hands of an effete cuckolder, the Miller depicts the ultimate unmanning and queering of his rival the Reeve, who sees himself depicted in the fictional carpenter John.

With the Miller's hilarious tale that defeats the Knight and unmans the Reeve, fabliau-telling reveals itself as a dominant rhetorical strategy in expressing hostility between men, one that the Reeve now employs to his own advantage. When the Miller finishes his tale, the Reeve expresses his desire to defeat him in the game of storytelling. Declaring to the Miller that "ful wel koude I thee quite" (3864) and promising to "somdeel sette his howve" (3911), the Reeve exposes his antagonism toward the Miller; by using the brute force necessary to achieve such a goal ("For leveful is with force force of-showve" [3912]), the telling of tales takes on the physicality of an armed contest. Moreover, the Reeve explicitly plots to establish his supremacy over the Miller through the Miller's own genre: "And, by your leve, I shal hym quite anoon; / Right in his cherles termes wol I speke" (3916–17). Fighting fire with fire, trading fabliau for fabliau, the Reeve hopes to acquit himself of the Miller's queering insults and to position the Miller as queered through the sexual dynamics and conquests of the tale.

In "The Reeve's Tale," the miller Symkyn, with his brutish masculinity, is unmanned and queered for the delight of the Reeve and the embarrassment of the Miller. To accomplish this objective, Chaucer first accentuates Symkyn's phallic masculinity through the character's penchant for knives, swords, and other blades: "Ay by his belt he baar a long panade, / And of a swered ful trenchant was the blade. / A joly poppere baar he in his pouche" (3929–31). The location of the "poppere"—a small dagger—in Symkyn's "pouche" indicates that his blades blatantly serve as metaphors for his penis. Indeed, Chaucer reiterates the connection between phallic blades and Symkyn's penis by locating another weapon in the miller's nether regions, the "Sheffeld thwitel...in his hose" (3933). Underscoring the iron phallus of Symkyn's aggressive masculinity—and its threats—in a subsequent passage detailing the dangers to any man sufficiently foolhardy to flirt with his wife, the Reeve again describes Symkyn's readiness with blades:

> Was noon so hardy that went by the weye
> That with hire dorst rage or pleye,
> But if he wolde be slayn of Symkyn
> With panade, or with knyf, or boidekyn. (3957–60)

For Symkyn, preserving his masculinity lies in preserving the honor and sexual fidelity of his wife. The many phallic blades close at hand serve as tools in preserving her honor, as well as keeping his masculinity safe from the threats of cuckoldry. It would appear that, unlike John in "The Miller's Tale," Symkyn is handily capable of preserving his position within heteronormative sexuality.

Furthermore, if Symkyn is concerned with maintaining his wife's fidelity through the assistance of his many phallic blades, he also attempts to maintain his masculinity by avoiding the queering touch of other men. Complementing the heavy repetitiousness in the litany of Symkyn's swords, Chaucer twice underscores Symkyn's aversion to the touch of another man: "Ther was no man, for peril dorste him touche" (3932); and "Ther dorste no wight hand upon hym legge, / That he ne swoor he sholde non abegge" (3937–38). Symkyn perceives men and male homosociality as a threat, both in his fear of cuckoldry and in his violent distaste for the male touch. The repetition of this key detail foreshadows its significance in the fabliau's climax when Symkyn learns of his humiliation: not only does a man cuckold him, but the same man touches him as well.

Through the repetitiousness of the introductory lines that mention Symkyn's blades seven times, Chaucer appears to foreshadow that the conclusion of the fabliau will include a bloody knife fight. Indeed, given the Reeve's propensity for accelerating the narrative of "The Miller's Tale" by illustrating not one clerk's dangerous liaison with another man's wife but two such amorous adventures, the many knives appear to be a counterpoint to Absolon's iron rod. The Miller's parody of sodomy seems likely to become, under the Reeve's reconstruction of the tale, a different kind of metallic penetration—a brutal and bloody stabbing, rather than a mock enactment of anal intercourse. To use a familiar metaphor from the world of drama, the audience expects a gun introduced in the first act to be shot in the third; the careful reader of Chaucer's tale would likely expect at least one of these seven blades to appear in the fabliau's denouement.

The tale's resolution, however, fails to depict the knives promised in the introductory lines. The two young scholars satisfy their sexual desires with Symkyn's wife and daughter, cuckolding him and depriving him of heteronormative control of female sexuality in his household. Surprisingly, the violence promised by Symkyn's swords fails to materialize when Aleyn discloses to Symkyn his amorous exploits with his daughter. Chaucer, however, does follow through on his initial characterization of Symkyn as one who hates to be touched. When Aleyn inadvertently confesses his copulations to Symkyn, Chaucer details the human touch that unmans Symkyn: "And by the millere in he creep anon, / And caughte hym by the nekke, and softe he spake" (4260–61). The ensuing violence springs both from Symkyn's unmanning in the loss of control of female sexuality and from his unmanning by physical contact with another man. Stunned by Aleyn's words, the miller reacts violently, but, astoundingly, without any of his phallic blades. The blades disappear, as does the promise of penetration, leaving Symkyn with no revenge against the clerks except a few punches. Without his metaphorical penises, Symkyn is not merely cuckolded; he is castrated and cast out from the world of heteronormative privilege where the phallus promises such privilege. In terms of the fabliau's engagement with issues of social class, Symkyn's ambitions to marry his daughter well and thus to advance his own social position are likely thwarted in the premature loss of her virginity. The Reeve's depiction of the miller Symkyn, designed to insult the pilgrim Miller, includes this insult specifically designed to show a miller unarmed, unmanned, and sexually laughable. Through the depiction of the queer unmanning of Symkyn the miller, the Reeve stresses that his deployment of the fabliau has avenged himself against the Miller: "Thus have I quyt the Millere in my tale" (4324).[28] Fighting with the rhetorical force of the fabliau, the Reeve attempts to reconstruct his own queered manhood back into the heteronormative order by assaulting the Miller's with a similar queering rhetoric.

The Queering Tales of the Friar and the Summoner

After witnessing the homosocial aggression between the Miller and the Reeve play out through the emasculating threat of cuckoldry, the Friar and the Summoner likewise deploy queering fabliaux to act out their hostilities toward each other. The Friar's attack may be linked to the initial description of the Summoner in "The General Prologue," a description that carries the possibility of the Summoner's and the Pardoner's homosexuality. Paul Olson describes the pair as "male lovers" in which the "Pardoner who frees people from penalty for sin plays a female role while the summoner who binds the recalcitrant plays the male."[29] Regardless of the reasons for the Friar's vitriol—whether homophobia, clerical squabbling, or personal animosity—the attacks of both men create a world in which masculinity is threatened by homosociality; the "anal orientation" that Mary Godfrey observes in both narratives serves as a threat and an insult to the speaker's enemy and rival.[30]

In his "Prologue," the Friar launches his attack against summoners. Before any words are spoken, Chaucer describes the animosity the Friar holds for the Summoner: "He made alway a maner lourying chier / Upon the Somonour, but for honestee / No vileyns word as yet to hym spak he" (1266–68). The Friar does not long maintain his scowling expression yet silent mouth. Disguising his attack on summoners as mere play by calling his words twice a "game" (1275 and 1279), the Friar attacks the sins of summoners by linking their abuses of authority to fornication and unbridled sexuality: "A somonour is a rennere up and doun / With mandementz for fornicacioun, / And is ybet at every tounes ende" (183–85). Although Harry Bailly attempts to impose peace between the two ("Telleth youre tale, and lat the Somonour be" [1288]), the Summoner refuses Harry's palliative words and declares to the pilgrims that his words will soon repay the Friar in kind: "Nay. . .let hym seye to me / What so hym list; whan it comth to my lot, / By God, I shal hym quiten every grot" (1290–92). The queerly masculine battle begins, and fabliaux again serve as the rhetorical weapons of choice.

The Friar's attack on the Summoner ends with the summoner in his tale damned to hell, but the attack begins with the suggestion that the summoner of his tale engages in a homoerotic relationship with his demonic friend. When the two men meet and decide to ride together, they quickly pledge friendship to each other, and Chaucer describes their newly formed intimacy with a telling hint of homoeroticism: "Everych in ootheres hand his trouthe leith, / For to be sworne bretheren til they deye. / In daliance they ryden forth and pleye" (1404–406). Although this scene does not explicitly depict homoerotic activity, Chaucer's use of both "daliance" and "pley" builds an undertone into this scene in which the friendship carries the electric charge of sexuality.

An interpretation of the erotic undertones to the relationship between the Friar's summoner and fiend depends on the sexual connotations both of "daliance" and "pley." In the Chaucerian canon, "daliance" appears eleven times, and of the ten instances other than the one quoted earlier, it carries the distinct connotation of sexual courtship and flirtation seven times.[31] In "The Wife of Bath's Prologue," "daliance" first appears as part of heteronormative courtship (260). Along with "richesse" (257), "shap" (258), "fairnesse" (258), and "gentillesse" (260), "daliance" is a quality that men desire in women. Later, Alison describes "daliance" as part of the courtship ritual that led to one of her many marriages: "Til trewely we hadde swich daliance, / This clerk and I, that of my purveiance / I spak to hym and seyde hym how that he, / If I were wydwe, sholde wedde me" (565–68). The word carries a similar meaning in "The Physician's Tale," in which the chaste Virginia refrains from appearing "at feestes, revels, and at daunces, / That been occasions of daliaunces" (65–66) in order to preserve her purity. In the short poem "To Rosemounde," which concludes with his own signature, Chaucer describes "daliaunce" as part of his flirtatious life when he thrice laments to Rosemounde that "ye to me ne do no daliaunce" (8, 16, 24). "Daliaunce" is found only once in "The General Prologue," and, appropriately enough, it refers to the Friar's own sexual licentiousness. The Friar, of course, is no sexual innocent:

> A FRERE ther was, a wantoune and a merye,
> A lymtour, a ful solempne man.
> In alle the ordres foure is noon that kan
> So muchel of daliaunce and fair langage.
> He hadde maad ful many a mariage
> Of yonge wommen at his owene cost. (208–213)

In these seven examples, "daliaunce" clearly carries a connotation of sexual flirtation. The remaining three references to "daliance" in Chaucer's works—in the "Prologue" to "The Tale of Sir Thopas" (704), the "Prologue" to "The Canon's Yeoman's Tale" (592), and *The Legend of Good Women* (F 356)—indicate the word's valence as sociability and social conversation. Nevertheless, the preponderance of evidence for Chaucer's use of the word "daliance," especially in its contextual connection to the Friar's own sexual transgressions, suggests a sexual understanding of its use in "The Friar's Tale."

In a manner similar to "daliance," the semantic range of "pley" certainly covers the sexual, as when in *Troilus and Criseyde* Pandarus tells Criseyde that he "koude. . .tell a thynge to doon yow pleye" (II: 121). In this line, Chaucer strikes several registers of the word "pleye," suggesting amusement, dramatic performance, and sexual intercourse. For Chaucer, both "daliance" and "pley" connote sexuality, even if they do not always denote it. The combination of both words in "The Friar's Tale," along with the fact that the Friar is surely incorporating the apparently queer friendship between the Summoner and the Pardoner in his tale, subtly indicates that the relationship between the summoner and the fiend exceeds the bounds of the heteronormative. In addition to the queer homosociality of this scene with its dalliance and play, the Friar also insults the Summoner through the comic climax of the fabliau, in which the old woman delivers the summoner to the devil both purposefully and inadvertently.[32]

In accordance with the Reeve's response to "The Miller's Tale," the Summoner feels greatly angered and insulted by "The Friar's Tale" with its combination of queer and unholy allegations. Chaucer describes him as barely able to control his rage: "This Somonour in his styropes hye stood; / Upon this Frere his herte was so wood / That lyk an aspen leef he quook for ire" (1665–67). Enraged, crazed, and quaking, the Summoner sees his tale as an opportunity to repay the Friar for the perceived insults of the preceding tale: "Syn ye han herd this false Frere lye, / As suffreth me I may my tale telle" (1670–71). Indeed, the Summoner is so upset by "The Friar's Tale" that the obscene elements, reserved for the fabliau proper by the Miller, the Reeve, and the Friar, prematurely seep into his "Prologue" with its description of a nest of friars in Satan's anus. The Summoner describes an angel who leads a friar to Satan and then commands the archfiend:

> "Shewe forth thyn ers, and lat the frere se
> Where is the nest of freres in this place!"
> And er that half a furlong wey of space,
> Right so as bees out swarmen from an hyve,
> Out of the develes ers ther gonne dryve
> Twenty thousand freres on a route,
> And thurghout helle swarmed al aboute,
> And comen agayn as faste as they may gon,
> And in his ers they crepten everychon. (1690–98)

In response to "The Friar's Tale," in which a summoner and a demon share a fraternal alliance with quiet undertones of sexuality, the Summoner presents a tableau of such a relationship pushed to its utmost extreme. The fiend of "The

Friar's Tale" becomes Satan himself, and the delicate hints that the relationship between the summoner and the demon bears some of the markers of sexual flirtation are transformed into the utmost parody of sodomitical intercourse. The penetration is not merely that of the male member, it is that of the male's entire body and his whole fraternal order. Building upon the Friar's depiction of an illicit relationship between an earthly religious hypocrite and a hellish fiend, the Summoner trumps the Friar before he even begins his tale.

The Summoner outplays the Friar in his "Prologue," but he reserves a final insult with queer innuendo for the tale itself. Thomas, in preparing to share his flatulence with Friar John, advises him "Now thanne, put in thyn hand doun my bak, /...and grope wel bihynde. / Bynethe my buttok there shaltow fynde / A thyng that I have hyd in pryvetee" (2140–44). The obvious question to ask is, of course, what does Friar John hope to find in the posterior nether regions of another man? His absolute greed leads him to "grope" Thomas's anus, when he should be "groping" the man's conscience, the very practice for which Friar John criticizes the curates ("Thise curatz been ful necligent and slowe / To grope tendrely a conscience / In shift" [1816–18]). Failing his duties as a friar, John finds himself excavating the buttocks of his flock rather than tending to their spiritual needs, and the discharge of flatulence is his just reward. Representing the Friar as John, the Summoner unmans his fellow pilgrim and enemy, the Friar, by depicting his allegorical equivalent attempting to fulfill his desires in a man's anus. In the pairs of queerly aggressive fabliaux, as swapped by the Miller and the Reeve and the Friar and the Summoner, the aggressive force of fabliau, coupled with the queering threats of cuckoldry, homosexuality, and sodomy, consistently highlight the ways in which men seek to exclude other men from heteronormative privilege.

When Women Queer, or How Heteronormative is Female Desire? The Fabliaux of the Cook, the Merchant, and the Shipman

In the male queer fabliaux, we see Chaucer's focus on aggressive men competing against one another with allegations of homosexual queerness in order to remove their enemies from the privileged position of heteronormativity; in contrast, the female queer fabliaux—"The Cook's Tale," "The Merchant's Tale," and "The Shipman's Tale"—evince little concern with masculine aggression and insults in the frames of these tales, and this lack of male aggression corresponds with a lack of homosexual imagery within the tales. That these tales focus less specifically on homosexuality, however, does not accord with less of a focus on queerness.[33] As distinct from the male queer fabliaux and their focus on male desires, the female queer fabliaux explore the limits of masculine heteronormativity in relation to female desires: rather than the homosexual jokes, images, and anxieties of the queer male fabliaux, we see in the female queer fabliaux a foreshadowing of Alison of Bath's call in her "Tale" for women's "sovereynetee / As wel over hir housbond as hir love, / And for to been in maistrie hym above" (1038–1040). Furthermore, building upon Lochrie's distinction between cuckoldry as an economic transaction between men and adultery as a woman's own activity, it becomes apparent that the three female queer fabliaux are more concerned with the humorous pleasures of women's adultery than with the aggressive humiliations associated with cuckoldry. Their queering edge arises from the desires of female characters inside the tale rather than from male aggression outside of it. Male humiliation motivates the four male queer fabliaux, but female sexuality as a desired end for its own humorous sake provides the impetus for these three tales. Another way to consider the difference among the fabliaux is that the male queer fabliaux establish a pilgrim as the butt of the joke; the female queer fabliaux contain jokes told for the fun of the telling, but no fellow pilgrim need receive the brunt of their aggressive humor. Masculine heteronormativity, constructed as controlling female desire and agency in "The Miller's Tale" and "The Reeve's Tale," crumbles in these tales, but without the blatant barbs of specifically homosexual queerness directed to a fellow pilgrim.

"The Cook's Tale," "The Merchant's Tale," and "The Shipman's Tale" are all told by male pilgrims who are aware of the limits of masculine heteronormativity but who are not engaged in aggressive tale-telling with other male pilgrims. The Cook appears to enjoy the telling of tales for the fun they provide, and in a notable contrast to the previous tale-tellers who exploited a sense of play to insult their enemies with malicious earnest, Roger rejects the potential seriousness of play and endorses a vision of play as its own end. When the Host tells him that "A man may seye ful sooth in game and pley" (4355), Roger responds, "sooth pley, quaad [bad] pley" (4357). Similar to the Cook, the Shipman's words also indicate that he seeks only ribald amusement with his tale, not to attack a fellow pilgrim with it:

> "And therfore, Hoost, I warne thee biforn,
> My joly body schal a tale telle,
> And I schal clynken you so mery a belle,
> That I schal waken al this compaignie.
> But it schal not ben of philosophie,
> Ne phislyas, ne termes queinte of lawe.
> Ther is but litel Latyn in my mawe!" (II: 1184–90)[34]

The Cook and the Shipman appear rowdily good-natured in their enjoyment of the Canterbury game. They do not seek to insult a fellow pilgrim and are thus uninterested in the aggressive tendency wit latent in the genre, but the fabliau is still an appropriate generic choice for their tales of bawdy humor.

The Merchant is likewise uninterested in narrative attacks. His "Prologue" highlights the fact that his fabliau will serve as an ironic commentary on the Clerk's story of Patient Grisilde, but the Merchant does not attack the Clerk personally. Indeed, if there were to be a butt of "The Merchant's Tale," it would likely be the Merchant himself due to his own marital troubles. When the Merchant agrees to tell his tale after the host's request, he replies, "Gladly...but of myn ownee soore, / For soory herte, I telle may namoore" (1243–44); these words indicate his deliberate move to deny an identification in his tale between January and himself and, thus, to separate his identity from that of his cuckolded character. The Merchant's melancholy "Prologue" may suggest a more melancholic tale, but his fabliau nevertheless offers ample comic reason to join him in lamenting marriage. The Cook's, Shipman's, and Merchant's motivations for telling fabliaux differ somewhat, but the shared motivation behind the Miller's, Reeve's, Friar's, and Summoner's fabliaux—humiliating and homosexually queering a rival male—is noticeably missing.

Free from exterior pressures of male–male aggression, the Cook's, Merchant's, and Shipman's depictions of adultery do not depict the male humiliation so evident in "The Miller's Tale" and "The Reeve's Tale"; these fabliaux focus more on the queering humor of a woman's adultery than on the humiliations of cuckoldry. The fragmented form of "The Cook's Tale" makes drawing definitive conclusions difficult, but that Perkyn Revelour's friend's wife is a prostitute virtually precludes that she could humiliate her husband through cuckoldry; since her occupation is widely known, he can hardly be concerned with fears of infidelity. Although prostitution may not be an ideal venue to express female sexual agency, it likely provides this character with more autonomy than Alison in "The Miller's Tale" and Symkyn's wife and daughter in "The Reeve's Tale," whose "seductions" strike some readers as bordering on rape.[35] "The Merchant's Tale" and "The Shipman's Tale" are even more definite in the absence of male humiliation: although May in "The Merchant's Tale" and the merchant's wife of "The Shipman's Tale" are adulteresses, January and the merchant do not suffer humiliation in the same manner as John in "The Miller's Tale" and Symkyn in "The Reeve's Tale" because neither man ever learns the truth of his deception. The heteronormative privileges of January and the merchant, at least from their own perspectives, are safely preserved by their ignorance at the conclusions of these tales.

This is not to suggest, however, that these female queer fabliaux are entirely free from homosocial aggression. Within the tales themselves, as in

"The Merchant's Tale" when January must literally face his squire's copulation with his wife, masculine competition nonetheless appears. Although the Merchant may not be engaged in an aggressive verbal combat with another man, the tale reflects his own queer anxieties about his place within heteronormativity due to his troubled marriage. Further, "The Cook's Tale" and "The Shipman's Tale" both contain latent male competition in their triangulated relationships of desire. These three fabliaux celebrate feminine transgression from normative constructions of fidelity in marriage, but recognizing their own flirtations with queer fears highlights Chaucer's polymorphous constructions of desire within his fabliaux. The female queer fabliaux depict men heterosexually queered out of their heteronormative privilege, but they do not contain queering allegations that bleed beyond the boundaries of the narratives. That the fabliaux as a group all focus on queering—whether heterosexually or homosexually—stresses the queer dynamics of Chaucerian fabliaux, in which sexual normativity is revealed to be the consistent goal of satire and ridicule.

In another telling contrast between the male and the female queer fabliaux, the latter delight in female sexuality in a manner in which the former do not. Whereas women serve as a means for other men to humiliate and embarrass their husbands in "The Miller's Tale" and "The Reeve's Tale" and play only supporting roles in "The Friar's Tale" and "The Summoner's Tale," women's desires, not men's desires, direct the plots of "The Merchant's Tale" and "The Shipman's Tale." The gruesome depictions of January's sexual performance (1821–65, 1946–66) align the audience's sympathies with May, and Chaucer then describes her plans to find her own sexual satisfaction:

> But sooth is this, how that this fresshe May
> Hath take swich impression that day
> Of pitee of this sike Damyan
> That from hire herte she ne dryve kan
> The remembrance for to doon hym ese. (1977–81)

May thus emerges as the protagonist of the tale as she moves to satisfy her own sexual desires. Likewise, the merchant's wife of "The Shipman's Tale," apparently caught by her husband in adultery, turns the tables on him with her subsequent articulation of their marital contract: "I am youre wyf; score it upon my taille, / And I schal paye as soon as ever I may" (415–16). May and the merchant's wife take a more active role in their adultery by making decisions about how and why to pursue their affairs and then concealing them from their husbands. Freed from the constraints of attacking their fellow pilgrims, "The Merchant's Tale" and "The Shipman's Tale" pay closer attention to a woman's desire for sexual and economic satisfaction than to a man's desire for revenge. These narratives focus not on homosexually queering men, but on celebrating the power of women to queer men from masculine heteronormative privilege. How heteronormative, then, is female desire? For the cuckolded husbands, female desire distressingly subverts male privilege; if normativity is predicated upon male desires, as the patriarchy of medieval culture indicates, female desire acting on its own volition, in and for itself, disrupts prevailing constructions of normativity.

Chaucer's fabliaux flirtatiously play with the queer when men fight and attempt to define their relationships to heteronormative ideology, but such tensions change in tone and content when other men tell fabliaux for the sheer sake of the genre's licentious fun by celebrating female sexuality. But what happens when the character most closely aligned to a fabliau ethos tells a tale of romance? When Alison of Bath narrates her romance, she has certainly learned the lesson of queering genres from the dueling narrative battles before her, and her great innovation lies in cloaking the aggression and hostility of her fabliau sensibility within the rarefied environs of the romance. This fabliau sensibility assists the Wife of Bath in her queering game of genres designed to realign male and female sexual and power positions, which is the subject of this chapter's next section.

Queering Genres, Battering Males: The Wife of Bath's Narrative Violence

Why does the Wife of Bath tell a romance?[36] This question is virtually a critical cliché, but for good reason: "The General Prologue," the pilgrims' prologues, and the narratives preceding her tale establish the expectation that Alison will tell a tale suited to her social class and vocation. As even the most casual reader of *The Canterbury Tales* cannot help but observe, the speaker of a tale generally chooses a genre that reflects his or her character: in the majority of the tales, the speaker's economic class or vocation relates at least peripherally to the genre of his/her tale.[37] The Wife of Bath, however, disrupts this pattern: although her "Prologue" establishes her as a bawdy and raucous figure, on a similar economic level of such other fabliau-tellers as the Miller and the Merchant, she breaks from her socioeconomic position to tell a romance rather than a fabliau. Furthermore, Alison's "Prologue" and "Tale" are virtually surrounded by fabliaux.[38] They must follow the texts of the introductory Fragment I, which contains the Miller's and the Reeve's fabliaux, and they immediately precede the fabliaux of Fragment III, "The Friar's Tale" and "The Summoner's Tale." Given her social position, her bawdy temperament, and her place in the overarching narrative of *The Canterbury Tales*, it seems much more likely that Alison would tell a fabliau than a romance.[39]

Indeed, scholarship has established that readers who are surprised by the Wife of Bath's romance and who expect her to tell a fabliau are perceptive to Chaucer's own authorial editing: "The Shipman's Tale," a fabliau, appears to have been Chaucer's first choice for Alison's tale, which he later replaced with a romance.[40] Helen Cooper observes the generic appropriateness of the fabliau for Alison and argues that the choice of a romance humanizes the bawdiness of her character: "The fabliau of 'The Shipman's Tale' that was apparently once intended for her, with its venal wife getting the better of her unsuspecting husband, would have been a more obvious fit. By giving her a romance, Chaucer adds another side to her character: she is an incurable romantic."[41] A more moderate view of Alison describes her as "an equalitarian moral revolutionary."[42] But can we really see the Wife of Bath either as an incurable romantic or as any type of moralist? Her utilitarian, sexually rapacious and economically motivated views of sex and marriage reveal her to be a lusty yet hard-minded woman, not a helpless romantic aquiver with lofty ideals of love.[43] Given her earthiness and her hungry focus on fulfilling her sexual appetites, Chaucer appears to be preparing Alison to narrate a tale matching her own lascivious lifestyle, but she then pulls the rug out from under her audience's feet.

Through this toying with readerly expectations of genre, Chaucer explores the tensions and fault lines of the courtly genre of romance when it is spoken by a character more appropriately located in the world of fabliau. The two genres oppose each other in virtually every feature: romances depict stories of courtly love and chivalry, set in the past, with noble characters engaging in noble actions; fabliaux offer tales of unlicensed sexuality, set in the present, with base characters acting basely. Crucial to my argument about Alison's manipulation of generic tropes is the fact that, within the fictions of the pilgrimage, men control all genres, including the fabliau (whose ethos she represents) and the romance (the genre she chooses), because only men have told tales prior to her. Alison defeats the romance and the men who represent a romantic ethos through the generic force of fabliau, and she assails the masculine bias both of romance and of fabliau to achieve this goal. By reconfiguring the tropes of romance and fabliau, she creates a safe space for women within the fabliau while simultaneously queering and ridiculing male desire within both genres.

Alison's deployment of genre as a rhetorical weapon indicates that the ostensibly simple matter of selecting a genre can reveal ulterior, if not downright hostile, motivations and that Chaucer exploits the generic aggression between fabliau and romance for its full comic potential, as well as for its subversiveness. As Laura Kendrick observes, Chaucer's use of the romance instead of the fabliau allows Alison to undermine patriarchal ideology much more powerfully than if she had told a fabliau: "By changing the sex of fatherly authority, the Wife of Bath reverses the usual order of things in the pathetic fiction of her gentle romance; in this way, she puts herself and all women on top in a more seriously subversive way than she might have done with the momentary comic reversal of a fabliau fiction such as 'The Shipman's Tale.' "[44] Building upon previous scholarly considerations of the nexus between the Wife of Bath and the fabliau and romance traditions, I articulate the ways that Alison constructs the genres of fabliau and romance in a manner to suit her own purposes in undermining patriarchal privilege. The Wife of Bath gains power both as a member of the storytelling audience and as a teller in her own right with her aggressive rhetoric. Through her participation in the construction of generic tropes, she privileges certain aspects of fabliau and undermines tropes of romance. Rather than waging her war with predetermined weapons, ones that would have been fashioned by the male tale-tellers prior to her and that would thus ultimately undermine her anti-patriarchal agenda, she creates new weapons through her aggressive reformulations of romance and fabliau. In her newly constructed genres, male narrative and rhetorical authority is queered such that masculinity itself no longer accords one immediate ideological privilege.

Replicating the generic tension between fabliau and romance through his depiction of bawdy Alison telling a courtly romance, Chaucer deploys not merely the oppositional relationship between fabliau and romance but the satirical edge of the fabliau as well. Melissa Furrow emphasizes the combative relationship between the two genres, noting that "Fabliau exists in a sort of adversarial relationship to romance, borrowing some of its trappings to make the kinship clearer: the same versification, the love-triangle, a judicious sprinkling of love vocabulary and conventional description, an occasional very specific parody of authorial boasts in prologues and concluding lines."[45] The fabliau and the romance thus appear to run on parallel tracks with the fabliau taking the low road of common characters indulging in bodily and bawdy intercourse while the romance takes the elevated road of aristocratic and courtly characters expressing ideal and pure love. From its lower position on these theoretical tracks, the fabliau, with its satirical edge, hurls its earthly contumely at the rarefied world of the romance.[46] Through its merciless satirizing of love, fabliau wields a harshly and humorously critical attack against its generic opposite, the romance. When put side by side, however, fabliau not only reveals the emptiness of romance; it has the potential to queer it as well. As romances privilege male desire, fabliaux often, although not always, undercut the heteronormative bias of masculine agency by placing a woman on top, both literally and figuratively.

As a representative of such a fabliau sensibility, the Wife of Bath adopts the rhetorical strategies of the fabliau to ridicule the pretensions of the romance, joining the force of rhetoric to the form of fabliau in order to express her disdain for a rarefied vision of love.[47] Although coming from a generic rather than a rhetorical perspective, my critical stance harmonizes with Barrie Ruth Straus's argument that Alison's "speech articulates the phallocentric conditions of the discourse within which she and her readership are constituted, and provides a critique of these patriarchal foundations of language."[48] The lusty Wife's deployment of genre is vocalized through rhetorical strategies; the combination of genre and rhetoric allows her to deflate the pretense of romance in the light of her own experiences with heterosexual relationships. As she refashions the fabliau and the romance, Alison can speak freely about the joys of sex and the limitations of love and reconstruct a feminine agency that has been mostly ignored by the previous tale-tellers.

To vocalize her views on sex and love, Alison exploits the possible freedoms of fabliau, a genre that offers female characters greater agency than does the romance. As Angela Weisl notes, the masculine bias of romance limits the potential of woman: "For all of its possibility for women, romance has a built-in 'glass ceiling.' Women may gain a measure of subjectivity and control, but they are ultimately controlled, either literally by the men (or male power structures) in the romance, or by the genre itself, while, oddly, controlling the genre, in the sense that without her, the romance cannot work as romance."[49] While fabliaux do not always offer a paradise of female agency to their protagonists, the outlook is generally more optimistic than in romance. Norris Lacy judiciously comments that fabliaux must be judged individually, that the genre has no overarching pro- or antifeminine ethos: "it is neither possible nor particularly important to decide whether the fabliaux are more antifeminist, or less so, than other genres. . . . What is crucial in dealing with the fabliaux. . . is to recognize and respect the autonomy of individual texts."[50] Such an approach is essential for Chaucerian fabliaux, in which women may be treated as chattel (as in the Miller's and the Reeve's fabliaux) or as their own independent sexual agents (as in the Merchant's and the Shipman's fabliaux). The Wife of Bath, a clarion voice of sexuality, belongs squarely in the latter camp of female protagonists. When Alison aligns herself with both Venus and Mars ("For certes, I am al Venerien / In feelynge, and myn herte is Marcien. / Venus me yaf my lust, my likerousnesse, / And Mars yaf me my sturdy hardynesse" [609–612]), she does not establish correlations either between Venus and the love of romance or between Mars and the violence of fabliau. Rather, lusty Venus and violent Mars converge in her fabliau spirit; with this alliance between Venus's unchecked sexuality and Mars's aggression, Alison mocks the pretensions of romance while zealously pursuing her own sexual agenda.[51]

Alison deflates the pretensions of romance by highlighting a critical difference in the attitudes toward love and sex between the romance and the fabliau: romances typically combine chaste love with the promise of sex, but fabliaux provide sexual activity with very little love—neither courtly nor romantic. Although one can certainly think of romances that feature sex and of fabliaux that include love, nevertheless, without digressing into the complete history of both genres, this generalization in terms of their entire narrative trajectories is undoubtedly true in relation to the Canterbury narratives—both the romances and the fabliaux—that precede Alison's. Alison is often viewed as a hopeless romantic due to her many marriages and her telling of a romance, yet it is critical to separate her views of love from her views of sex. She is a vocal and vociferous supporter of sexual relations, but her advocacy of love is much more muted: being married five times may suggest romantic love, but it certainly does not prove it. Critical responses to Alison have at times downplayed her rampant sexuality, as when Mary Carruthers suggests that the "important spoils [of the marriage bed] for her are neither children nor sensual gratification but independence."[52] Alison's frequent attention to female genitalia, however, suggests that she views the marriage bed as a means to achieve both independence and sensual gratification. The effort to desexualize Alison appears also in Catherine Cox's analysis of her glossing, as she concludes that Alison's " 'bele chose' is her 'pleye' of language, not the play of her female anatomy."[53] Could it not be the play of both?

By locating Alison within a feminized fabliau tradition, we uncover the greater importance of sex than love for her; from this perspective, we can view her romance in a way that does not require the delightfully vulgar heroine to become the proponent of an overidealized view of love. Alison endorses the position that marriages should be ruled by women, despite the admonitions of such critics as James Winny that "To see the Wife simply as the exponent of an arch-feminist view of womanly sovereignty in marriage...is to accept an unadventurously literal reading of a richly imaginative work."[54] On the contrary, decoding Alison's deployment of the generic tension between romance and fabliau underscores her comic brilliance and her strong proto-feminism, allowing us to see more clearly how she articulates the virtually impossible goal of female agency in a world of nearly unchecked medieval misogyny.[55] By queering male desire out of heteronormativity and into ridiculousness in both genres, Alison leaves male sexuality no narrative foothold in either genre for her fellow Canterbury pilgrims.

Alison's Feminist Reconstruction of the Fabliau and Queering of Male Desire in Her "Prologue"

Although readers have many excellent reasons to expect Alison to tell a fabliau rather than a romance, Chaucer has a queering reason for her not to tell a bawdy tale. The fabliaux preceding Alison's "Prologue" serve as the location of an aggressive form of male sexual desire; female sexual desire, if depicted at all, appears in a secondary role. Indeed, as previously mentioned, male sexual desire is so privileged that its fulfillment can take the appearance of rape. Alison of "The Miller's Tale" soon acquiesces to Nicholas's advances, but her initial resistance proves troubling to some readers, as does the fact that the female characters of "The Reeve's Tale" do not consent to intercourse with the clerks. Prior to Alison's "Prologue" and "Tale," fabliau appears to be a man's genre for the pilgrims of *The Canterbury Tales*. Alison's savvy storytelling, however, inverts the generic construction of fabliau as masculine by claiming for herself the sexual pleasures of a fabliau ethos. Likewise for romance, Palamon's and Arcite's male sexual desire is privileged over Emily's in "The Knight's Tale" and, although "The Miller's Tale" undercuts the genre of romance in its degradation and parody of courtly love into fabliau sex, male desire still asserts itself as the privileged agent. Through Alison, Chaucer allows female agency to queer genres and to batter back against the narrative violence inflicted upon women in the preceding romances and fabliaux. Thus, Alison's queerness emerges, somewhat paradoxically, in her unapologetic enjoyment of heterosexual intercourse, and the queering force of her rhetoric depends largely on positioning her male audience into a position of narrative emasculation, in which the power of masculinist generic rhetoric has been stolen from them.

In the fabliaux prior to Alison's "Prologue" and "Tale," masculine desire, as expressed both through the sexual conquest of female characters and through the humiliation of the male rival for a woman, reveals itself through sexual conquest. In response, Alison reconfigures sex as a privileged space of female agency by reclaiming its generic sensibilities as belonging to a feminine sphere. Certainly, Alison's views of sexuality align her voice with the fabliau, and her concentration on sexuality over romantic love contributes greatly to the fabliau spirit of her "Prologue." Having mastered five previous husbands and preparing for the sixth when he appears, she vows that "For sothe, I wol nat kepe me chaast in al" (46), a pledge that in itself removes her from the refined and idealized worlds of courtly romance and distances her from the generic ideal of woman in romance as exemplified by Emily in "The Knight's Tale" and Custance in "The Man of Law's Tale."[56] Her candid descriptions of the commercial aspects of marital sexual relations reveal a woman who sees through the promises of courtly love featured in romance:

"I wolde no lenger in the bed abyde,
If that I felte his arm over my syde,

> Til he had maad his raunson unto me;
> Thanne wolde I suffre hym do his nycetee.
> And therfore every man this tale I telle,
> Wynne whoso may, for al is for to selle." (409–414)

This blatant consumerist impulse of self-prostitution in marriage showcases the Wife of Bath's exploitative views of sexuality; she sees through the poetry of courtly love to the raw economics underneath.[57] "The Reeve's Tale" establishes the potential of economic gain for men through unbridled fabliau sexuality, as Maline shares with Allen the secret of the stolen grain; Alison reconceptualizes this aspect of the fabliau within her self-construction in her "Prologue." Beyond the economic dimension of this scene, Alison queers the masculine ethos from the contours of romance by subverting male sexual control. Male desire may not be queered here, as it remains heteronormative, but female desires—whether sexual or economic—now are asserted as well, a factor that was ignored in all tales prior to hers.

Alison's economic motivations for sexual activity are but one sign that she sees love as so much trifling nonsense, and a quick survey of her "Prologue" demonstrates that she consistently privileges fabliau sex over romantic love as a tactic in queering heteronormativity. She envies Solomon because of the "myrie fit" (42) he finds on each of his wedding nights ("As wolde God it leveful were unto me / To be refresshed half so ofte as he!" [37–38]). This wish suggests that Alison's sexual relationships with her husbands are of greater concern to her than her love for them, as does her repeated insistence that men must pay their marital debts: "Why sholde men elles in hir bookes sette / That man shal yelde to his wyf hire dette?" (129–30). Her "instrument" (149), which she promises to use "As frely as my Makere hath it sent" (150), demands constant attention, and Alison is determined that "Myn housbonde shal it have bothe eve and morwe, / Whan that hym list come forth and paye his dette" (152–53). Unfortunately, a bountiful supply of husbands does not necessarily correlate with a fulfilling sex life, and Alison suffers no compunction in detailing the sexual failures of her previous husbands:

> "The thre were goode men, and riche, and olde;
> Unnethe myghte they the statut holde
> In which that they were bounden unto me.
> Ye woot well what I meene of this, pardee!
> As help me God, I laughe whan I thynke
> How pitously a-nyght I made hem swynke!" (197–202)

Publicly humiliating these men for their inadequate sexual performances, Alison laughs at their failures to fulfill their sexual obligations to her.

Through this queering focus both on male humiliation at the hands of female sexuality and its concomitant emasculation of male desire, Alison's garrulousness in detailing her husbands' failings in the marital bed denies male sexuality its privileged position within masculinist heteronormativity.

The blunt focus on penises and vaginas also marks the highly sexualized charge of Alison's fabliau world.[58] Her focus on marital relationships stresses the anatomical over the emotional, as she records her husbands' compliment that "And trewely, as myne housbondes tolde me, / I hadde the beste *quoniam* myghte be" (607–608). In harmony with this positive endorsement of her genitalia, she praises the male member when she describes her husbands as those whom she "pyked out the beste, / Bothe of here nether purs and of here cheste" (44a–b). Purse and chest ostensibly refer to her husbands' wealth, but the location of the purse in the nether regions suggests a euphemism for the male genitalia, especially since purse and pouch serve as metaphoric descriptions of the male groin in other Chaucerian passages.[59] Throughout Alison's "Prologue," the fabliau elements of sexuality focus on female desires rather than masculine ones. Due to the failure of male desire to assert itself, it atrophies through generic disuse. In the fabliau world of Alison's "Prologue," the genre has been so thoroughly queered that male sexual agency withers in retreat.

No hint of courtly love, except in parodies, appears within the fabliaux preceding the Wife of Bath's "Prologue," but Alison reconfigures the borders between romance and fabliau by situating courtly love, as depicted in "The Knight's Tale," as a masculine arena now exploitable and queerable by women within her "Prologue" celebrating a fabliau sensibility. In the Wife's world, men represent easily exploitable emotional patsies caught up in the swirl of love:

> "They had me yeven hir lond and hir tresoor;
> Me neded nat do lenger diligence
> To wynne hir love, or doon hem reverence.
> They loved me so wel, by God above,
> That I ne tolde no deyntee of hir love!
> A wys womman wol bisye hire evere in oon
> To gete hire love, ye, ther as she hath noon." (204–210)

This passage stresses the ease with which Alison wins men's love, but it does not indicate that she loves them in return; rather, she disparages their affections. We again see her concern with economic gain by ensnaring a man, but she does not mention her emotional involvement in the process. Here masculine romantic love belongs to but is not reciprocated by a fabliau woman; she will exploit it, but not return it.

Even when Alison mentions love in reference to her own sexual life, it seems more likely that she nonetheless means what today we would interpret as "sex."[60] In one of her self-serving moments of approving written authority, Alison quotes Scripture to assert her right over her husband's body: "I have the power durynge al my lyf / Upon his propre body, and noght he. / Right thus the Apostel tolde it unto me, / And bad oure housbondes for to love us weel" (158–61). Deciphering Alison's meaning in the word "love" here is tricky, but reading with, not against, her fabliau character would indicate that she means intercourse rather than emotional involvement or, at least, that she invokes both sexual and affective registers of the word. Because her claim to her husband's body is tied to a man's paying of his marital debt, a sexual rather than emotional interpretation of love builds strongly upon her fabliau conception of heterosexual relationships.[61]

Alison rarely mentions her love for men, but if she does, she privileges sex over love when she describes how she loves with no discretion but follows her own bodily appetites: "I ne loved nevere by no discrecioun, / But evere folwede myn appetit" (622–23). The Wife establishes that her bodily cravings lead her to love, but these fleshly appetites do not discriminate and become another sign of her irrepressible sexuality. She proceeds to describe her egalitarian nature in the pursuit of men: "Al were he short, or long, or blak, or whit; / I tok no kep, so that he liked me, / How poore he was, ne eek of what degree" (624–26). Of all the many men in her life, Alison speaks of love only in relation to Jankyn. She reports that she "hadde of hym so greet chiertee" (396) and "took [him] for love, and no richesse" (526). Still, the love that she describes here is strongly tied to his sexual performance, as she reports that "Whan that he wolde han my *bele chose*, / That thogh he hadde me bete on every bon, / He koude wynne agayn my love anon" (510–12). Her descriptions of him enflame her desires more than her love, even when directed at his legs and feet: "me thoughte he hadde a paire / Of legges and of feet so clene and faire / That al myn herte I yaf unto his hoold" (597–99). The lascivious pleasures of her gaze reconstruct and queer the masculine bias of scopophilic pleasures, as Jankyn loses the privileges of the male subject and metamorphoses into a feminized object.

In fabliaux, marriages often fail to maintain any standard of conjugal bliss, and the Wife of Bath's marriage to Jankyn similarly highlights the comic valence of fabliau marriages that queer heteronormative masculinity when they fight over his misogynist reading.[62] The description of the battle first stresses its violence:

> "I with my fest so took hym on the cheke
> That in oure fyr he fil bakward adoun.
> And he up stirte as dooth a wood leoun,

And with his fest he smoot me on the heed
That in the floor I lay as I were deed." (792–96)

The brutal physicality of the fight subsides and its humor emerges when Alison, after having been knocked unconscious, promises to forgive Jankyn before she dies. Jankyn falls for her trick, and, instead of receiving the promised kiss of atonement and reconciliation, is rewarded with the battle's renewal: "And yet eftsoones I hitte hym on the cheke" (808). Luring Jankyn in for a sucker punch, Alison changes the tone of the scene from the horror of domestic violence to the humor of fabliau fun. This comic violence establishes Alison's rule in her fabliau household; she is the winner and thus the ruler, as Jankyn concedes "Myn owene trewe wyf, / Do as thee lust the terme of al thy lyf; / Keep thyn honour, and keep eek myn estaat" (819–21). The comic valence of this scene as fabliau is obvious, but, as I discuss later, Chaucer here foreshadows Alison's final rejection and queering of romance with the rhetorical "sucker punch" of her closing curse to end her romance. And though this scene is comic, its valence as earnest, as the typically Chaucerian play that conceals serious motivations, should not be overlooked, as Jankyn is thoroughly queered from his heteronormative privilege while his wife assumes mastery over their home.

In addition to describing her own life with the generic tropes of the fabliau, the Wife of Bath suffuses her worldview with fabliau thoughts and themes that queer masculine privilege. One particular fabliau theme that Alison alludes to in her "Prologue" is the threat of cuckoldry, which women bring to marriages with old men:

"The clerk, whan he is oold, and may noght do
Of Venus werkes worth his olde sho,
Thanne sit he doun, and writ in his dotage
That wommen kan nat kepe hir mariage!" (707–710)

Chaucer uses this theme as the central conflict in "The Merchant's Tale," as May cuckolds Januarie. The humor that Chaucer finds in cuckoldry further establishes Alison's place in a fabliau and queering world of sex. Indeed, in the metaphor of a man lighting his phallic candle in another man's lantern, Alison demands that sexual activity be abundantly shared: "Ye shul have queynte right ynogh at eve. / He is to greet a nygard that wolde werne / A man to lighte a candle at his lanterne" (332–34).[63] Building on this lesson, the Wife points out that "He shal have never the lasse light, pardee. / Have thou ynogh, thee thar nat pleyne thee" (335–36). An adulterous wife does not necessitate that a husband will receive less sex himself, but the husband is again queered of his heteronormative privilege of regulating female sexuality. The relevance of this passage to Alison's own life is revealed both when she confesses that she finds "many a myrthe" (399) while "walkynge out by nyghte" (397) and when she asks, "Is it for ye wolde have my queynte allone?" (444).[64] The answer, though left unstated except in the outrageous sarcasm of the following lines, strips men of their patriarchal (and generic) control of female sexuality.

The crucial difference between Alison's fabliau ethos and those of the Miller and Reeve is her reconfiguring of the fabliau spirit as a celebration of female rather than male sexuality. Through this construction of Alison as representing a fabliau ethos and then by giving this fabliau wife a tale of romance, Chaucer prepares the reader for his satire of the trappings and pretensions of the entire courtly genre. In this instance of a romance being narrated by a woman with a fabliau sensibility, the humor of her fabliau ethos trumps the niceties of the romance. Moreover, we should be prepared for just such a tactic on Alison's part, as she warns her fellow pilgrims that she is toying with them. We know that play stands as her chief goal in telling her story: when the Pardoner asks Alison to "teche us yonge men of youre praktike" (187), she replies that, although she will be happy to do so, she hopes that they will not take offense at her words. Her tale, after all, is mere play:

> "But yet I praye to al this compaignye,
> If that I speke after my fantasye,
> As taketh not agrief of that I seye,
> For myn entente nys but for to pleye." (189–92)

We must read her romance as play rather than as an actual reflection of her own desires, as a decided effort at humor and fun in which she reconfigures the meanings of the romance genre. Within the play of the tale, however, she conceals the queering truth of her reformulated genres. Given the fabliaux that surround her "Tale" and the fabliau spirit of rampant sexuality throughout her "Prologue," the true fun of the Wife of Bath's romance is spotting her fabliau spirit degrading the tale and queering the male as she tells it.

The Subversion of Romance and the Triumph of Fabliau: Alison's Queering Genres

The genre play evident in "The Wife of Bath's Tale" establishes a queering dissolution of hermeneutic stability.[65] In the opening of her romance, Alison vacillates between romance and fabliau, and the fabliau elements appear poised to highjack the tale. The romance begins appropriately with

"In th'olde dayes of the Kyng Arthour, / Of which that Britons speken greet honour" (857–58). Alison then hybridizes her romance with fairy tale elements: "Al was this land fulfild of fayerye" (859), and she also includes fabliau elements through the multitude of friars. Sexually motivated friars and other such religious figures are stock characters in fabliaux, and the vast number of friars in this tale ("As thikke as motes in the sonne-beem" [868]) appears to be moving the tale from fairy-tale romance to fabliau. Chaucer further underscores the potential generic move to fabliau through the sexual threat posed by these friars: "Ther is noon oother incubus but he, / And he ne wol doon hem but dishonour" (880–81).[66] A brigade of fornicating friars belongs clearly to the world of fabliau, but Alison then proceeds with her romance. She refrains her fabliau spirit from taking over the romance, but it lurks in the background of the tale; the reader senses that these friars or some other representation of Alison's fabliau sensibility should emerge before she finishes her romance to queer the violent incarnation of male desire as represented by the rapist knight.[67]

After the intrusion of these fabliau friars, Alison returns to the romance with the violence of rape. In "The Miller's Tale" and "The Reeve's Tale," fabliau sexuality threatens women with sex that can very closely resemble rape; here Alison reconfigures the meaning of rape and genre by situating the threat of sexual violence within the world of romance. Given this opening violation of a woman, the romance turns out to be not quite as misogynist as one might expect: the women of Arthur's court decide the knight's fate, he searches for the secret of what women most desire, a woman extricates him from his dire dilemma, and they marry despite his extreme hesitations. Marc Glasser outlines the changes in this scene between the tale and its Middle English analogues, concluding that "Chaucer's 'Tale' contains greater coercion to marry than any of the analogues. This increased coercion is appropriate for a tale told by the Wife of Bath because her 'Prologue' shows that her marriages have been relationships in which each spouse has struggled to dominate the other."[68] This increased coercion strongly queers the rapist knight, as his agency becomes more and more constricted throughout the narrative.

In the process of queering the knight, his new wife presents him with the famed marital dilemma—to have her ugly and faithful or beautiful and adulterous; he cedes the decision to her, and the romance ends in a marriage of supposed equality.[69] This ending, however, does not correspond with Alison's own experiences, as she won mastery over—not equality with—Jankyn. After Jankyn concedes that he should follow her pleasures (819–21, quoted previously), Alison reports that "After that day we hadden never debaat. / God helpe me so, I was to hym as kynde / As any wyf from Denmark unto Ynde" (822–24). In contrast, the knight's bride cedes her authority to the point of life and death ("Dooth with my lyf and deth right as yow lest" [1248]) and succumbs to the point of complete subservience ("And she obeyed hym in every thyng" [1255]). From the perspective of her queering "Prologue," could the pushy Wife of Bath really see this ending of her romance as appropriate, just, or praiseworthy? Given the many similarities between her "Prologue" and "Tale," with their knowing wives and ignorant husbands, why does the ending of the "Tale" diverge so meekly into exhortations to female subservience? After constricting and queering male agency as punishment for rape to the point that he cedes patriarchal privilege to his new wife, the woman's decision to cede her authority back to him is, at the very least, disappointing to anyone wary of rapists wielding the ideological power of heteronormative privilege.

The final lines of "The Wife of Bath's Tale" appear not only inconsistent with Alison's thought, but completely dichotomous as well, due to the tension between its encomium to wedded bliss and its curse of unyielding and uncooperative husbands. Alison speaks in two voices here, the mellifluous (if not saccharine) tones of romance and the strident tones of fabliau:

> "And thus they lyve unto hir lyves ende
> In parfit joye; and Jhesu Crist us sende
> Housbondes meeke, yonge, and fressh abedde,
> And grace t'overbyde hem that we wedde;
> And eek I praye Jhesu shorte hir lyves
> That noght wol be governed by hir wyves;
> And olde and angry nygardes of dispence,
> God sende hem soone verray pestilence!" (1257–64)

If we read the Wife of Bath's romance through the lens of fabliau, the hermeneutic focus switches from the romance's blessing of an unrealistically ideal marriage to the fabliau's curse. Louise Fradenburg declares that "The Wife of Bath's curse reinvokes the fabliau register, the world of the 'Prologue,' and thus undoes the tale's magic with the ugly truth of everyday reality."[70] Why, however, should we read this moment as registering an "ugly truth"? Alison prospers in her earthly world, reveling in her sexuality and never subjecting herself to patriarchal authority. The rejection of romance allows her to articulate a more realistic yet nonetheless satisfying account of the troubles women face with men: if men are not appropriately governed by their wives, if men do not contribute to women's sexual satisfaction, if men commit acts of violence against women, then men deserve nothing more than God's pestilence and to be queered both generically and narratively from their positions of privilege.

The fabliau register of the curse gives Alison her voice back, a voice she allowed to be highjacked by romance so that she could steal it back all the more forcefully at the tale's conclusion. Simply stated, the romance's blessing does not sound like the Alison of the "Prologue"; such lofty sentiments were never expressed by her in her fabliau-inspired description of the woes and sexual blisses that marriage may bring. The curse brings back Alison's voice in its direct and fearless call for Jesus's anathema. Chaucer uses the line "And eek I praye Jhesu to shorte hir lyves" (1261) to establish Alison's assessment of her romance because it is almost a direct quotation from her "Prologue": "O leeve sire shrewe, Jhesu shorte thy lyf! / Yet prechestow and seyst an hateful wyf / Yrekened is for oon of thise meschances" (365–67). The blessing of marriage belongs to Alison's story, not to her voice; the curse is her own. As such, we should accept it as her final words on her tale.

The Wife of Bath deploys the romance in order to undercut it at its conclusion, and by so doing, she queers the genre, with its concomitant male privilege, from heteronormativity. These goals are realized both through the fabliau sensibility she evinces throughout her "Prologue" and through her skills as a reader and glosser.[71] In the beginning of her "Prologue," we see that she can adopt Scripture to her own purposes with her famous opening declaration that "Experience, though noon auctoritee / Were in this world, is right ynogh for me / To speke of wo that is in mariage" (1–3). Alison proceeds to explicate biblical passages in a manner to suit her own purposes, as when she reports that Jesus criticized multiple marriages to the Samaritan woman; to this biblical account, however, the Wife of Bath plays dumb: "What that he mente therby, I kan nat seyn" (20). She chooses deliberately what she desires to understand, much preferring God's instruction "to wex and multiplye" (28), an order "[t]hat...kan I wel understonde" (29). Likewise, as she quotes Scripture to her own ends, Alison deploys the genre of romance to set up her own unique interpretation of it. Peggy Knapp argues, "The Wife sees textual production and interpretation as deeply aligned with institutional interests...In her view, glosses may lie by covering over unacceptable features in 'naked texts.'"[72] As she reconfigures the texts of Scripture to suit her needs, so she deploys the genre of romance to argue to her own purpose in the final moment. All the romance leads to the punchline—and the truth—of her curse. As Alison lures Jankyn to her fist during their fight, throwing him a sucker punch when he least expects it, she delivers her concluding curse in a similar manner: the punch that is Jankyn's due for his misogyny metamorphoses into the fabliau punchline of the curse. She seduces the primarily male audience of pilgrims into expecting a romantic end to her tale in which her riotous femininity appears tamed, only to wallop them with her final words.

A queering fabliau interpretation of the Wife of Bath's romance allows for a more optimistic view of Alison's transgressive capabilities. For many critics, the generic constraints of romance eventually ensnare the bawdy woman; Susan Crane elegantly summarizes the social bind for women that, in her opinion, ultimately captures Alison:

> The festive sexuality that pervades her performance celebrates the transgressive potential of women's sovereignty but also expresses sovereignty as seized power rather than sanctioned authority. Alison's restless metamorphoses, from antifeminist creation to romancer to clerical scholar and back to militant wife in her envoy, emphasizes that each tradition on which she draws denies women authority.[73]

R.W. Hanning likewise sees Alison, in the end, as conquered by her texts: "For all her advocacy of 'maistrye,' Alison of Bath demonstrates again and again the subjection of herself and her sex to the tyrannical harassment of text and gloss."[74] Fabliau, however, offers female agency more freedom than scriptural tradition or romance. One need think only of Chaucer's "The Merchant's Tale" or "The Shipman's Tale" to place Alison in the context of women striving and succeeding to satisfy their own sexual goals. Fabliaux may not be an ideal home for women, but in them, they are accorded a better chance of independently expressing and acting on their human sexual desires. As a participant in the construction of genres, Alison creates them to fulfill her desires; her reconceived genres that queer masculinity and promote feminine agency influence the remainder of *The Canterbury Tales* in more than a momentary reversal.

At the very least, scholars must no longer ignore, dismiss, or gloss over her curse. Robert Meyer argues that the end of Alison's romance concludes that "a relationship of mutual submission—fidelity, humility, and obedience—is what wise men and wise women should desire most" and summarizes that "A true ironist, [Alison] has protested the imperfections of love; a true romancer, she has articulated an ideal."[75] I do not see Alison as such a romantic figure, but I do agree that she is a true ironist, and it is in her ironic position protesting the falsities of love that she ends her tale. Her final words undercut the entire romance that has gone before and queer the genre of romance to meaninglessness.

The Friar's response to Alison supports this fabliau interpretation of her romance, as he senses that the play that she promised in her romance has disappeared. And indeed, her closing call for God's pestilence, in light of fourteenth-century concerns with the vast number of people lost horribly and gruesomely to the plague, suggests that her curse bears a shockingly aggressive rhetorical force, one that attacks with the violence of a nearly physical blow.[76] The Friar thus reminds her that "But, dame, heere as we ryde by the weye, / Us nedeth nat to speken but of game" (1274–75) before promising that "I wol yow of a somonour telle a game" (1279). In a typical

Chaucerian irony, the Friar's "game" in his tale is both hilarious in itself yet a serious attack against his enemy the Summoner. Alison's romance functions on a similar level: it is a romance with all of the trappings of the genre, but she switches from the play of fantasy to the utter seriousness of her curse both against husbands who would control the lives of their wives and against male pilgrims who are complicit in the privileges of patriarchy. The Friar's reminder that she only need speak in game strongly suggests that Alison leaves the play of her romance for the reality of her curse, a curse that the male audience, as represented by the sexually amorous Friar, sees directed at itself. The even greater irony of Alison's queerings of romance and fabliau is that the fabliau, a comic and vibrant genre easily construed as play, metamorphoses into a serious vision of the woman on top and man on a queered bottom. The humor and play of her fabliau spirit seduces the audience into believing the Wife capable of only fun and fantasy; through the return of her fabliau sensibility where it least belongs—in the courtly world of romance—the fabliau vision of female supremacy blossoms from momentary fun to lasting vision.

Crucial to Alison's success in her reformulations of the fabliau is that it metamorphoses into a more welcoming arena for female sexuality and queered masculinity in the subsequent fabliaux of the Canterbury pilgrimage. Although the Friar's and Summoner's fabliaux are mostly unconcerned with female sexuality, "The Merchant's Tale" and "The Shipman's Tale" build upon Alison's creation of the fabliau as a playing field of female sexual agency. As noted earlier in this chapter, May in "The Merchant's Tale" and the merchant's wife in "The Shipman's Tale" display greater control of their sexual objectives than the female characters of "The Miller's Tale" and "The Reeve's Tale." Alison rebuilds a fabliau ethos to suit her own needs, and Chaucer continues to depict how the pilgrims react to one another's tales by their mutual reworkings of generic conventions. As participating members of a genre community, the Merchant and the Shipman narrate tales congruent with the model of subversive feminine sexuality that Alison propagates. Her revisioning of the genre becomes the last word on the subject; at the very least, most female and queer readers have more to celebrate in Chaucer's later fabliaux than in the earlier ones, which suggests his attention to the evolution of the genre within the overarching narrative.

In the end, it appears that Chaucer allows the Wife of Bath to vocalize his own dislike for the romance tradition, to denounce it as so much ridiculousness through her curse. Chaucer's distaste for Arthurian romance may not be an overriding concern of his authorial stance, but it is certainly a noticeable one: D.S. Brewer comments, "Not narrator nor narrators but Chaucer the poet derides Arthurian romance—it is one of his constant and notable though minor traits."[77] Sarah Disbrow agrees, pointing out that

"The fact that only the Wife of Bath tells an Arthurian tale, and that the Arthurian references to Gawain and Lancelot in 'The Squire's Tale' and to the story of Lancelot of the Lake in 'The Nun's Priest's Tale' are ironic, provides further evidence that Chaucer rejected Arthurian romance in favor of epic and saints' lives when he came to make an unambiguous representation of heroism."[78] Two of the remaining romances of the pilgrimage—"The Squire's Tale" and Chaucer's "Tale of Sir Thopas"—ridicule male narrative authority, and "The Franklin's Tale" depicts a world of great gentility yet one in which male control of female sexuality is tentative and under duress. Reading the Wife of Bath's romance through her fabliau spirit, we see that this instance of Chaucer's Arthurian romance is the most ironic, as well as the most queering of heteronormative masculine identity, of them all.

Chaucer's fabliaux and the Wife of Bath's "Prologue" and "Tale" reveal the deep anxieties aroused by the queer, the fear of unmanning, and the intense antagonism underneath the surface of the homosocial. These pilgrims may not be able to play nicely, but therein lies the seething fun of the fabliau, based squarely on the fear of the queer and the slipperiness of heteronormative identity. And as Alison demonstrates, queering genres serves as an ideal tactic for expressing feminine agency within a dominantly masculine discourse. Queering genres, both fabliau and romance, allows these pilgrims to expose the perils of heteronormativity, which can rarely be adequately shored up against the onslaughts of the queer.

CHAPTER 4

QUEERING TRAGEDY: QUEER DESIRES AND
QUEERING GENRES IN CHAUCER'S
TROILUS AND CRISEYDE

The manifold pleasures of reading Chaucer's *Troilus and Criseyde* arise, in good measure, due to the lack of sexual stability and generic cohesion throughout the text. Readers seeking firm interpretive purchase, either through an understanding of the conflicting motivations of Troilus, Criseyde, and Pandarus in pursuing the game of love or through the expectations of generic form, will likely find their desires repeatedly frustrated; in the end, the reader must concede the vast unknowability of the narrative. In this chapter, I explore the ways in which Chaucer presents these pleasures through the amorphousness both of sexual and of generic desires. With Pandarus as a queer destabilizer of normativity in sexuality and in genre, *Troilus and Criseyde* confronts the reader with the limitations of prevailing sexual and narrative ideologies and ultimately highlights the arbitrariness of its characters' fortunes.

In the first section of this chapter, I analyze Pandarus as a representative of a queering sensibility in terms of his own sexual desires. To unravel the queer complexities of Pandarus's desires, I address the question of heteronormative analysis and undermine a "straight" reading of Pandarus through the destabilizing force of medieval conceptions of gender and sexuality. Once Pandarus is defamiliarized and deconstructed from ostensible masculine heteronormativity, the multiple layers of his speeches and silences further make possible a queer reading of the character. Reading both what he says and what he does not say, we see that Pandarus alternatively speaks and keeps silent about his desires; despite frequent allusions to these desires, they nevertheless remain occluded from full view. Hermeneutic scholarship has taught readers to pay close attention to the ways in which textual silences paradoxically speak, and Pandarus's silences at key moments in the text compel the reader to participate in the construction of his character. As part of this analysis, I also examine the queerness of Pandarus's gaze in which he brings sexual satisfaction to himself through the staging of scenes designed for his pleasure. What does Pandarus gain through his pandering of Troilus, and what does Chaucer gain by having the pander proceed so queerly? Ultimately, Pandarus's queer friendship, like Criseyde's love and all other earthly things, fails Troilus; this failure, however, provides the impetus for Troilus's apotheosis and subsequent realization of the futility of all earthly endeavors.

In this chapter's second section, I explore the ways in which Pandarus's sexual ambiguity corrupts generic codes, and, through this corruption, the reader is denied the comforts of a pat meaning to a polyvalent text. At the poem's conclusion, readers who desire a soothing moral to the complex emotional and spiritual conundrums engendered both by Troilus and Criseyde's love and by Pandarus's pandering discover the dissolution of generic form, which frustrates attempts to find easy meanings in earthly loves and human genres. As Pandarus's sexuality is unknowable, as the text's ostensible genre of tragedy is multiform to the point of meaninglessness, this insistent refusal of meaning punctures easy answers to the text's deep questions about the significance of life on earth and of death in the eighth sphere. If *Troilus and Criseyde* upholds Christian teleology in its closing demand that the reader embrace Christ, the path that Pandarus constructs to take us there is a queer one indeed.

Queer Pandarus? Silence, Sexual Ambiguity, and the Pandering of Courtly Love

Is Pandarus queer? I freely admit that I have uncovered no conclusive evidence to support an argument that he is queer, if by "queer" one means "homosexual."[1] Through the ensuing analysis, no smoking gun materializes to convince the critic resistant to the assertion that Pandarus may be read as homosexual; nonetheless, his flaunting of normativity encourages the reader to examine this character with a decidedly queer eye. I explore this issue here, although my objective is to prove neither that Pandarus loves Troilus in a sexual manner nor that their overtly homosocial relationship is latently homosexual.[2] The text neither presents them as lovers nor insists that their homosocial relationship be read as homoerotic. Rather, *Troilus and Criseyde* refuses to disallow a queer reading of Pandarus's desires, in terms of his relationships both with Troilus and with Criseyde. Obviously, Pandarus and Troilus do not have sex, yet a great deal of mutual male affection characterizes their intense friendship. The question of whether

Pandarus engages in a sexual liaison with Criseyde is even murkier, as many readers detect shades of incest in their interactions. Beryl Rowland interprets Pandarus as a bisexual pimp, which casts him directly within the realm of the nonnormative and the queer, both in terms of his sexual desires and in terms of his position vis-à-vis courtly love.[3] Reading Pandarus through a lens of queerness, although it offers vast insights into his character, fails to answer fully the many questions readers have about him, and it is this queer unknowability that readers must confront as they ponder his occluded desires.

Whom or what does Pandarus desire? *Troilus and Criseyde* does not present Pandarus as a successful lover, but desires—homosocial, heterosocial, and queer—remain firmly in the background of his relationships with both Troilus and Criseyde. As Carolyn Dinshaw notes, "Pandarus's activity...provides its own erotic satisfactions. It keeps him physically active, breathless, and sweaty: he leaps, he perspires, he moves back and forth between the two lovers."[4] And Pandarus frequently mentions his own sexual desires, alluding to but never discussing his personal interest in amatory affairs. A queer reading of Pandarus's relationships offers explanatory force for Pandarus's erotic energy and the ways in which it directs the action of Chaucer's plot: his pandering of Criseyde for the satisfaction of Troilus's desires in some manner address his own desires as well.

In terms of Pandarus's relationship with Troilus, Chaucer's view of male–male sexuality in late fourteenth-century England parallels in key ways his depiction of the narratival relationship. Male–male relationships were a matter of concern in the 1380s, given the latent homosocial and homoerotic problems associated with Richard's affinity (his concentric circles of male friends and advisors).[5] Anxieties over homosocial relations would seem almost inevitable in a society so strongly organized around male affinity, in which the problematic question of how to police the boundaries between acceptable and unacceptable forms of male closeness emerges. The argument that Chaucer depicts the relationship between a queer advisor and a young nobleman finds a contemporary parallel in the accusation that Richard II was led astray by "obscene intimacies" with his advisors. This contemporary homosocial relationship with possible sexual undertones provides a possible model for the male–male relationship in *Troilus and Criseyde*, as Chaucer would have known of this scandal through his political career. As Michael Hanrahan documents,

> Thomas Walsingham unmistakably establishes the sexual threat posed by Richard's favorites. During his account of Robert de Vere's royal appointment to the Duke of Ireland in 1386, Walsingham describes Richard and de Vere, the king's closest friend and confidante, as sharing "obscene intimacies"

("*familiaritatis obscoenae*"), an attack that implies that unmentionable vice, sodomy. Adam of Usk will later record a more overt reference to Richard's sodomy, when he includes the king's "sodomies" ("*sodomica*") among the causes of Richard's deposition. The charge of sodomy was never officially brought against Richard, but its occurrence in these Lancasterian chronicles betray the political agenda behind the allegations, namely, Richard's unfitness for rule.[6]

The parallel between the relationships of Richard II and Robert de Vere and of Troilus and Pandarus, then, is that the noblemen are led astray by close alliances with non-heteronormative friends.[7] Obviously, such fears as aroused by the relationship between Richard II and de Vere are not depicted in *Troilus and Criseyde*; no character ever accuses Pandarus of improperly influencing Troilus. Nevertheless, we see in the relationships both between Richard II and de Vere and between Troilus and Pandarus that de Vere and Pandarus wield a great deal of influence over their friends and that this influence contains strong hints of queerness. The Chronicles record the fear of de Vere's queerness, and a similar queerness appears in Chaucer's depiction of Pandarus.[8] Further, as Chaucer would have been aware of the relationship between de Vere and Richard II, so too would the likely audience of *Troilus and Criseyde*.[9]

Throughout the text, Pandarus's actions stress his desire to assist Troilus in his romance with Criseyde, but the motivations behind this desire remain unspoken. However, both through his relationships with Troilus and Criseyde and through the pandering he carries out between them, Pandarus's unspoken objectives and desires are also addressed. In the ensuing analysis, my goal is not to argue that Pandarus loves Troilus in response to latent homosexual desires, but that he loves both Troilus and Criseyde in a manner that reveals the limits of normativity in friendship, courtship, and family. In a world in which both heteronormative and queer sex were acts but did not construe personal identity, homosocial pastimes were extolled in some discourses while reviled in others.[10] Furthermore, the positive depictions of same-sex sexuality in classical sources provided medieval England with a view of homoeroticism that differed intrinsically from concurrent moral and legal considerations of the topic. As Stephen Jaeger observes of male–male relationships in the medieval world, "[Homosexuality] did not exist and using it thrusts an alien set of values onto a sensibility which is delicate and wants reconstruction on its own terms."[11] Furthermore, if homosexuality did not exist as a core truth of identity in the medieval period, as it is often used today, neither did heterosexuality. Consequently, I ask the reader to take on a new perspective: what happens to our vision of Pandarus if we read his desires as queer rather than as necessarily asexual? How do other moments of the text begin to metamorphose queerly? Certainly, I do not agree with Robert Levine that "Pandarus himself has no apparent sexual needs, unless they be the perverse ones detected by a minority of readers."[12] Pandarus mentions his affections repeatedly, so we should believe that they do indeed exist. If that point is granted, then what are these "perverse" desires Levine appears determined not to see?

Once such an opening into our analysis is granted—that the love Pandarus speaks of may carry queer undertones—certain passages of the text begin to appear increasingly nonnormative. The secretive nature of Pandarus's love reinforces the poem's demand for conjecture. Through the textual lacunae in which so little information is offered about Pandarus's paramour, readers are invited to create for themselves the identity of Pandarus's love. When Pandarus declares that, despite his own lovesickness, he will advise Troilus in matters of love, he refuses to divulge the identity of his beloved: "I love oon best, and that me smerteth sore; / And yet, peraunter, kan I reden the / And nat myself; repreve me na more" (I: 667–69).[13] We learn that Pandarus loves and that he feels lovesick for his beloved, but Chaucer provides the reader with no subsequent information about who this person might be. Later in the poem, the stanza that most specifically addresses Pandarus's lovesickness tells nothing about the object of his desire, about exactly whom he loves:

> That Pandarus, for al his wise speche,
> Felt ek his part of loves shotes keene,
> That, koude he nevere so wel of lovyng preche,
> It made his hewe a-day ful ofte greene.
> So shop it that hym fil that day a teene
> In love, for which in wo to bedde he wente,
> And made, er it was day, ful many a wente. (II: 57–63)

It appears that Pandarus's love is a blank slate upon which the character writes his own desires, but upon which readers may project their desires as well. Chaucer allows readerly interpretations to play freely here, in his refusal to limn a specific vision of Pandarus's beloved. As I will discuss, Troilus and Criseyde both make nodding references to Pandarus's phantom love, but these references never allow the reader to see this beloved in any corporeal incarnation. She is amorphous to the point of unreality for the reader and, thus, the question of her actual existence is less important than the question of why Pandarus does not attempt to develop his relationship with her. Refusing to advance his own game of love, Pandarus pursues his personal desires through the zealous play of a triangulated game of courtly love with Troilus and Criseyde. Whether his activities reflect sublimated desires for this phantom love or latent desires for Troilus and Criseyde, his desires are nevertheless the ones most insistently directing the unfolding of the narrative, not through the pursuit of his own consummation of heterosexual intercourse with his beloved but through the polymorphous play of pandering.

In these moments of silence about Pandarus's love, Chaucer appears keenly aware that through what is spoken and what is not spoken, a text creates meaning; in this instance, silence is just as important as speech to the formation of readerly interpretation. Theories of reading stress that texts will, almost inevitably, confront their audiences with the impossibility of definitive interpretation. As Pierre Macherey declares, "By speech, silence becomes the centre and principle of expression, its vanishing point. Speech eventually has nothing more to tell us: we investigate the silence, for it is the silence that is doing the speaking."[14] Likewise, Roman Ingarden observes the interpretive difficulties inherent in represented objectivities that nonetheless cannot escape "spots of indeterminancy":

> If an individual object is called "man," is intentionally projected in this naming, and is materially determined as such, then all of its (innumerable) properties are still not positively, unequivocally determined thereby... .And precisely because this object is simultaneously formally intended as a concrete unit containing an infinite number of fused determinations and, consequently, intentionally created as such, "spots of indeterminancy" arise within it, indeed an infinitely great number of them.[15]

Macherey's and Ingarden's analyses complement each other well, as they both underscore the limits of language—whether in silence or in representation—to foreclose the search for meaning to the words on a given page.[16] The silences and representations of *Troilus and Criseyde*, through their refusal to address definitively the heteronormative when one might expect it, afford one the opportunity to find the queer. Pandarus's speeches hint at answers, but the answers never come due to the accompanying epistemological failures of signification.

In Pandarus's relationship with Troilus, signification flows in the direction from Troilus to Pandarus but does not return in a mutual current of fraternal sympathy, even when Troilus attempts to discuss Pandarus's desires and to assist his friend, as his friend has assisted him. By concentrating his energies on Troilus's needs in love, Pandarus deflects attention from his own problems and further develops the homosocial bond between them. He positions himself as Troilus's confidant through their mutual predicaments in love, yet he convinces Troilus to share all the details of his (Troilus's) love while withholding all the details about his own:

> "Men seyn, 'to wrecche is consolacioun
> To have another felawe in hys peyne.'
> That owghte wel ben oure opynyoun,
> For bothe thow and I of love we pleyne.
> So ful of sorwe am I, soth for to seyne,
> That certeinly namore harde grace
> May sitte on me, for-why ther is no space." (I: 708–714)

Pandarus claims his right to know Troilus's secrets because they both suffer from the cruelties of love, yet he shifts his argument away from a mutual sharing of sorrows. The initial lines of this stanza suggest that the men should reveal their hardships to each other to ameliorate their respective situations. The closing lines of the stanza, however, foreclose any interest Troilus might have in Pandarus's love when Pandarus abruptly changes his attitude about their mutual plight and focuses exclusively on Troilus's lovesickness, directing attention away from himself. Indeed, when Troilus offers to return Pandarus's favors and to help his friend with his problems in love ("Now blisful Venus helpe, er that I sterve, / Of the, Pandare, I mowe som thank deserve" [I: 1014–15]), Pandarus refuses such assistance: "For Goddes love, I bidde the a boone: / So lat m'alone, and it shal be thi beste" [I: 1027–28]). Fracturing a mutual epistemology of each other's loves, Pandarus occludes his desires while Troilus's are exposed both to the pander and to the readers, for their mutual enjoyment.

In a move to deepen their homosocial yet asexual intimacy, Troilus questions Pandarus about his friend's past sexual history. Attempting to convince Pandarus that he (Troilus) can never forget Criseyde, Troilus shoots forth queries that touch upon the many mysteries of Pandarus's sexuality:

> "But tel me now, syn that the thynketh so light
> To changen so in love ay to and fro,
> Whi hastow nat don bisily thi myght
> To chaungen hire that doth the al thi wo?
> Whi nyltow lete hire fro thyn herte go?
> Whi nyltow love an other lady swete,
> That may thyn herte setten in quiete?" (IV: 484–90)

Troilus then redirects his attentions to his own problems in love, and the questions remain unanswered. That Chaucer leaves these questions so intriguingly open in the text demands the reader's engagement in answering them. In his refusal to answer his own authorial questions, Chaucer invites readers to create Pandarus according to their individual desires. Certainly, this passage tells us that Troilus *thinks* Pandarus's love is a woman, but no definitive information—a name or a blazon of her beauty—confirms Troilus's use of the pronoun "hire"; Pandarus's beloved thus remains a phantom vision of love. With no answers to Troilus's questions, moreover, the resulting obfuscation constructs Pandarus's desires as queer, as he refuses to articulate their participation within the realm of the normative. Indeed, regardless of the anatomical sex of Pandarus's love, his insistent silences construct this love as queer because no such silences are necessary between these friends.[17] In this instance, unnecessary silence correlates with the queer, since the love lies suspiciously out of view.

Such moments of silence that allow openings for queer interpretations occur with astounding and confounding frequency throughout the text. When Pandarus tells Criseyde about his love, again in extremely couched and coded terms, he quickly changes the subject and begins to joke with her:

> "Nece, I have so gret a pyne
> For love, that everich other day I faste—"
> And gan his beste japes forth to caste,
> And made hire so to laughe at his folye,
> That she for laughter wende for to dye. (II: 1165–69)

As Richard Green notes of this passage, "We may assume that Pandarus regards his love affair as a convenient social fiction, maintained with the style that befits a nobleman."[18] As Green suggests, why would Pandarus and Criseyde laugh when he confesses such great pain unless it is based upon an amusing social fiction readily known to be such? Is Pandarus's nonexistent lover an "open secret," a fraud tacitly accepted as a truth in the form of a social convenience?[19] Obviously, the many jokes and pleasantries divert Criseyde's attention from pursuing the subject at hand. Laughing so hard at his antics, she asks no more questions about his love interest. Pandarus's goal appears to be to change the subject so that he saves himself from revealing his queer desires, desires that involve Criseyde's sexual relationship with Troilus more than his own relationship with his phantom beloved.

Yet another moment that offers the opportunity to read Pandarus queerly appears when he assures Troilus that, if the young knight shares with him the identity of his secret love, Pandarus will not steal her away from Troilus. Pandarus promises that he would never do such a thing:

> "If God wol, thow art nat agast of me
> Lest I wolde of thi lady the bygyle!
> Thow woost thyself whom that I love, parde,
> As I best kan, gon sithen longe while.

> And sith thow woost I do it for no wyle,
> And sith I am he that thow trustest moost,
> Tel me somwhat, syn al my wo thow woost." (I: 715–21)

The closing words, "syn al my wo thow woost," foreclose Troilus's objections, but this line does not hold up to close scrutiny, as Troilus later questions Pandarus about his love (IV: 484–90; quoted previously). If Troilus knew even the barest details about Pandarus's beloved, he would not ask such basic questions about her later in the text. At this point, it once again appears that Pandarus's love is nothing more than a convenient social fiction. Again he mentions a love, supposedly someone Troilus knows, but again we find no clue to this person's identity. Chaucer tells the reader that Troilus knows whom Pandarus loves but withholds the information from the readers, who must then fill in the blanks for themselves. Furthermore, Pandarus's statement that he would not cheat Troilus of his love reveals the queer possibility that Pandarus is not as much sexually interested in a particular woman and heterosexual consummation as he is in his queer pandering, in playing roles beyond the heteronormative realm of courtly love.

Queerness also infuses Pandarus's role as pander in his willingness to deliver his niece to Troilus, and this pandering of blood relatives bleeds into Troilus's devotion to Pandarus. When Troilus offers to play the role of the pander for Pandarus, it appears that heterosexual desire will be appeased through trafficking in sisters and other female relatives:

> "And that thow knowe I thynke nought ne wene
> That this servise a shame be or jape,
> I have my faire suster Polixene,
> Cassandre, Eleyne, or any of the frape—
> Be she nevere so fair or wel yshape,
> Tel me which thow wilt of everychone,
> To han for thyn, and lat me thanne allone." (III: 407–413)

Despite this proposal, Troilus never serves in such a fashion for Pandarus, and neither man returns to this offer in the text. All of Pandarus's actions are directed for Troilus's pleasure alone, not for the advancement of Pandarus's own goals in a heterosexual relationship with any of the women whom Troilus might pander for him. Troilus's offer to pander his sisters and sister-in-law to satiate Pandarus's desires points to the patriarchal primacy of male desires within *Troilus and Criseyde*, but both Pandarus and Troilus— Pandarus in his actions, Troilus in his promise—rely on the decidedly queer course of pandering their female relatives.

More and more queer possibilities appear as Pandarus adumbrates a beloved who does not exist—at least this person does not exist for the reader who can never know him or her—in order to win his friend's confidence. When Pandarus confronts Criseyde with the news that Troilus desires to see her, immediately prior to the consummation scene, Criseyde defends her love for Troilus by asserting that Pandarus never loved anyone as she loves Troilus: "Hadde I hym nevere lief? By God, I weene / Ye hadde nevere thyng so lief!" (III: 869–70). Pandarus's intriguing and queer response is not that he has indeed loved a woman as much as Criseyde loves Troilus, but that he will prove his ability to love through his dedication to Troilus:

> "Now by my thrift," quod he, "that shal be seene!
> For syn ye make this ensaumple of me,
> If ich al nyght wolde hym in sorwe se,
> For al the tresour in the town of Troie,
> I bidde God I nevere mote have joie." (III: 869–75)

We might expect to learn of Pandarus's heterosexual romance in this passage, but this readerly desire is again frustrated by Pandarus's queerly insistent doting on Troilus. Offering no defense of his love, Pandarus's words reveal desires for Troilus and Criseyde and conceal them for the phantom beloved.

The argument that Chaucer's use of textual silence demands that the reader participate in the construction of meaning recurs throughout Chaucerian criticism. Although this time the observation is directed to a queer interpretation of Pandarus, it should nevertheless ring familiar to a scholarly audience familiar with critical debates surrounding this controversial passage:

> I passe al that which chargeth nought to seye.
> What! Gof foryaf his deth, and she al so
> Foryaf, and with here uncle gan to pleye,
> For other cause was ther noon than so.
> But of this thing right to the effect to go:
> Whan tyme was, hom til here hous she wente,
> And Pandarus hath fully his entente. (III: 1576–82)

Chaucer hints that Pandarus and Criseyde sleep together in this passage, and, in response, several critics argue that this passage makes the reader complicit in the process of creating the text's meaning.[20] For example, Louise Fradenburg argues that this passage "might be read, but I would argue could never definitely be read, as Pandarus's incestuous dalliance with Criseyde. . . .Chaucer's poem indeed treads the finest of lines between the perception of the occlusion of violence and the desire to participate in it."[21] I find that Chaucer pursues the same strategy with Pandarus's sexuality: it is so opaque, polyvalent, polymorphous, and contradictory that the reader must participate in its construction rather than passively accept it. A reader desiring to find queer possibilities in Pandarus, like the reader who sees incest between Pandarus and Criseyde, can do so precisely because the text refuses to forbid such a reading; a reader desiring not to see the queer possibilities of Pandarus's relationships with Criseyde and with Troilus can likewise find sufficient ambiguity in these passages to foreclose such interpretations. From both perspectives, Pandarus's nonnormative desires are evinced through his relationships with both Troilus and Criseyde, such that whether he actually sleeps with Criseyde (or wants to sleep with Troilus) becomes a secondary point to the overwhelmingly, insistently obfuscatory nature of his unknowable desires.

Pandarus's rhetorical tropes complement his speeches and silences about his mysterious love that reveal unspoken and queer desires for Troilus and Criseyde. Through the juxtaposition of contrasting entities in which unlike persons or things complement one another, Pandarus creates unities of ostensibly oppositional forces. For example, Pandarus declares both that "A fool may ek a wis-man ofte gide" and "A wheston is no kervyng instrument, / But yet it maketh sharppe kervyng tolis" (I: 630–632). He then summarizes his thoughts about the relationship between contraries:

> "By his contrairie is every thyng declared.
> For how myghte evere swetnesse han ben knowe
> To him that nevere tasted bitternesse?
> . . . .
> Eke whit by blak, by shame ek worthinesse,
> Ech set by other, more for other semeth,
> As men may se, and so the wyse it demeth." (I: 637–39, 642–44)

For Pandarus, an entity is both recognized and improved through contact with its contrast: the bitter exposes the sweet, the white makes explicit the black, shame complements worthiness.[22] Building upon this argument for wholeness through contrast, both Pandarus and Troilus speak of their relationship in binary terms that they use to represent the wholeness of their friendship. Pandarus declares that "for trewe or fals report, / In wrong and right iloved the al my lyve" (I: 593–94). Through true and false, wrong and right, Pandarus's love for Troilus is constant. Similarly, Troilus explains how deeply Pandarus affects the totality of his own life:

> Tho Troilus gan doun on knees to falle,
> And Pandare in his armes hente fast. . .
> "Now, Pandare, I kan na more seye,

But, thow wis, thow woost, thow maist, thow art al!
Mi lif, my deth, hol in thyn hond I leye.
Help now!" Quod he, "Yis, by my trowthe, I shal." (I: 1044–1045, 51–54)

The sum of Troilus's existence—his life and his death—is within Pandarus's power. As Elaine Tuttle Hansen notes, "[t]he homo-erotic cast to this scene is intensified not so much when Troilus embraces Pandarus as when he speaks words to Pandarus that are elsewhere directed to the lady, laying his life in Pandarus's hands and seeking his mercy."[23] The conflation of gendered oppositions makes possible a queer reading: through Troilus's employment of speech traditionally directed to a female for a dialogue with a male, the queer thematics of the poem are evident through the erasure of sexual and gender polarities. Pandarus is addressed as a female, and, consequently, gender divisions become obscured and queered.

The relationship between Troilus and Criseyde itself serves as yet another locus where Pandarus inserts his own queer desires. Certainly, Pandarus sees himself included in the sating of desire that Troilus and Criseyde's relationship promises. In a statement of triangulated desire congruent with Eve Sedgwick's theorization of homosocial desire,[24] Pandarus openly predicts the gratifications available to him through Troilus and Criseyde's affair:

"Wherfore I am, and wol ben, ay redy
To peyne me to do yow this servyse;
For bothe yow to plese thus hope I
Herafterward; for ye ben bothe wyse,
And konne it counseil kepe in swych a wyse
That no man shal the wiser of it be;
And so we may ben gladed alle thre." (I: 988–94)

Beginning with a promise to advance Troilus's love, Pandarus concludes that all three will be "gladed" by the affair. The triangulation of this desire both obscures its queer possibilities (since Pandarus indicates that Troilus's and Criseyde's desires are his primary concern) and makes them possible (since his desires are addressed as well). Queerly, determinedly, Pandarus obfuscates and reveals his desires through the pandering he performs.

Pandarus's goal is not merely to assist Troilus to win Criseyde's love, but to stress his queer role in the process and to make the relationship dependent as much upon his pandering as upon the lovers' actions. Pandarus does not let Troilus forget that it is through his actions that Troilus succeeds:

"And have it brought to swich plit as thow woost,
So that thorugh me thow stondest now in weye

> To faren wel; I sey it for no bost,
> And wostow whi? For shame it is to seye:
> For the have I bigonne a gamen pleye
> Which that I nevere do shal eft for other,
> Although he were a thousand fold my brother." (III: 246–52)

Through Pandarus, Troilus finds sexual satisfaction; the panderer renders himself indispensable to his friend, guaranteeing his place in the young knight's affections. And since Pandarus's own affections are so intimately intermingled with Troilus's through the adoption of the role of pander, the love between Troilus and Criseyde serves as a queer proxy for Pandarus's own adumbrated yet never revealed desires.

If Pandarus's silences and speeches reveal his amorphously queer desires, so too does his gaze. Pandarus deftly orchestrates both Troilus's and his own gazes so that he can create an outlet for his queer affection. Sarah Stanbury argues that Troilus's and Criseyde's gazes ultimately reflect back upon themselves as viewers whereas Pandarus's gaze is able to construct the reality of the poem: "[Pandarus's] gaze is utterly unlike the gazes of Troilus and of Criseyde in books 1 and 2 that collapse space to send the view back on the altered body of the perceiver. Pandarus's gaze seems to have no body, or rather to proceed from such a position of power that he is master of his own fabrications."[25] However, Stanbury does not address the ways in which Pandarus constructs the visual relationship between Troilus and himself; her analysis does not consider the ways in which the gaze can be directed between men, too. In this queer Trojan world, Pandarus's queer desire is manifest in the scenes in which he directs how, when, and where Troilus looks.

Although Pandarus is creating a scene in which Troilus will look upon Criseyde, he explicitly instructs Troilus to pay more attention to him than to Criseyde when the knight passes below her window:

> "And thow shalt fynde us, if I may, sittynge
> At some wyndow, into the strete lokynge.
> And if the list, than maystow us salue;
> And upon me make thow thi countenaunce." (II: 1014–1017)

Since, as Stanbury argues, both Troilus's and Criseyde's gazes affect themselves more than the person upon whom they are looking, Pandarus's construction of Troilus's gaze suggests that he is preparing the knight to succumb to the power of his own gaze. By having Troilus look at him in a highly artificial setting that the pander himself creates, Pandarus fashions an opportunity for himself to be the spectacle of Troilus's gaze and, thus, to have Troilus's gaze construct him (Pandarus) as the object of Troilus's desire.

As Troilus looks on Criseyde and physically feels the effect of his stare ("And of hire look in him ther gan to quyken / So gret desir and such affeccioun, / That in his herte botme gan to stiken / Of hir his fixe and depe impressioun," I: 295–98), as Criseyde sees Troilus and feels drunk with pleasure ("Criseÿda gan al his chere aspien, / And leet it so softe in hire herte synke, / That to hireself she syede, 'Who yaf me drynke?' " II: 649–51), Pandarus recreates Troilus's gaze with himself as its object to create the same physical effect of desire.

Pandarus's queer plan comes to fruition when Troilus passes beneath Criseyde's window as she and he watch. Pandarus observes Troilus first: "Pandare hym aspide / And seyde, 'Nece, ysee who comth here ride!' " (II: 1252–53). Pandarus is more attuned to, in large part because he directs, Troilus's actions. However, what is most significant in this passage is the effect that Troilus's gaze has both on Criseyde and on Pandarus. Chaucer narrates that Troilus looks only at Pandarus, not Criseyde: "And up his look debonairly he caste, / And bekked on Pandare, and forth he paste" (II: 1259–60). The narrator then reports that "To God hope I, she hath now kaught a thorn, / She shal nat pulle it out this nexte wyke" (II: 1272–73). Although the narrator merely hopes that Criseyde has been appropriately affected by Troilus's gaze, he describes definitively how Pandarus reacts to Troilus's stare: "Pandare, which that stood him faste by, / Felte iren hoot" (II: 1275–76). Why does Pandarus feel "iren hoot" here if he does not participate at all in the sexual energy of the scene? Pandarus's "iren hoot" reaction to Troilus suggests strongly both that the pander creates an outlet for his queer desire through his construction of Troilus's gaze and that he finds a level of sexual gratification through the process. Intriguingly, Chaucer also employs a hot iron in "The Miller's Tale" when Absolon wreaks his vengeance upon Nicholas ("And [Absolon] was redy with his iren hoot, / And Nicholas amydde the ers he smoot" [3809–810]). Absolon burns Nicholas's bottom with a hot iron; Pandarus feels iron hot at the approach of Troilus. In "The Miller's Tale," same-sex desire is parodied; in *Troilus and Criseyde*, it is adumbrated. For Chaucer, hot irons metaphorically point to queer desires, at least in these two instances.[26] Throughout *Troilus and Criseyde*, the gaze provides both the creation of and the satisfaction of desire; Pandarus's queer gaze fits just such a pattern of scopophilic pleasure.

By depicting Pandarus's polymorphous and queer sexual desires with such intriguing complexity and secrecy, Chaucer deepens his philosophical and spiritual examination of earthly love. At the narrative's conclusion, Troilus learns a lesson about the ephemerality of human love, that in the bliss of the eighth sphere, "What nedeth feynede loves for to seke?" (V: 1848). Similar to Criseyde's love, Pandarus's intense friendship, in the end, offers little solace, little comfort, little love. That Pandarus's affections bear with them elements of queer desire adumbrates Troilus's rejection of all incarnations of human and physical love. As Leah Freiwald observes, "because it ironically parallels the love affair..., the friendship of Troilus and Pandarus adds a further dimension to Chaucer's theme of the frailty and vanity of earth-bound affection."[27] Uncovering the queer undercurrents to Pandarus's desires, to Troilus and Pandarus's friendship, and to Troilus's and Pandarus's relationships with Criseyde thus allows us to see fully Chaucer's dismissal of the earthly in favor of the eternal.

In light of Ricardian anxieties over queer homosocial bonds and their impact upon the king's affinity, Chaucer's oblique gestures toward a similar such relationship highlight yet another example of his famous slipperiness, his shadowy adumbration of but seldom direct engagement with contemporary political issues. Thus, it is necessary to look below the surface of the text for the full picture of sexuality that emerges. In his reading of "The Pardoner's Tale," Steven Kruger concludes,

> reading texts like "The Pardoner's Tale" as part of a process of writing queers (and women and Jews) back into the Middle Ages, we can begin to understand the ways in which a dominant medieval European culture—self-defined as Christian, heterosexual, masculinist—depended for its self-definition upon a rigorous writing-out of Judaism and Islam, of women's experience, of the sexually other.[28]

Both writing in and writing out Pandarus's queerness through its subtextuality, Chaucer's sexually ambiguous panderer unsettles gender categories and sexual roles. Such a destabilizing gesture may in the end function to privilege the heteronormative romance between Troilus and Criseyde that is at the heart of the narrative, but it nonetheless provides yet another example of the ways in which medieval sexuality refuses to adhere to modern constructions of gender and sexuality.

If queerness is therefore a symbol of yet another failure, of the insignificance of human affairs in relation to the divine, Pandarus's manifold queerness—in regard to his own occluded desires and to his latent and triangulated desires for Troilus and Criseyde—demands the reader to engage with the unknowability and the vast confusions engendered by nonnormative desires. And, as I argue in the following section of this chapter, Pandarus's queer desires undermine the promise of generic stability in much the same way that they subvert heteronormativity. The reader who approaches *Troilus and Criseyde* with the hope of a generic hermeneutic through which to make sense of the plot's unfolding will face a queering genre, as much as they face Pandarus's queering and indecipherable desires.

Pandarus and the Queering of Tragic Teleology

The abundance of hints to queer and nonnormative desires in *Troilus and Criseyde* highlights the potentially frustrating openness of the text itself, in which we can never fully know the answers. Consequently, whether Pandarus desires Troilus and/or Criseyde sexually is less important than the fact that the poem refuses to foreclose a queer interpretation of Pandarus, that the character embodies desires so protean and shifting that they can only be described within the range of the queerly nonnormative. Through Chaucer's decision to celebrate transgression in Pandarus, the poem offers a queer subjectivity the opportunity to read an often heteronormatively interpreted text with an eye to the multiplicities of sexual desire. The importance of Pandarus's queerness lies not merely in its very appearance, however, as queer silences and gazes alone would accomplish little in terms of queering the text itself. In this section of the chapter, I turn to the question of the ways in which queer Pandarus undermines generic stability. If we read *Troilus and Criseyde* as a tragedy, as Chaucer encourages us to do, this hermeneutic, in the end, is insufficient to account for the vast disparity among the narrative fortunes of the three main characters in terms of the text's teleologically (and anachronistically) Christian conclusion. Whose tragedy is it, anyway?

As Chaucer's queer Pandarus refuses to signify simply, so too do the text's generic codes deny the reader a firm interpretive foothold. The genre of *Troilus and Criseyde* is a timeless critical conundrum, as the generic possibilities are many and at times contradictory. Although Chaucer labels it a "tragedye" (V: 1786), critics have suggested that such other genres as romance, Boethian comedy, Boethian tragedy, epic, mock epic, and novel better describe the text.[29] In his guide to the poem, Barry Windeatt discusses the influences of additional generic traditions, including history, drama, lyric, fabliau, and allegory.[30] In light of this panoply of generic possibilities, it is judicious to concede that a definitive answer of any single genre will fail to satisfy fully the question of the generic identity of *Troilus and Criseyde*. Through the fracturing multiplicity and interplay of generic forms, Chaucer surpasses the limits of any single genre in his most ambitious work. In contrast to *The Canterbury Tales*, with its dazzling parade of genres in a mostly linear progression of differing forms, *Troilus and Criseyde* provides a kaleidoscopic vision in which genres are intermingled and intermixed in its presentation of a stunningly disparate yet ultimately coherent amalgam.[31]

By labeling *Troilus and Criseyde* a tragedy yet by interjecting materials of other generic traditions, Chaucer establishes that the meaning of tragedy, if not of genre itself, is one of his poetic themes. The text ponders the meanings of multiple tragedies, not the meaning of a monolithic view of tragedy, as Troilus, Criseyde, and Pandarus suffer individually, although in varying degrees, in the dénouement. This trifold tragic focus allows Chaucer to explore the generic form of tragedy and its concomitant philosophical, romantic, and spiritual issues more subtly than in the somewhat simplistic *de casibus* structure of the narratives of "The Monk's Tale."[32] Given the amorphous status of tragedy in the Middle Ages, Chaucer's experimentation with the genre showcases his authorial innovation: as Henry Kelly demonstrates, Chaucer was "the first vernacular poet to write tragedies,"[33] reviving and reinventing a literary tradition that belonged to classical authors more than to Chaucer's vernacular contemporaries. *Troilus and Criseyde* addresses tragedy neither in terms of Aristotelian theories of hamartia and hubris nor in the style of Senecan slaughters. Kelly's extensive study of Chaucer's conception of tragedy argues persuasively that "Chaucer's primary source for his understanding of tragedy was Fortune's rhetorical question in Boethius's *Consolation of Philosophy*: 'Quid tragediarum clamor aliud deflet nisi indiscreto ictu Fortunam felicia regna vertentem?'" (1997: 50).[34] For Chaucer, tragedies are unique and specific and investigate the ways in which individual characters interact with a Boethian conception of Fortune: Troilus's tragedy is not Criseyde's, and hers is not his, although the same text tells both tales.

Boethian Fortune catalyzes Chaucerian tragedy, but this force in itself is insufficient to explain the full relevance of tragedy for Chaucer. After Fortune toys with humanity throughout the narrative, Christian teleology appears, in *deus ex machina* fashion, to give an affirmative afterglow to Troilus's suffering and, in effect, to condemn Criseyde in her narrative end. We see in this instance that, for Chaucer, Fortune ultimately connects with Christianity to imbue a pagan love story with spiritual meaning. The manifold meanings of the tragedies of *Troilus and Criseyde* mutate again through the additional perspective of Pandarus, as the figure of the queer, the textually ambivalent marker of polymorphous and unbridled freedom, suffers his own tragic ending that nonetheless tacitly suggests an alternative to the prevailing tides of death.

From the beginning of *Troilus and Criseyde*, Chaucer explores conceptions of Boethian tragedy in which Fortune's play with humanity inevitably overturns the aspirations of individuals. The poem thus begins appropriately enough, lamenting the double sorrow of Troilus:

> The double sorwe of Troilus to tellen,
> That was the kyng Priamus sone of Troye,
> In lovynge, how his aventures fellen
> Fro wo to wele, and after out of joie,

> My purpos is, er that I parte fro ye.
> Thesiphone, thow help me for t'endite
> Thise woful vers, that wepen as I write. (I: 1–7)

The hallmarks of Boethian tragedy are apparent: Fortune's wheel spins, and Troilus travels from unhappiness to happiness, but then back again to sorrow. The excessive emotionality of the stanza's final line establishes for the reader the expectation of a truly mournful narrative. As Gayle Margherita rightly observes, "Of all the difficult beginnings in Chaucer's poetry, these opening lines of the *Troilus* are perhaps the most troubling. The generic and ontological problematics of history and memory are here linked to melancholia, to the body, and to death. It is therefore not surprising that the rest of the poem seems committed to forgetting that past."[35] But if the blunt and tragic focus of these opening lines confronts the reader both with a troubling beginning and, as Margherita suggests, with a desire to escape and to forget this beginning, we need a mechanism for such a dual readerly effect to enjoy the unsettling pleasures of the tragedy and then to resist the trauma of memory. As I argue, Pandarus serves as the mechanism of escape from the constraints of this heterosexually inscribed yet queerly precipitated tragedy of romance.

Despite the troubling nature of the poem's opening lines and their evocation of a range of tragic elements, a tragic view fails to account completely for the conclusion of the narrative. By labeling *Troilus and Criseyde* a tragedy but pointing to the liminal space between tragedy and comedy, Chaucer denies that tragedy can adequately represent his narrative and suggests that the text also offers the transformative hope of comedy: "Go, litel bok, go, litel myn tragedye, / Ther God thi makere yet, er that he dye, / So sende myght to make in some comedye" (V: 1786–88). Writing not exclusively within the genre of tragedy but within the mutable borders between tragedy and comedy, Chaucer complicates efforts to interpret *Troilus and Criseyde* under the sole aegis either of tragedy or of comedy and directs the reader to ask more specific questions of the meaning of the text's multiple conclusions. Each of the three main characters needs to be analyzed not merely in relation to tragedy, but in relation to the space between tragedy and comedy. Furthermore, such an analysis must also pay attention to the heterosexual romance that precipitates the apparent tragedy of Troilus's death, as well as the implications of tragic and comic hermeneutics for understanding the fates of Criseyde and Pandarus.

Along with the interplay of tragedy and comedy, the heterosexual romance between Troilus and Criseyde also bears important implications on generic considerations, as the genre of romance likewise serves as a crucial structure for the text. Andrea Clough theorizes that, despite the apparent incongruity between tragedy and romance, *Troilus and Criseyde* can be understood as a "romance tragedy":

> [I]n *Troilus* [Chaucer] developed a [new] type [of tragedy], only hinted at in Boccaccio's work: the combination of formal tragedy with full-length tragic romance. For it was Chaucer's unique achievement to perceive the analogy between the fall of lovers and the Fall of Princes, and by applying the conventions of formal tragedy to the subject of ill-fated love, he created a new type, a hybrid form, which I label "romance tragedy."[36]

As Clough suggests, the intermingling of romance and tragedy need not provide a reason to dismiss the predominantly tragic cast of *Troilus and Criseyde*. Combining the elements of romance and tragedy through the machinations of a queer panderer, Chaucer reworks the relationship between these genres and further complicates the effects of Pandarus's queering presence. In a narrative chain reaction, Pandarus's actions set in motion a romance, which in turn catalyzes a tragedy in Troilus's death, which in turn sparks Troilus's comic realization in the eighth sphere. The root of all of these genres is Pandarus, without whom no romance, tragedy, or comedy could develop for the lovers. Pandarus plays a vital role in the creation of tragedy, comedy, and romance, and this vital role suggests that he symbolizes as meaningfully as Troilus and Criseyde in any attempt to determine a generic meaning for the text.

Before analyzing Pandarus's role in the construction of generic meaning, a brief overview of Troilus's and Criseyde's fortune in terms of Boethian tragedy and comedy will be helpful. Monica McAlpine locates alternate Boethian perspectives on the meaning and importance of human life in the differing fortunes of Troilus and Criseyde.[37] Through his laughter in the eighth sphere, Troilus discovers ironic and comic detachment from worldly affairs and thus becomes the protagonist of a Boethian comedy; Criseyde, in her decision to remain safely with Diomede and to protect her earthly existence, ultimately suffers the dismal fate of a Boethian tragedy through her short-sighted focus on self-preservation. That is, if Troilus's movements from woe to well to woe mark him as a tragic hero, his increased spiritual (and anachronistically Christian) understanding of the pettiness of human affairs indicates that he, in the end, matures into a comic perspective; Criseyde, on the other hand, represents a tragic heroine condemned to a lack of spiritual awareness. When the narrative emphasizes the promise of Christian teleology in its closing stanzas, Troilus's Boethian tragedy of fortune metamorphoses into a Christian comedy, whereas Criseyde's narrative destiny suggests a darker, less revelatory conclusion.[38]

Certainly, Troilus realizes the ultimate ephemerality of earthly love upon dying and escapes the full despair of tragedy. After he departs from the vain desires of the Trojan world and "His lighte goost ful blisfully is went" (V: 1808), Troilus laughs in the eighth sphere, amused by the follies of his friends and himself:

> [He] fully gan despise
> This wrecched world, and held al vanite
> To respect of the pleyn felicite
> That is in hevene above; and at the laste,
> Ther he was slayn his lokyng down he caste,
>
> And in hymself he lough right at the wo
> Of hem that wepten for his deth so faste. (V: 1816–22)

Rejecting the wretched world he has left, Troilus laughs both at himself and at the ultimate meaninglessness of life on earth; this laughter is predicated upon his "respect of the pleyn felicite / That is in hevene above." Sarah Stanbury argues that "Troilus's laughter stems from his recognition of separateness, a recognition that even as observer he is disconnected from the 'blynde lust' that motivates human activity."[39] Freed from the earthly torments that contributed to his ostensibly tragic death, Troilus finds a comic answer to the question of life's meaning. The discordant, if not bizarre, vision of Troilus laughing at his own dead body emphasizes his recognition of the foolishness of human concerns with life and death in the light of heavenly rewards. (This laughter is even more surprising when compared with Troilus's earlier plan for eternal lamentation over Criseyde: "Whan I am ded, I wol go wone in pyne, / And ther I wol eternaly compleyne / My wo, and how that twynned be we tweyne" [IV: 474–76]). Troilus's laughter could be interpreted as mocking or derisive, but that he laughs at himself and his mourners suggests more a compassionate chuckle at human misperceptions than a scornful dismissal of their concerns. With Troilus's laughter, the tragedy of earthly death metamorphoses into the comedy of spiritual understanding and the eternal promise of Christian teleology for a select group of pagans. Although the surviving Trojans can only see the tragedy of his death, Troilus perceives the heavenly comedy that constructs human existence on earth.

Due to her failure to realize the ultimate ephemerality of human life, Criseyde's various movements between woe to well culminate on earth rather than in the heavenly environment of the eighth sphere: preserving her life beyond all other concerns, she fails to discern the grander truths of spiritual existence, the truths that Troilus realizes to be so humorous. In this tragically limited perspective, she suffers in the narrative future as much as

Troilus suffers prior to his apotheosis. The reader learns that the future lies bleakly before Criseyde, as she herself laments the loss of her reputation:

> "Allas, of me, unto the worldes ende,
> Shal neyther ben ywriten nor ysonge
> No good word, for thise bokes wol me shende.
> O, rolled shal I ben on many a tonge!
> Thoroughout the world shal my belle be ronge!
> And wommen moost wol haten me of all.
> Allas, that swich a cas me sholde falle!" (V: 1058–1064)

We never see in *Troilus and Criseyde* the depiction of the hatred and contumely that Criseyde fears, but by foreshadowing the ignominiousness of her own fate, Criseyde damns herself to her own tragic conclusion.[40] And if the dénouement of *Troilus and Criseyde* does not depict her ultimate fate, Chaucer nevertheless underscores Criseyde's future death when the narrator first introduces her:

> For now wil I gon streght to my matere,
> In which ye may the double sorwes here
> Of Troilus in lovynge of Criseyde,
> And how that she forsook hym er she deyde. (I: 53–56)

Remembering these lines at the narrative's conclusion, the reader is confronted with a bleak outlook on the fate of earthly romantic love, with both lovers dead after much earthly suffering. The contrasting perspectives of Boethian tragedy and comedy allow a nuanced understanding of the graded difference in their fates, but that they both experience death (whether in or beyond the text) showcases the overall tragic cast of *Troilus and Criseyde*. Boethian Fortune lets neither of the two lovers escape her wheel, even if Troilus achieves the solace of comedy to offset the bitterness of his own demise.

Presenting a predominantly tragic view of the heterosexual romance of courtly love, Chaucer simultaneously denies the reader a firm grasp of the text's meaning through the confusions of tragedy, comedy, and romance. Elaine Tuttle Hansen demarcates the ways in which Chaucer's authorial strategies rely on the interplay of narrative technique, romantic agency, and courtly love, suggesting that "the narrative technique here calls attention from the outset to the question of agency and power in heterosexual relations, to the confusion within courtly ideology over precisely this issue, and to the problems of male sexuality in particular, which the conventions of romantic love both conceal and exacerbate through the emphasis on role reversal."[41] These narrative issues belong primarily to Pandarus, and it is through them that he serves his role as the mechanism of escape from the tragedy of romance: he muddles the agency of romance both in heterosexual affairs and in queer desires; he exploits confusions over courtly ideology to advance his game of love; and he takes advantage of the possibilities of role reversal (as in his famous "contraries" speech, I: 624–51) to manipulate the actions of other characters. As the text moves to closure through the fates of Troilus and Criseyde, this sense of closure is undermined by Pandarus. If *Troilus and Criseyde* offers an ultimately Christian view of teleology in which the reader learns a moral lesson through the contrasting fortunes of Troilus and Criseyde, Pandarus refuses to fit neatly into any generic or hermeneutic meaning.

The pleasure of Christian teleology (with its promise of salvation) is thus fractured by the failure of narrative teleology (through the queering genre play of Pandarus). Through the simple act of lengthening *Troilus and Criseyde* over his source material, Chaucer latently brings the issue of teleology into the text. Clare Kinney affirms, "The supplementation of a source or the constant recapitulation of a fiction's original ground plan are maneuvers which resist narrative closure. Teleology is challenged by the dilation of the text."[42] Through the expansion of *Troilus and Criseyde* over the previous versions of the tale, Chaucer creates in Pandarus a character whose primary purpose is the disruption of teleology through the pleasures of dilation. As the instigator of heterosexual romance to satisfy his own queering desires, Pandarus latently questions the meaning of tragedy, comedy, and romance, and, through this process, resists the moral asserted at the narrative's conclusion. As the "third wheel" without whom no tragedy, comedy, or romance could transpire, Pandarus's actions precipitate any meaning the narrative can develop. These generic disruptions result in a tension between Pandarus's secular and the narrator's Christian values, as Nancy Reale notes: "Pandarus's talent for and pleasure in arbitrarily asserting meaning for actions, words, emotions, and intentions, or, put another way, his creation of a world in the absence of divinely fixed values, eventually unnerves Chaucer's appreciative but less bold narrator, who turns to the certainty of a Christian perspective."[43] The talent that Pandarus displays in creating is no less apparent in his actions, words, emotions, and intentions than in his deconstruction of generic stability across the tragic/comic/romantic divides. As the queer instigator of the romance that leads to the deaths of the lovers, the comic perspective of Troilus, and the tragic fate of Criseyde, what is Pandarus's responsibility for the tragedies that befall Troilus and Criseyde?[44]

In the final analysis, even an interpretation of Troilus's death as a Boethian comedy and Criseyde's end as a Boethian tragedy fails to provide a sufficiently strong structure for the end of the tragicomedy of romance, as the insistent openendedness of *Troilus and Criseyde* refuses to communicate monologically. Through an analysis of the conflicting domains of the sacred and profane in Troilus's death, Claudia Papka argues that *Troilus and Criseyde* celebrates the rejection of a simple meaning, declaring:

> And just as Troilus's transcendence finally destabilizes our interpretation of him in a way his simple death could not, so Chaucer, by explicitly introducing a "sacred" ending to a "profane" text, seems to be providing a neat condemnation of "feyned love" but is in fact introducing an epistemological gap into the poem.... We desire continuity because we are afraid of individuality, but in Troilus and in *Troilus*, Chaucer shows us the inevitability of transgression, and the impossibility of closure—indeed, he seems to celebrate it.[45]

This epistemological gap—the shattering of a simple reinstantiation of Christian teleology in this pagan world—arises not merely in relation to Troilus but in relation to Pandarus as well, as the panderer makes closure impossible by instigating the failed romance that in turn catalyzes the failure of knowledge. If Troilus demonstrates the "inevitability of transgression," as Papka judiciously observes, Pandarus, as the puppet-master behind the majority of Troilus's actions, must also accept accountability for the transgressive lack of closure in the text.

When we examine his final lines (both those in which the narrator describes him and in which he speaks), it becomes apparent that Pandarus suffers his own epistemological gap—and thus creates yet another one for the reader. The two attributes with which Chaucer most consistently characterizes Pandarus—activity and prolixity—noticeably disappear:

> This Pandarus, that al thise thynges herde,
> And wiste wel he seyde a soth of this,
> He nought a word ayeyn to hym answerde;
> For sory of his frendes sorwe he is,
> And shamed for his nece hath don amys,
> And stant, astoned of thise causes tweye,
> As stille as ston; a word ne kowde he seye.
>
> But at the laste thus he spak, and seyde:
> "My brother deer, I may do the namore.
> What sholde I seyen? I hate, ywis, Cryseyde;
> ....
> And fro this world, almyghty God I preye
> Delivere hire soon! I kan namore seye." (V: 1723–32, 1742–43)

The last lines of both stanzas powerfully reiterate that Pandarus, the honey-tongued huckster of heterosexual romance and queer desire, is bereft of the power of language. "The reduction of Pandarus to impotent silence provides a neatly ironic contrast to the earlier brilliance of his rhetorical performances, but it does not serve to complete [his] story," as Monica McAlpine observes.[46] Coupling Pandarus's promised silence with his description as now standing "[a]s stille as ston," Chaucer makes apparent that Pandarus is shocked into a new sense of powerlessness in which his words and actions fail him. As the image of Troilus laughing at his own funeral highlights his comic understanding of the vanity of human pursuits, Pandarus's silence complements Troilus's laughter in that both silence and laughter convey to the reader that a profound change has transpired in the respective characters. In the depiction of Pandarus's refusal to speak, we find not a firm sense of closure but an eternal dilation. The reader can only remember a silent Pandarus as a suspicious anomaly, if not an outright oxymoron.

Intriguingly, these lines also highlight the difference between Pandarus's and Troilus's narrative endings in that Pandarus enacts what Troilus predicted as his own fate. Troilus earlier declares that he would have to be transformed into a stone to forget Criseyde ("Thowe moost me first transmewen in a ston, / And reve me my passiones alle, / Er thow so lightly do my wo to falle" [IV: 467–69]); Troilus also suggests that a loss of words would be fatal to him ("Nay, God wot, nought worth is al thi red, / For which, for what that evere may byfalle, / Withouten wordes mo, I wol be ded" (IV: 498–500).[47] Enacting Troilus's fate, Pandarus embodies the narrative conclusion that his friend foresaw as his own. Before Troilus's tragedy metamorphoses into comedy in the eighth sphere, Pandarus suffers the tragic fate of the heterosexual romance he set in motion. Troilus and Criseyde both foresee and bewail their respective fates, but Troilus escapes his as Pandarus enacts it. As for Criseyde, the reader is given no reason to think that she likewise escapes the fate that she predicts for herself. Troilus thus miraculously eludes his predetermined end through anachronistic Christian teleology, while Pandarus embodies Troilus's suffering by serving as the young man's tragic surrogate. In this manner, the queer character assumes responsibility for the tragedy he precipitates.

Chaucer's decision to complete his depiction of Pandarus with the character's disavowal of speech cannot easily be construed into a definite meaning, as we simply do not have sufficient information to conjecture whether Pandarus remains silent and gives up pandering or quickly reverts to his former ways. But in this moment, Pandarus makes a choice to end his activity and his speech, a choice as startling and as narratively necessary, in its own way, as is Criseyde's decision to remain with Diomede. Choice, then, is the issue at this moment. Viewing *Troilus and Criseyde* through the lens of Aristotelian natural philosophy, Jennifer Goodman concludes that the text creates a world in which human agency is not crippled by natural or divine forces, despite the thorny issues of predestination and divine omnipotence: "God, as our creator, knows how we will choose. But our choices are our own. They belong to the realm of freedom which God gives us along with our natures. Troilus and Criseyde's paths diverge because, like all of creation,...they have natural places to which they are drawn."[48] Fortune's wheel turns, but the characters make choices along the way that ultimately position them within a framework of Christian teleology, even if this teleology fails to account for the fate of the three primary characters.

The issue of choice is a crucial one in interpreting *Troilus and Criseyde*, yet it cannot be wholly extracted from the tragic works of Fate and Fortune. As Troilus concludes in his musings over human choice and predestination, "So mot it come; and thus the bifallyng / Of thynges that ben wist bifore the tyde, / They mowe nat ben eschued on no syde" (IV: 1076–1078). These characters make choices that bear repercussions on their lives, but these choices correspond—perhaps coincidentally, perhaps miraculously—with their teleological destiny. *Troilus and Criseyde* refuses to answer the question of choice versus destiny, instead highlighting their frustrating interplay. Herein lies Chaucer's confused and conflicting view of Christian teleology: why does Troilus gain eternal comic insight rather than Criseyde or Pandarus? In terms of the poem's anachronistic Christianity, Troilus's earthly love for Criseyde borders on the sinful in that it specifically attributes a divine meaning to an earthly love, as when Troilus compares Criseyde to a saint while apostrophizing to her house: "And farwel shryne, of which the seynt is oute!" (V: 553). In defense of Troilus, he remains true to Criseyde, and his amatory steadfastness to her may in some way position him for his comic revelation. But Pandarus is as true to Troilus as Troilus is to Criseyde, yet he suffers in silence by serving as Troilus's surrogate in the poem's conclusion. Further, if Pandarus anachronistically "sins" by trafficking in women, Troilus's willingness to act in just the same manner demonstrates the limits of his own moral compass (III: 407–413; quoted previously). In the end, Troilus's apotheosis is not a reward for living justly or for making the right choices: it is arbitrary. All of the characters' choices emphasize that they are pursing their own earthly—rather than spiritual—objectives throughout the narrative. Christian teleology gives meaning to Troilus's death, but he deserves it no more than Criseyde or Pandarus. Here we see perhaps the ultimate example of heterosexual male privilege, as comic salvation is miraculously offered to one who deserves it no more than anyone else.

In terms of choice versus Boethian Fortune and opposed to Troilus's miraculous salvation, Pandarus represents neither tragedy nor comedy but dilation, transgression, and resistance. Evading teleological closure both in the Christian and narratival realms, Pandarus stands between Troilus's and Criseyde's narrative fates, but he does not balance them. Rather, he signifies to the reader as queerly in the conclusion of the text as he did in the heterosexual romance he created, suggesting desires never expressed, creating love and spiritual meaning from which he is, in the end, excluded. In the final analysis, we cannot know Pandarus through his queer desires or through his relationships to Christian and narrative teleologies. Due to the fracturing of narrative genre and his queering desires, Pandarus demands that the reader acknowledge, if not embrace, a lack of closure. Between Troilus's laughter and Criseyde's self-damnation obstinately stands Pandarus's final declaration of silence. As always, Pandarus's queer silences speak louder than his words and now point to the limits of Christian and narrative teleology through their arbitrary calls for meaning and closure, as his obfuscations also point to the limits of heterosexual identity.

In *Troilus and Criseyde*, then, queerness represents a refusal to participate within codes of normativity, whether those codes involve courtly love, Christian teleology, or generic meaning. Pandarus, the most active and volitional of the characters, in the end strongly resists any attempt to interpret his desires and his fate. By highlighting the epistemological gap elicited by a Christian teleology that does not construct his own destiny, Pandarus queerly demonstrates that the individual cannot always be conscripted into an ideological framework. He does not overturn the ideological system of courtly love or of anachronistic Christian teleology, but in his resistance to meaning, he queerly points to their limits as they attempt to impose order upon a world of confused and confusing desires.

CHAPTER 5

QUEERING ARTHURIAN ROMANCE:
GENRES, GODGAMES, AND SADOMASOCHISM
IN *SIR GAWAIN AND THE GREEN KNIGHT*

Peggy Knapp observes that "In one text, [*Sir Gawain and the Green Knight*] tells two quite different stories—one about a great knight, recounted in the genre of romance, the other about a penitent Christian, recounted in the genre of exemplum or moral fable."[1] The *Gawain*-poet's genre play, located on the border between romance and exemplum, creates a text that consistently destabilizes its meaning in a similar manner as its sexual play destabilizes Gawain's heroic and Christian identity.[2] In addition to focusing on genre as a key tactic in this poetic mission, I also analyze the *Gawain*-poet's insistent deployment of games as a strategy of deception, in which genre serves as a crucial trick in a larger authorial game. To understand the *Gawain*-poet's play of genre, we must see how it works within the play of the godgame, a ludic concept that explores the meanings of games played by opponents with vastly different understandings of their strategies and significance. For the *Gawain*-poet, genre and sexuality are playful strategies in a serious moral game, so it is through a lens of play and game that genre and sexuality should be investigated. The first section of this chapter explores the genres of romance and exemplum through the hermeneutic of the godgame in a theologically normative interpretation of the text that sees Gawain's spiritual growth as the chief aim of the narrative.[3] The second section interprets the godgame's play of genre and sexuality as a queering strategy designed to trap Gawain and the reader sadomasochistically into a renewed relationship with Christianity: through the latent generic presence of the saint's life, *Sir Gawain and the Green Knight* reveals itself as a disciplining and disciplinary text that demands readerly abandon rather than resistance.[4] From this perspective, I argue that both Gawain and the reader are queered into a better understanding of Christianity through the dynamics of a sadomasochistic relationship with the Christian divine.

Gawain and the Godgames of Romance and Exemplum

For the *Gawain*-poet, genre is an authorial game with a strict moral purpose, and to address this issue, it is first necessary to explore medieval and modern concepts of play and game. Games and play abound in *Sir Gawain and the Green Knight*, and through his depictions of such amusements, the *Gawain*-poet investigates the ways in which they reveal the knight's understanding of his individual identity as a Christian. Through the intersecting dynamics of Arthur's chivalrous court of play and the Green Knight's gaming challenge to it, the Green Knight brings a crisis of self-definition to Gawain: this game forces Gawain to confront his personal limitations and to gain a better understanding of his place within a Christian world. The ample scholarship on Gawain and game covers this territory extensively;[5] in this section of the chapter, I expand on previous scholarship by providing a structural analysis of the game's many levels, by locating the romance within the tradition of the godgame, by analyzing the critical juncture between play and game crucial to the godgame, by examining the overlap between the godgames of the Green Knight and of Christianity, and by exploring the ways in which the textual godgame of the beheading contest merges with the meta-textual godgame of genre. Christianity is figured, not merely as the narrative's default worldview, but as an active player in this fascinating game. The Green Knight's godgame of chivalry (and the genre of romance) ultimately merges with the Christian godgame of spirituality (and the genre of exemplum), forcing Gawain to confront his limitations in these two key aspects of his identity.

Games, at their simplest, must involve a goal, rules, and participants willing to achieve the goal while adhering to the rules. Bernard Suits theorizes that all games incorporate objectives, rules, and attitudes into their structure:

> To play a game is to attempt to achieve a specific state of affairs (prelusory goal), using only means permitted by rules (lusory means), where the rules prohibit use of more efficient in favour of less efficient means (constitutive rules), and where the rules are accepted just because they make possible such activity (lusory attitude).[6]

The players accept the rules and requirements of the game, for whatever reason they have decided to enter into it; engagement with the game should entail following the rules. Robert Wilson suggests that the lusory attitude is the incorporation of the rules into the players' mindset, "the internalization of the rules."[7] In addition to a goal and rules, most games also have stakes; although these stakes may be minimal (the joy of winning) or large (money, prestige, glory), their presence in a game indicates that the game matters to the players, that it typically bears some personal significance to them.

In many analyses of game and play, the two terms are treated interchangeably, as if "game" and "play" are synonyms of each other. A quick distinction between game and play, however, is that games bear a structure of rules, goals, and stakes, but play need have none of these constitutive elements. Johan Huizinga provides a concise (and oft-quoted) definition of play:

> Summing up the formal characteristics of play we might call it a free activity standing quite consciously outside "ordinary" life as being "not serious," but at the same time absorbing the player intensely and utterly. It is an activity connected with no material interest, and no profit can be gained by it. It proceeds within its own proper boundaries of time and space according to fixed rules and in an orderly manner. It promotes the formation of social groupings which tend to surround themselves with secrecy and to stress their difference from the common world by disguise or other means.[8]

This definition of play, remarkable for its simplicity and apparent completeness, underscores that play incorporates a much looser structure than game, so much looser that play may be more of an attitude than an activity.[9] Brad Stone, for example, comments that "play does indeed require a certain attitude to enter it."[10] By distinguishing between game as structure and play as attitude, we see the dynamics of the Green Knight's game more clearly. Simply put, although game and play often complement each other, games are not always fun if the stakes become too high (such as life or death); play, on the other hand, should always contain an element of amusement and whimsy.

The godgame, through its conceptualization of game players with vastly different understandings of their game, highlights the chasm that often appears between game and play. It details the confusion purposefully generated by some game-masters who hold complete control over the other player. As Robert Wilson outlines,

> A godgame occurs in literature when one or more characters creates an illusion, a mazelike sequence of false accounts, that entraps another character. The entrapped character finds himself entangled in the threads of (from his point of view) an incomprehensible strategy plotted by another character who (thus) takes on the roles both of a game-maker, since he invents rules for the other character to follow, and of a god as well. In the latter sense, the

master of the game is godlike in that he exercises power, holds an advantageous position, will probably be beyond detection (even understanding) and may even be, so far as the entrapped character is concerned, invisible.[11]

When the game-master has such superior—and at times supernatural—advantages, the pawn-player experiences chaos within the nevertheless highly structured game that the adversary creates.[12] The person called to play the game, who is more played with than playing, nevertheless is ensnared in a situation that demands immediate engagement. Although the godgame may appear to be a game primarily for the god-figure and an ordeal for the pawn-player, the pawn-player generally "wins" the game through the experience of the game-maker's labyrinthine but ultimately instructional game. The purpose of the godgame is to force the player to confront the mystery of existence and thus to ponder deep questions of life and living; John Fowles suggests that the godgame reveals "a series of human illusions about something that does not exist in fact, absolute knowledge and absolute power."[13] If we add "absolute virtue" to Fowles's list, the relevance of the godgame to Gawain begins to emerge.

One of the chief features of the godgame is its ambiguous division of play and game. The godgame exploits the fault line between play (as fun) and game (as structure) in order for the game-master to deliver a pedagogical experience to the pawn-player. Although players such as Gawain typically expect games to be fun—as when he laughs following the Green Knight's departure with his severed head, a moment when we would expect Gawain not to treat the game as play (463–64)—the game structure, in effect, tricks the pawn-player to expect a sense of play that it never delivers.[14] In contrast, the game-master may play the game, in the sense of enjoying it, even though he or she may need to pursue it seriously, as when Bertilak pursues his daily hunts in the exchange game. The shifting dynamics of play in a godgame underscore that each moment must be analyzed carefully in terms of who is playing and enjoying the game at what moment, and who is being played with.

The godgame may appear an anachronistic hermeneutic for medieval literature: despite Fowles's interest in medieval literature (especially in *The Ebony Tower*), his conception of the godgame applies directly to his own twentieth-century literature, not that of fourteenth-century England. Nevertheless, the godgame is a particularly appropriate tool for analyzing *Sir Gawain and the Green Knight* due to medieval Christian views of play.[15] Two medieval exegetical traditions—one that treats play as a *de facto* moral test and another that depicts Jesus as a game player—correspond sufficiently with the structure of the godgame to warrant its use as a hermeneutic structure for medieval literature.[16] As godgames typically test or instruct the pawn-player to some greater truth or insight, the medieval view of play as a moral test allows play to serve as a crucial indicator of the pawn-player's identity. How s/he plays the game reveals who s/he is. And as godgames require a divine or supernatural game-player, the tradition of depicting Jesus as a player in the heavenly game of salvation supports an analysis of the divine features of medieval literary games.

Describing it as a morally ambiguous arena, Thomas Aquinas examines play in a manner that highlights its moral haziness and constructs it as a latent moral test. After concluding that moderate play is moral, Aquinas addresses the question of whether an excess or a deficiency of play is sinful. In Articulus 3, "Utrum in superfluitate ludi possit esse peccatum," Aquinas concludes: "Et sic patet quod excessus in ludo est peccatum mortale."[17] That too much play is sinful may not be surprising, but Aquinas concludes in Articulus 4, "Utrum in defectu ludi consistat aliquod peccatum," that a lack of play is also sinful. Although too little play emerges as less of a sin than an excess ("defectus ludi minus est vitiosus quam ludi superexcessus"), insufficient play is nevertheless a sin as well and, therefore, play should not be avoided altogether.[18] Such a view is not reserved to exegetes, as Dante likewise stresses that the play of laughter reveals a man's character and should therefore be engaged in moderately. In the *Convivio*, he depicts play and mirth as a necessary tempering of spirits that protects the dignity of a man and, correspondingly, the modesty of a woman:

> E che è ridere se non una coruscazione della dilettazione dell'anima, cioè uno lume apparente di fuori secondo sta dentro? E però si conviene all' uomo, a dimostrare la sua anima nell'alegrezza moderata, moderatamente ridere, con onesta severitade e con poco movimento della sua faccia; sì che [la] donna che allora si dimostra, come detto è, paia modesta e non dissoluta.
>
> (And what is laughter save a coruscation of the delight of the soul, that is to say, a light appearing outwardly according as it exists within? And therefore it is fitting that a man, in order to show his soul moderate in merriment, should laugh in moderation, with a dignified severity, and with slight movement of his features; so that the lady who is then revealed, as said above, may appear modest and not dissolute.)[19]

Aquinas and Dante accord play and laughter an essential status in the life of humanity because it tests one's ability to find the proper balance between excess and deficiency; play and humor delight if engaged in moderately, but they offend if engaged in excessively. Thus, in a similar manner to the godgame, which tests the pawn-player through his/her play of the game, medieval thinkers describe play as a crucial moral arena in which one can prove oneself worthy of praise or of scorn. From this basis, in which play reveals character, the godgame metamorphoses the latent moral significance of play and game into a blatant challenge.

Aquinas and Dante allow us to see play as a *de facto* proving ground for humanity, which makes it appropriate for use in a godgame; the tradition of depicting Jesus as a game-player gives us further cause to analyze *Sir Gawain and the Green Knight* within the framework of the godgame. In such medieval drama as the "Harrowing of Hell," Jesus plays a game when He prepares to bring mirth and joyous games to the souls suffering in hell:

> The feynde theym wan with trayn,
> Thrugh fraude of erthly fode;
> I haue theym boght agan
> With shedying of my blode
> And now I will that stede restore
> Which the feynde fell fro for syn;
> Som tokyn will I send before,
> With myrth to gar thare gammes begyn.[20]

Jesus's salvation of the souls trapped in hell is thus construed as the starting point of a game; the heavenly play of salvation contrasts with the diabolical play of the devil, Herod, and the crucifiers depicted in earlier scenes of the sequence.[21] Jesus's game, nothing less than salvation prepared by a benevolent and loving God, demands its players to participate and to adhere to the rules of Christianity with faith, not knowledge. The *Gawain*-poet, obviously well schooled in biblical knowledge, deploys this tradition of Christian play within the gaming world of the Arthurian court.

Before proceeding to an analysis of the games and genres of *Sir Gawain and the Green Knight*, a final significant aspect of games should be noted. In addition to rules, goals, and stakes, games must be playful *for someone*. As mentioned previously, the seriousness of some games entails that they are not always fun for the players. If a game is not fun for the players, its sense of play is most often reserved for the spectators. The fun of the Green Knight's game, fraught as it is with danger and humiliation for Gawain, is enjoyed both by the characters who face no real danger and by the readers. Scott Troyan notes that the concern with games and play is not limited to the narrative level of the poem but actually structures the work to pull the reader into the game:

> Not only does the text tell the story of a game, it involves the audience as a part of the game by utilizing a series of metaphors imitating some sense of revelation. Signs, words, and other things bespeaking truth in *Sir Gawain and the Green Knight* are ubiquitous reminders of the game that by causing one to reflect on the text, by provoking one to work through the various

linguistic games and levels of reflection generate help to enlighten one regarding his or her own self.[22]

This text demands that the reader enter the game, and the game afoot is to decipher the significance of the games to Gawain's conception of himself. The game is played for the reader, but its fun conceals a message of Christian seriousness that the *Gawain*-poet exposes not through pedantry but through play.

The brilliance of *Sir Gawain and the Green Knight* is that, although the godgame forces Gawain to confront the impossibility of flawless virtue, this realization comes to the reader with a sense of play and festivity. As audience of the text, we are both inside and outside its medieval world of festival, as were its original auditors: the play and laughter of festival conceal a deep message of Christian truth that displaces festival fun as it simultaneously provides such fun. Mikhail Bakhtin describes such a mixture of the sacred and the profane as "Christmas laughter," in which "spiritual content. . .combined with worldly tunes."[23] In the romance's humorous yet spiritual world, set in the season of Christmas revelry, laughter combines with Christianity such that the two are blurred until the poem's end and then even beyond. As Morton Bloomfield notes, the poem is "fundamentally humorous, although by no means unserious."[24] The godgames of the Green Knight and of Christianity provide a structure of fun and amusement in order to probe questions of fundamental significance to Christian identity, knightly virtue, and a fallen earthly world. In the following sections of this chapter, I examine these issues first by examining the rules and strategies of the godgames and genres, then by investigating the stakes of the games to determine what in addition to Gawain's head is in jeopardy throughout the game, and last by exploring how the secular godgame of chivalry and the genre of romance transforms into a Christian godgame of virtue and the genre of exemplum. After this normative analysis is completed, the groundwork will be successfully established to turn to the queering implications of the *Gawain*-poet's genres.

The Rules and Strategies of the Godgames and Genres

As evidenced by a hacked-off head that can be picked up by its body, the game that the Green Knight commences at Arthur's court is no ordinary one. The genre of romance, however, treats the unexpected as the expected, and this feature of the romance traps Gawain, as he falls deeper into romantic illusions of self and chivalry. Moreover, the Green Knight goes to great lengths to hide both the rules and the true meaning of his chivalric godgame, keeping Gawain's attention focused on decapitations rather than on his spirituality. The rules of this game, at their simplest, are that Gawain will strike a blow against the Green Knight and accept a blow from him one year later.[25] The Green Knight asks Gawain to repeat the rules of their game, and Gawain does so:

> "That bede the this buffet, quat-so bifallez after,
> And at this tyme twelmonyth take at the an other
> Wyth what weppen so thou wylt, and wyth no wygh ellez
> on lyue." (382–85)

The Green Knight is pleased to hear Gawain correctly repeat the rules and thanks him in advance for the blow he will receive. Before proceeding to the next step of the game, the Green Knight stresses the importance of the game's rules by referring to them as a covenant: "And thou hatz redily rehersed, bi resoun ful trwe, / Clanly al the couenaunt that I the kynge asked" (392–93). On a structural level, these rules represent the entire game that the Green Knight and Gawain agree to play.[26]

During the Christmas festivities at Bertilak's court, Gawain agrees to the second explicit set of rules of the chivalric godgame, and the rules of this game also bear the markings of a legal covenant. As J.A. Burrow notes, this scene mirrors that of the first fitt in which "Christmas festivities lead up to a point at which the hero makes a *contract* with his adversary."[27] The *Gawain*-poet employs a shift in the host's tone from frivolity to earnest in order to indicate that Gawain does not understand the full ramifications of this "new" game:

> "Yet firre," quoth the freke, "a forwarde we make
> Quat-so-euer I wynne in the wod hit worthez to yourez
> And quat chek so ye acheue chaunge me therforne
> Swete, swap we so, sware with trawthe
> Quether, leude, so lymp, lere other better." (1105–109)

The *Gawain*-poet stresses the seriousness of the game when the two men repeat the terms of this agreement: "To bed yet er thay yede, / Recorded couenauntez ofte; / The olde lorde of that leude / Cowthe wel halde layk alofte" (1122–25). Gawain readily agrees to this "new" game, declaring "Bi God...I grant thertylle, / And that yow lyst for to layke, lef hit me thynkes" (1110–11). Perceiving the entire contract as new, Gawain joins this game without realizing its connection to the first.

We see the skeletal structure of the chivalric godgame and its connection to the genre of romance in Gawain's and the Green Knight's agreements over the rules, but the rules of another godgame—a Christian one, connected to the genre of exemplum—are in play as well. The "rules" of this Christian godgame are latently expressed on the pentangle shield that highlights Gawain's supposed virtues.[28] Gawain's shield displays more guidelines that he must follow, and his inability to adhere to these rules emerges as the focus of the Christian godgame. The pentangle affirms Gawain's perfection, that "he watz funden fautlez" (640), but perfection is a principle that can never be maintained in a fallen world. The knight has supposedly earned the praise that the pentangle signifies, and the *Gawain*-poet underscores that his reputation is deserved: "Gawan watz for gode knawen, and as golde pured, / Voyded of vche vylany, with vertuez ennourned / in mote" (633–35). After a catalogue of the pentangle's five virtues, the *Gawain*-poet reiterates that "Now alle these fyue sythez, for sothe, were fetled on this knyght" (656). The dramatic action that follows tests this assertion of virtuous reputation and proves that it represents an impossibility. From the outset of the game, the rules—both of the Green Knight and of romance, as well as of the pentangle shield and of exemplum—trap Gawain in a labyrinth from which no human being (except a saint) could successfully escape.[29] The pentangle incorporates Gawain's future realization of human limitations into the very structure of the game.

Rules provide the basic structure of games and genres, but textual strategies and authorial manipulations provide much of their interest and excitement. The strategies that the *Gawain*-poet employs enhance the complexity both of the godgames for Gawain and of the genres for the reader. Bertilak's chief strategy lies in exploiting the chasm between game and play; he tricks Gawain into thinking the exchange game is mere playful fun, while he himself engages in the game seriously. The depictions of the three hunts, with their emphasis on the graphic details of chasing and killing prey, showcase the host's zealous engagement in his chivalrous game. In contrast, Gawain sees the exchange game as delightful frivolity, as when he joins in the play at Bertilak's castle: "Thus wyth laghande lotez the lorde hit tayt makez, / For to glade Sir Gawayn with gomnez in halle / that nyght" (988–90).[30] On each of these days, the *Gawain*-poet contrasts the host's action and Gawain's inaction: "Thus laykez this lorde by lynde-wodez euez / And Gawayn the god mon in gay bed lygez" (1178–79); "This day wyth this ilk dede thay dryuen on this wyse, / Whyle oure luflych lede lys in his bedde" (1468–69); "Sir Gawayn lis and slepes / Ful stille and softe al night; / The lorde that his craftez kepes, / Ful erly he watz dight" (1686–89). The crucial difference in their strategies is that Bertilak actively plays the game through his hunting, in contrast to Gawain's passive dalliances in bed. Through this contrast, the *Gawain*-poet highlights that the game encompasses all aspects of Gawain's stay at Bertilak's court, yet Gawain only recognizes that he is playing it when he exchanges winnings with his host. Gawain delights in the recreation of play, but does not engage in it with an eye to its serious ramifications. The reader is likewise ensnared: do we identify with our lazy yet chivalric protagonist and the pleasures of romance, or are we prescient enough to foreclose this identification by realizing the impending moral force of the exemplum?[31]

On a textual level, the daily exchanges bring to the surface a deeper level of Bertilak's strategy—the sacrifice, a ploy that enables him to win the game.[32] In fact, the sacrifices of the daily exchanges assist the host in imbuing the game with a sense of delightful play that deceives Gawain to its full significance. When Gawain swaps winnings with his host at the end of the first day of their game, their reunion is a happy one ("When Gawayn wyth hym mette / Ther watz bot wele at wylle" [1370–71]). The spoils of the day—venison for Gawain, a kiss for the host—are amicably shared, and the terms of the game are repeated for the following day.[33] In each of the scenes in which Gawain and his host confirm their pact, the *Gawain*-poet emphasizes the playful nature of the meetings, but the lightness of these interactions obscures to Gawain that these encounters bear deep relevance to the manner in which he will soon view himself.[34] (These meetings also underscore the fact that Gawain plays games he does not fully understand when he is drinking wine.[35]) Certainly, the exchanges trick Gawain into thinking that he is winning the game.[36] For a mere six kisses, Gawain receives venison, a boar, and a fox pelt. If these trophies were insufficient to convince Gawain of his daily successes, however, the host enthusiastically encourages Gawain to see himself as the victor:

> The lorde sayde, "Bi saynt Gile,
> Ye ar the best that I knowe!
> Ye ben ryche in a whyle,
> Such chaffer and ye drowe." (1644–47)

Blinding Gawain to the importance of this game, the host allows him to "win" these rounds in order to defeat him subsequently. Gawain knows only mirth and play at his host's court, but this apparent comfort sets the stage for his incipient defeat; allowing Gawain to enjoy this round of the chivalric godgame—to enjoy it as play—prepares him to lose in the end. Again, the same strategy applies to the reader: if we delight in the play of romance and courtly festivity, we miss the forthcoming lesson of the exemplum.

Bertilak's strategy of tricking Gawain with the supposed fun and play of the game is mirrored by his wife's similar strategy in her daily seductions. The *Gawain*-poet portrays the lady's entrance into Gawain's bedroom and her promise to imprison him as a jest. Playing her game of love with laughter and amusement, the lady tricks Gawain throughout their encounters into playing a game he does not wish to play. Relying on laughter to carry him through a potentially precarious situation, Gawain fails to realize that the lady is ensnaring him in the overarching structure of the Green Knight's game. Although we cannot discount his discomfort in these moments of the text, humor and laughter nonetheless sweep Gawain along into the chivalrous godgame. Congruent with this dismissal of Gawain's discomfort is one of the chief ironies of *Sir Gawain and the Green Knight*: the lady tricks Gawain into thinking that they are playing his game, not hers. She states her reasons for coming to his chamber as:

> "I com hider sengel, and sitte
> To lerne at yow sum game;
> Dos, techez me of your wytte,
> Whil my lorde is fro hame." (1531–34)

As we learn at the game's end, the lady here knowingly conceals her part in the larger game while requesting Gawain to teach her the game of courtly love. Gawain is tricked both by laughter and fun, as well as by her compliments to his knightly knowledge.[37]

The intricate strategies of Bertilak and the lady highlight a glaring failure on Gawain's part: he devises no strategy to assist him in the game. In response to Bertilak's and the lady's schemes that trick Gawain at every turn, Gawain's only "strategy" is to cheat by withholding the girdle, a strategy that is doubly ironic in light of his insistence that the two men adhere strictly to the rules of their game. When his host asks Gawain from whom he received his kisses, the knight insists that such information is beyond the scope of their agreement: "'That watz not forward,' quoth he, 'frayst me no more. / For ye haf tan that yow tydez, trawe non other / ye mowe'" (1395–97). The *Gawain*-poet further emphasizes Gawain's duplicity by contrasting it to the Green Knight's integrity to the terms of their agreement.[38] When Gawain asks his host for a guide to the Green Knight's chapel, he responds with words that ironically highlight Gawain's deceit: "'In god faythe,' quoth the godmon, 'wyth a goud wylle / Al that euer I yow hyght halde schal I redé'" (1969–70). The host remains true to the terms of engagement, but the games—and how Gawain plays them—highlight his inability to meet the standards of his pentangle and, thus, his failure to be the man whom the pentangle affirms him to be. The gap between the promises of the pentangle shield in an exemplum and Gawain's actions in a romance undermine his knightly identity. Gawain's cheating discloses his failure to be who he thinks he is; as a strategy, it fails to help him either to win the game or to preserve his honor. Comparable to Gawain, does the reader deploy any strategy in interpreting the text? Falling to the pleasures of romance, most readers succumb to narrative seduction with little clue that they will soon be in need of a moral defense.

Does the Christian godgame of exemplum display a discernible strategy? As the ultimate controlling force of the narrative, Christianity trumps Bertilak's godgame by turning the threat of his romantic and magical godgame into a pedagogical lesson and an exemplum for an already virtuous knight. The strategy of Christianity is that it can reconceptualize and reconfigure magical actions to Christian ends. Certainly, the *Gawain*-poet highlights the specifically Christian elements of this godgame. While searching for the Green Knight's castle, Gawain repeatedly prays for divine assistance:

> And therfore sykyng he sayde, "I beseche the, lorde,
> And Mary, that is myldest moder so dere,
> Of sum herber ther heghly I myght here masse,
> Ande thy matynez to-morne, mekely I ask,
> And therto prestly I pray my pater and aue
>   and crede." (753–58)

This prayer is answered immediately, as Gawain discerns Bertilak's castle; the knight then thanks Jesus and St. Julian for his safe delivery to Bertilak's court: "and heghly he thonkez / Jesus and sayn Gilyan, that gentyle are bothe, / That cortaysly had hym kydde, and his cry herkened" (773–75).[39] Gawain finds Bertilak's court as the answer to his prayer, and the *Gawain*-poet writes that Jesus "herkened" the knight's plea. The presence of the Christian Divine is certainly more occluded than in the scene from the "Harrowing of Hell" cited earlier, but it is nonetheless present in the poem, directing Gawain's actions and answering his prayers. Since Jesus, Mary, and Julian bear responsibility for Gawain's presence in Bertilak's castle, we can see them as players in this game, as participants in the unfolding dynamics of the Christian godgame.

The Stakes of Godgames and Genres

Games and play—those of the Arthurian court, of the Green Knight, and of Christianity—advance the narrative so that Gawain displays his virtuous identity through his pentangle shield and armor; the godgame of the Green Knight (the beheading game and the exchange game, aligned with the romance tradition) and the godgame of Christianity (the "rules" of the pentangle, providing the moral requirements of the exemplum tradition), however, expose the incongruities between external reputation and internal identity. Gawain, tricked by his own reputation, must learn who he is based upon a better understanding of Christianity. "Gawain assumes an identity as a member of a general type, that is, the identity of a knight.

Within this general type, he is individualized by...the pentangle painted on his shield," argues Stephanie Hollis.[40] Knight and individual, courtier and unique self, Gawain has yet to explore fully the limitations of both senses of his self; he must face the obstacles inherent in straddling two worlds. Because the Green Knight's godgame and the pentangle both represent impossible challenges that will undermine Gawain's identity yet lead him to a deeper understanding of his Christianity, the knight's identity—as the knightly hero of a romance and as the Christian protagonist of an exemplum—emerges as the stakes of the godgame.

From the very beginning, the Green Knight's chivalric godgame ties itself to the identity of the Arthurian court as expressed by the game and play of romance and chivalry. The Arthurian courtiers enjoy play, game, and festival as part of their chivalrous lifestyle, and their adherence to chivalry serves as a means of self- and group-definition. Victoria Weiss notes: "Both Gawain and his fellow Arthurian courtiers cling to definitions of chivalry which remain unreal and, like games with their functional, if at times, arbitrary, rules, give both Gawain and his friends the mistaken idea that the game of chivalry is a complete resource for solving any problem life can present to a nobleman."[41] Since chivalry is both a game and a marker of the court, the Green Knight's challenge becomes a test of identities constructed upon chivalrous ideals. The identity of the Arthurian court is at stake throughout the Green Knight's godgame, and the delightfully ironic aspect of the godgame is that their identity is predicated upon play: through Gawain's attempts to play the Green Knight's unplayable game, he fails to maintain his heroic and chivalric identity.

The Green Knight appears in answer to Arthur's request for a marvel after the lavish descriptions of Arthur's court and its play (37–95); his entrance, however, disrupts the courtiers' play with a game devoid of any real merriment for them. The *Gawain*-poet presents dueling conceptions of play's implications: that of the Arthurian court's festival world (which enjoys play as its own end) and that of the Green Knight's godgame (which bears with it deep seriousness in its threats of death). The Green Knight's bizarre intrusion and deadly Christmas game put a damper on their revelries, as his arrival is greeted by a stunned silence; nonetheless, the courtiers light-heartedly return to their play after his departure. Arthur attempts to put the preceding events within the context of normal Christmas revelry by telling Guinevere that "Wel bycommes such craft vpon Cristmasse, / Laykyng of enterludez, to laghe and to syng, / Among thise kynde caroles of knyghtez and ladyez" (471–73). Indeed, Arthur can now eat his dinner since he has found the marvel he summoned. The play of the court then resumes with little concern for the Green Knight's appearance: "Wyth alle maner of mete and mynstralcie bothe, / Wyth wele walt thay that day, til worthed an ende / in londe" (484–86). The Arthurian identity of the courtiers, as defined by play, festival, and chivalry, appears remarkably unaffected after the Green Knight's challenge.

During the Green Knight's initial challenge, Gawain's identity conforms to that of the rest of the court. We see him sitting beside Guinevere at the feast until he replaces Arthur as the Green Knight's combatant. As the representative of the court, Gawain's attitude toward the game reflects the determined nonchalance of his king and courtiers. When the Green Knight leaves, Gawain and Arthur express with their laughter a light-hearted response to a serious game: "The kyng and Gawen thare / At that grene thay laghe and grenne" (463–64). Arthur and Gawain appear determined to view the game as play, but this game should not be considered play because the stakes are too high. The Arthurian chivalric identity still holds, despite the dangers that have just threatened their lives; indeed, they eagerly return to the fun of play at the beginning of the second fitt: "Gawan watz glad to begynne those gomnez in halle" (495).[42] In the whole of the first fitt and the beginning of the second, the *Gawain*-poet emphasizes the playful stability of the Arthurian court; the courtiers refuse to acknowledge the deadly implications of play and game despite the Green Knight's threat to decapitate Gawain a year hence. Even when Gawain leaves for certain death, a sense of play dominates Arthur's court. Arthur's spirits appear as merry on All Saint's Day as on the previous New Year's when he celebrates Gawain's imminent quest: "And [Arthur] made a fare on that fest for the frekez sake, / With much reuel and ryche of the Rounde Table" (537–38). Gawain likewise appears remarkably cheerful about his impending fate and bluffs away any fears he might have, as the *Gawain*-poet reports that "The knyght mad ay god chere, / And sayde, 'Quat schuld I wonde? / Of destinés derf and dere / What may mon do bot fonde?' " (562–65). For Arthur and Gawain, who still do not realize the stakes of the game, the Green Knight's game has not yet necessitated their reevaluation of a playfully chivalrous identity.[43]

Gawain appears to have a firmly developed sense of self at this point in the narrative: he knows that he is a knight of the Arthurian court, and he believes he adheres to the codes of chivalry. It quickly becomes apparent, though, that Gawain's identity is not as stable as the knight himself believes it to be, and Gawain's armor underscores this instability of identity. John Leyerle observes that costumes play an important role in defining the hero: "The hero has a costume, often armor of magical origin and power. This costume tends to be used for trickery or even deception.... These costumes are important because they symbolize the metamorphosis inherent in the hero's assumption of the role he is to play."[44] It appears, however, that, if anyone is tricked by the significance of Gawain's armor, it is Gawain himself. I have already explained how the pentangle shield serves as a set of guiding principles in the game, but Gawain's armor and the shield also serve as a statement of knightly identity. Gawain dons his armor and takes up the pentangle shield in preparation for his journey, and, in so doing, makes clear claims about his virtues and, thus, his identity.[45] The *Gawain*-poet spends four stanzas describing Gawain's armor, his horse and its trappings, and the pentangle shield (566–669); the sheer bulk of poetic lines addressing Gawain's attire suggests its importance to the thematic unfolding of the narrative.[46] Clothes and armor serve as Gawain's tools for declaring his knightly virtue, but only through his journey will he learn that his sartorial trappings are actually traps in the Christian godgame. And as Gawain is blinded by his own self-representation through his armor, he is likewise tricked and trapped by the Green Knight/Bertilak's costume changes. Both men play their roles as actors in the unfolding drama with the necessary costumes and props, but Gawain accepts his performance as a true statement of identity, failing to realize both that his identity cannot be adequately represented by his armor and that the Green Knight's appearance is a facade as well. The game ends when Bertilak allows Gawain to see through both of their costumes, revealing himself as a much more benevolent figure and Gawain as a much more human one. Gawain discards his original identification as knight of the pentangle and assumes a new identity as knight of the green girdle; when all of the costumes of romance are stripped and the true Christian identities of exemplum are assumed, the game concludes.

The game must be pursued because the court's chivalric reputation is at stake, and Gawain's sense of his knightly honor demands that the agreement be fulfilled. Arriving at Bertilak's court, Gawain initially showcases the stability of his playfully chivalric sense of self. When he enters the unknown court after his long journey, it ironically appears that he still seeks festival fun, not realizing that the game is ongoing and despite the life-threatening experience in which games have embroiled him. Gawain quickly returns to his playful self: he falls in with the amusements of the court "wyth spechez of myerthe" (860) and enjoys the feast his host offers him (887–98). In response to the many delights surrounding him, Gawain immediately overindulges with alcohol: "That mon much merthe con make, / For wyn in his hed that wende" (899–900). Entering his host's castle, Gawain finds a court dedicated to play, one remarkably similar to Arthur's court of one year ago. The irony of the *Gawain*-poet's art is that, as Gawain will discover, although he finds himself in a new court, he is still engaged in the same game. Furthermore, he is still trying to *play* a game that he could never enjoy, and his chivalrous identity still lies in jeopardy as the stakes of the game. These moments underscore the persistence of romance as Gawain's primary hermeneutic for all of his experiences and his insistent—yet incomplete—identification of the genre of his adventure.

In the end, the question of Gawain's identity in light of the rules both of chivalry/romance and of the pentangle/exemplum becomes the game's only focus, especially when the Green Knight admits that the stakes of the game were minimal, that Gawain's life was never truly in jeopardy, whether he accepted the green girdle or not:

> "Fyrst I mansed the muryly with a mynt one,
> And roue the wyth no rof-sore, with ryght I the profered
> For the forwarde that we fest in the fyrst nyght,
> And thou trystyly the trawthe and trwly me haldez,
> Al the gayne thow me gef, as god mon schulde.
> That other munt for the morne, mon, I the profered,
> Thou kyssedes my clere wyf—the cossez me raghtez.
> For bothe two here I the bede bot two bare myntes
>   boute scathe.
> Trwe mon trwe restore,
> Thenne thar mon drede no wathe.
> At the thrid thou fayled thore,
> And therfor that tappe ta the." (2345–57)

If Gawain had given up the green girdle in the third set of exchanges as the rules of the game demanded, the Green Knight would have merely pretended to strike Gawain a third time—as he did with his first two blows—rather than decapitate him.[47] The Green Knight's godgame, then, appears to have always had a foregone conclusion. Whether Gawain withholds the girdle or not, the Green Knight never intends to kill him: if Gawain keeps the green girdle, he lives due to its magic; if he gives it to his host, the Green Knight skips the third stroke.[48] Instead, Gawain fails to adhere both to the chivalric rules of the Green Knight's godgame of romance and the pentangle rules of the Christian godgame of exemplum. The Green Knight's game, which first appears as a test of strength, discloses itself not to be an agonistic competition but a revelatory experience.

Indeed, the trappings of the godgame retrospectively reveal themselves throughout the Green Knight's game when Bertilak admits to Gawain that the true stakes of his godgame were to test the reputation of the Arthurian court. Plotted by the supernatural Morgan to antagonize Guinevere, this game reveals truths about the human condition, ultimately in an uplifting manner, by forcing Gawain to realize the insufficiency of human virtue. He is little more than a pawn throughout the game, but his experiences with the game revitalize his sense of self and, through his newly acquired humility, his understanding of Christian virtues. And when we realize that both the Green Knight's and

Gawain's heads were never really at stake in their game, the true stakes become apparent. The stakes of the Green Knight's game, as he admits at its end, are the chivalric reputation of the Arthurian court ("For to assay the surquidré, yif hit soth were / That rennes of the grete renoun of the Rounde Table" [2457–58]); these lines remind the reader that the Green Knight earlier established Gawain's reputation as a stake in the game when he admonished him to accept the challenge, "other recreaunt be calde the behoues" (456). The stakes for the other earthly players of the game—his wife and Morgan—are nonexistent.[49] They control the game, and they cannot lose. Indeed, they have nothing to lose because nothing of theirs enters the game in any way such that it is threatened. With the stakes so low for them, these characters can truly play the game; for Gawain, the stakes are too high for him to play both because he does not know his life is not in danger and because he cares deeply about his chivalric reputation. Thus, we hear the Green Knight's laughter at the game's end in contrast to the silence of Gawain's apparent dishonor. And, as I discuss subsequently, the reader is left with the contradiction between Gawain's silence and the courtiers' laughter, an interpretive conundrum that forecloses a secure meaning from both the romance and the exemplum.

Defeat in Romance, Victory in Exemplum: Gawain and the Vagaries of Genre in the Christian Godgame

All games must end, and the end of the godgame entails Gawain's hesitant acceptance of Christianity's teleological causality and ultimately providential purpose. Gawain, who has not adopted a strategy (except cheating) throughout the game, decides on one before entering the Green Knight's chapel. As he called upon Christian divinities to help him find Bertilak's court, he now determines a strategy to assist him in the game by ceding all authority to God: "Ful wel con Dryghtyn schape / His seruauntez for to saue." (2138–39). Rather than praying for divine assistance to advance the game, as he did earlier, Gawain now submits to God's will; in terms of strategy, Gawain switches from a blind faith in his reputation as an Arthurian knight to a dedicated faith in God. Within the Christian godgame, this is the only strategy possible. The earlier prayers were directed at the specific physical requirements for Gawain to fulfill his chivalric quest and to effect the next plot development of the romance; these new prayers highlight that Gawain has resigned himself to God's will and accepts whatever God ordains, revealing a sense of Christian sacrifice that adheres to the exemplum tradition. Of course, Gawain still wears the green girdle for protection, but he shows an incipient awareness of God's role in his destiny.

This strategy succeeds for Gawain when he is forced to confront his failings. The question of who Gawain is and who he should be stands at the height of the game when the Green Knight interrogates Gawain's chivalric identity after the Arthurian knight flinches before the axe. In the face of death, Gawain loses control of his courtly persona, and the Green Knight then comments mockingly: "Thou art not Gawayn...that is so goud halden, / That neuer arghed for no here by hylle ne be vale, / And now thou fles for ferde er thou fele harmez!" (2270–72). Yet again, Gawain must face both that he is not the knight whom others expect but also that he is not the knight whom he expects himself to be. As he agrees with the Green Knight not to flinch a second time, he acknowledges that the chivalric code of courage must be maintained by keeping his head on the chopping block despite his fear of losing it: "I schunt onez, / And so wyl I no more; / Bot thagh my hede falle on the stonez / I con not hit restore" (2280–83). Ironically, Gawain does not lose his head—although he thinks he will—because the magic girdle protects him; despite the fact that the lady tells him about the girdle's power, he believes he will die.

Gawain's chivalric identity as a romance hero is forever altered by his failures in the game, and he confesses that "For care of thy knokke cowardyse me taght / To acorde me with couetyse, my kynde to forsake, / That is larges and lewté that longez to knyghtez" (2379–81). We see here Gawain's failure to adhere to the mores of his "kynde," which represents both his own inner nature and his social connections to the chivalrous realm. Gawain learns that he is not of this "kynde," as he thought he was. At this moment, his identity as knight of the pentangle fractures. The humiliation that Gawain experiences proves that he is not the knight he thought he was: as Derek Pearsall notes in regard to the *Gawain*-poet's art, "To show a fictional character capable of being embarrassed and humiliated...in the way that Gawain is embarrassed and humiliated is a new art of the interior self...that is being disentangled from the fictions of chivalry that had prevailed."[50] The Green Knight's game strips Gawain of his former chivalric identity and forces him to find a new spiritual identity based upon humility.

The Green Knight's chivalric godgame of romance is resolved at this point, but its connection to the Christian godgame of moral exemplum is still unclear to Gawain. Here we must look at the double bind that the green girdle creates for Gawain, both in terms of the Green Knight's and of the Christian godgames. Gawain withholds the girdle from Bertilak, an obvious breach of the game's rules, but he also withholds the girdle from his confessor, an apparent breach of the rules of Christianity. Does Gawain confess the girdle or not? Ad Putter summarizes the paradox of this scene:

1. Gawain's confession includes the fact that he intends to keep the girdle. This hypothesis is refuted by the priest's complete absolution, which the

priest could only have given if Gawain had restored the girdle to its rightful owner.
2. Keeping the girdle is a sin, but Gawain omits any mention of it. This is plainly contradicted by the *Gawain*-poet's statement that Gawain confesses *all* his sins, "the more and the mynne."[51]

Putter then suggests that "the passage simply ceases to make sense if it is approached on the assumption that the green girdle is a moral problem. It becomes readable only if we allow the girdle to slip from our conscience, just as Gawain has done."[52] Given the *Gawain*-poet's wide-ranging knowledge of Christianity and the complex structure of the poem, however, it seems safe to assume that the poet intends the reader to see the parallel in the bind of the green girdle both in terms of the rules of chivalry and of the rules of Christianity.

Both the rules of chivalry/romance and of Christianity/exemplum demand that Gawain give up the girdle, but he fails to adhere to either rule system. Remember, too, that Gawain rejects God's grace to accept the green girdle: "And he nay that he nolde neghe in no wyse / Nauther golde ne garysoun, er God hym grace sende / To acheue to the chaunce that he hade chosen there" (1836–38). Rather than finishing his task through God's grace without the girdle, as he first promises, Gawain sins by putting his faith in earthly magic rather than divine guidance. The godgame of Christianity here subsumes the godgame of the Green Knight, as Gawain falls further from the virtuous rules of the pentangle shield by failing in his confession. The absolution that Gawain receives for his confession, that "sette hym so clene / As domezday schulde haf ben dight on the morn" (1883–84) ironically underscores that Gawain does indeed face his Judgment Day tomorrow. He is only "so clene" as any human can be within a medieval Christian worldview, as the green girdle, as we learn, represents his love of life. Mortality is one of the results of original sin; Gawain's only sin is fearing his death.

Although Gawain cheats by withholding the girdle and sins by withholding his confession, the Christian godgame allows Gawain expiation of his sins through Bertilak's dispensation. After Gawain survives the three strokes, the Green Knight serves as his confessor:

"I halde hit hardily hole, the harme that I hade.
Thou art confessed so clene, beknowen of thy mysses,
And hatz the penaunce apert of the point of myn egge,
I halde the polysed of that plyght, and pured as clene
As thou hadez neuer forfeted sythen thou watz fyrst borne." (2390–94)

The lexicon of confession and absolution emphasizes that Gawain has sufficiently atoned for the very human sin that he "lufed [his] lyf" (2368). The confession that Gawain withheld, in terms of both godgames, appears to be another instance of cheating, and all cheating is now forgiven. Cheating in a secular and courtly game of romance leads to his cheating in the spiritual game of life, salvation, and exemplum, but the forgiving nature of the Christian godgame allows Gawain to metamorphose into a better Christian through his very failures.

Having survived his visit to the Green Knight's chapel, Gawain now establishes his Christian identity for himself. He puts on the green girdle as a symbol of the failures caused by his excessive pride and, in so doing, defines himself as an individual who has learned a lesson about the impossibility of perfection and the need for humility. Gawain is no longer a man defined by his knightly identity in ways that he himself does not understand; rather, he establishes a symbol for himself which, at this moment in the text, is unique to him:

> "Bot your gordel," quoth Gawayn, "God yow foryelde!
> That wyl I welde wyth guod wylle, not for the wynne golde
> ....
> Bot in syngne of my surfet I schal se hit ofte
> ....
> And thus, quen pryde schal me pryk for prowes of armes,
> The loke to this luf-lace schal lethe my hert."
> (2429–30, 33, 37–38)

Through the assumption of this new livery, Gawain is spiritually reborn; rather than a signifier of his position at the chivalrous court, his clothes become an emblem of his identity as a fallen Christian (and, thus, as a moral exemplar) when he returns home.[53]

By refashioning himself with the symbol of his faults, Gawain ascribes to himself a new identity which signifies that his pride has been conquered. As Lynn Johnson comments,

> [Gawain] defines himself, now, as a man and signifies his acceptance of the remedy for the human condition, penance, by wearing what is a memorial token of his failure....By Gawain's new attitude toward the green girdle, the poet suggests that Gawain has moved beyond the literal—and, hence, superficial—code of temporal chivalry to a recognition of his position within the framework of spiritual chivalry.[54]

Johnson's conception of spiritual chivalry (tested by the Christian godgame and exemplum) underscores the failure of earthly chivalry (tested by the

Green Knight's godgame and romance) to address adequately the complex circumstances a human and fallen knight must face. Gawain's assumption of the green girdle speaks his identity from his own vision of himself as a man who has overcome his past defects of character, who will look to the lovelace to ensure the defeat of his problematic pride. The Green Knight will no longer be able to laugh at Gawain because the Arthurian knight now bases his vision of himself upon Christian principles of humility.

The Green Knight's game bears the makings of a godgame in that a supernatural character creates a labyrinthine but ultimately beneficial game from which the human character learns a valuable lesson. This game, however, also appears to be a practical joke in which the green girdle serves as the punchline, with a masculine and heroic knight adopting a flimsy and feminine accessory.[55] Here again we see the duality of the game as both fun in itself and serious in its implications: the girdle is funny as a sign of Gawain's humiliation for having failed to adhere to the rules of the game, but Gawain's assumption of the girdle as a sign of his new identity simultaneously underscores the serious implications of the godgame. Without the game, he would not have learned this lesson in Christian humility. Again, the game must be fun for someone—if not the players, then the spectators. As the readers/spectators, the audience generally finds the girdle punchline to be one of the funniest moments of the text.

Gawain, who delighted in play at Arthur's and Bertilak's courts, now disavows such pleasantries and thus reconstructs his identity by rejecting past pleasures. With Gawain's rejection of his former self, the Green Knight invites him to return and play at his castle ("And ye schal in this Nwe Yer agayn to my wonez, / And we schyn reuel the remnaunt of this ryche fest / ful bene" [2400–402]). The Green Knight's invitation to Gawain to join him at his castle for festivities is repeated approximately fifty lines later in the text (2467–70), and this doubling of the invitation underscores that Gawain's refusal to participate in the play of the Green Knight's court is a rejection of a playfully chivalrous identity. Gawain scorns the offer both times it is put forth ("Nay, for sothe" [2407]; "And he nikked hym naye, he nolde bi no wayes" [2471]). His refusal specifically rejects the company of the women of Bertilak's court who have ensnared him in their game: "And comaundez me to that cortays, your comlych fere, / Bothe that on and that other, myn honoured ladyez, / That thus hor knygt wyth hor kest han koyntly bigyled" (2411–13). With the green girdle on his side, Gawain disavows the chivalric play of romance.

Leaving the social world of the Arthurian court exposes the incongruity between Gawain's chivalric and spiritual selves. By putting on the girdle as a proclamation of his moral failure ("Loken vnder his lyfte arme, the lace, with a knot, / In tokenyng he watz tane in tech of a faut" [2487–88]),

Gawain becomes a model of virtue upon his return to Arthur's realm when the other courtiers adopt the symbol of his adventures. As the *Gawain*-poet decribes the court eagerly welcoming Gawain home, he first stresses the solemnity of Gawain's adventures as he speaks to the court:

> He tened quen he schulde tell,
> He groned for gref and grame;
> The blod in his face con melle,
> When he hit schulde schewe, for schame. (2501–504)

Gawain's confession, however, is met with a chorus of laughter: "alle the courts als / Laghen loude therat" (2513–14). A.C. Spearing locates acceptance and forgiveness of Gawain and his misadventures in the courtiers' laughter: "When the court laugh at his story, their reaction is a healthy one, and should guide our own, for they see that he is giving excessive importance to a minor failing in an impossibly difficult task."[56] Welcoming Gawain back, the court embraces their knight with laughter and offers him comfort for the ordeal he has experienced. At the end of the game, Arthur and his knights find a new identity that recognizes the impossibility of perfect human virtue. Along with the courtiers, we the readers can also laugh, thanking Gawain for the moral lesson he has learned for all. We can enjoy the benefits of his humiliating yet instructional game through the liminal space of readerly identification, thankful that we need not suffer as painfully as he does.

Through Gawain's example, the courtiers learn that their knight of the pentangle could not adhere to perfect virtue and that neither can they. When Arthur and his knights adopt the green girdle as a symbol of the court, they assume a more realistic and human definition of themselves. Gerald Morgan sees this moment as the move to a new courtly identity: "By accepting the girdle as a badge (2513–22) the court once against insists upon the identification [between themselves and Gawain], and this is surely not a cause for shame. Gawain's fault serves not so much to qualify knightly renown as to define it."[57] Gawain newly defines knighthood for himself and his companions; through the godgames, the Green Knight and Christianity test the court's reputation and lead them to an understanding of its human limitations and, also, its human potential. The beneficial aspects of the Christian godgame of exemplum ultimately expel the painful elements of Gawain's humiliating experience of romance.

The court's laughter brings the reader back to the revelry at the poem's beginning, but this time the laughter is based upon the realization of human imperfection rather than seasonal revelry. The end of the game highlights the good produced by Gawain's deception: his moral failure brings with it the court's recognition that human perfection is an impossibly high standard for a fallen world. The *Gawain*-poet's theme—that good can emerge from sin and trickery, that hope exists for a postlapsarian world—appears in hindsight to have been promised by the opening lines of the poem, which recount the glorious birth of Britain from the treacherous fall of Troy. As one man's deception led to the devastation of Troy but also to the foundation of Britain,[58] Gawain's trickery leads to the devastation of his sense of self but also to the reformulation of his self and a moral lesson for his fellow courtiers. The godgames of the Green Knight and of Christianity do so with fun and laughter throughout for the reader, if not always for Gawain, who must play a game he never fully understands until he wins it by losing.

And parallel to Gawain, the poem's medieval auditors and modern readers find themselves trapped in the poem's meta-textual godgame—the one the *Gawain*-poet creates for his audience. To teach his social superiors a Christian lesson, the *Gawain*-poet uses the protective disguises of allegory and of gaming laughter so that he may speak freely, humorously, yet also sternly. The multiple layers of performance that the *Gawain*-poet embodies, the "performing self" that Ann Astell describes as "lead[ing] his audience first to recognize the fictive situation as one analogous to their own, and then to accept[ing] its moral teaching as applicable to themselves," creates a protective poetic freedom as confusing and impenetrable as his creation the Green Knight.[59] By tricking the audience with the generic trappings of romance yet providing a moral tale of Christian penitence, the *Gawain*-poet enacts once more the deception that so mortifyingly deceived Gawain. This time, however, the trick moves from the textual to the meta-textual, from the characters to the audience. For today's readers as much as for yesteryear's auditors, the *Gawain*-poet's godgame ends, and the joke is on us.

Interpreting *Sir Gawain and the Green Knight* as a romance with the moral force of an exemplum, we experience genre play that leads the reader to a reconceptualization of his/her Christianity. But such a dynamic is only one portion of the story of this romance, and in the remaining portion of this chapter, I analyze the queering and sadistic impetus of this genre play. Surely, *Sir Gawain and the Green Knight* offers narrative pleasures with which few texts can compare, but it combines these pleasures with deep-felt pains for Gawain and for readers, if they identify with Gawain. Mixing this pain both with the pleasures of promised salvation and with the threats of a latent queerness, the *Gawain*-poet's play with genre and sex questions the meaning of suffering within a fallen Christian world and the proper Christian relationship to a God who demands this suffering. In addition to a romance and an exemplum, how does *Sir Gawain and the Green Knight* metamorphose if we read it as a saint's life, with a focus on the queer pleasures of suffering for Christ?

Reluctant Masochism, Saints' Lives, and the Sadistic Godgames of *Sir Gawain and the Green Knight*

"What is the meaning of the meeting of violence and sexuality in such excessive and abundant language?" Reading these words, a scholar of fourteenth-century English literature might well imagine that they apply to *Sir Gawain and the Green Knight* in its graphic violence of decapitation and eviscerations, in its sexual play of courtly seductions and flirtatious queerness, and in its semiotic instability in which words and images dance around meanings but refuse to symbolize clearly. The question, however, belongs not to an exegesis of *Sir Gawain and the Green Knight* but to Gilles Deleuze in his analysis of the progenitors of sadomasochistic literature, the Marquis de Sade and Leopold von Sacher-Masoch.[60] My goal in this portion of the chapter is to explore the connection among sadomasochism, saints' lives, and the textual and meta-textual godgames in *Sir Gawain and the Green Knight*, as the *Gawain*-poet expresses his interest in the confluence of violence, sexuality, and excessive language both in the bizarre games that Gawain must play and in his own godgame of genre.

Recent scholarship, notably the work of Robert Mills and Louise Fradenburg, examines the sadomasochistic tensions of medieval art and literature, often in regard to the painful pleasures of suffering in saints' lives.[61] In the foundational text of modern masochism, Leopold von Sacher-Masoch's *Venus in Furs*, the protagonist Severin reveals that early Christian martyrs served as role models for his masochistic sexual development: "Precisely, the martyrs were supersensuous beings who found positive pleasure in pain and who sought horrible tortures, even death, as others seek enjoyment. I too am supersensual, madam, just as they were."[62] In this assessment, martyrs are viewed as sensuous beings who paradoxically embrace torture as a means to the ecstasies of martyrdom and sublimated sexual pleasure. By embracing their gruesome deaths, martyrs elevate their relationship with God over all earthly pursuits and thus demonstrate their ultimate understanding of the ephemerality of human life and the eternal blisses of the divine sphere. When viewed against a backdrop of latent martyrdom in which Gawain is offered but refuses the delights of Christian self-sacrifice, it becomes apparent that Gawain's adventures teach him the spiritual benefits of a saintly masochism. Because he fails to understand the ecstatic pain of the martyrs and the ways in which their examples should guide him, Gawain becomes a "reluctant masochist" who must learn, despite his fear and resistance, to embrace the pain of the bizarre game that disciplines him into subservience to the divine will. Within this conception of the Arthurian world, reluctant masochism and queer desires structure the confusing game that the *Gawain*-poet deploys to trap both his protagonist and his readers into an awareness of their human sinfulness.

Gawain's reluctant masochism surfaces in and complements the sadistic godgame he must play, and it is imperative that scholarship address the cruel valence of the games of *Sir Gawain and the Green Knight*. For if the godgame is ultimately morally and spiritually uplifting, it nonetheless arrives at such a salutary objective only after great cruelties. My goal with the remainder of this chapter is not to refute the preceding normative reading of the poem by now offering a queer one; rather, the manifest pleasures of a normative reading exist side-by-side and complement the latent pleasures of the queer. The complexity of *Sir Gawain and the Green Knight* lies in its presentation of traditional Christian morality within the framework of an excessive and overly determined romance that not only bears the generic stamp of an exemplum but the narratival model of a masochistic saint's life as well. These generic excesses create a world in which both Gawain and the reader are trapped until God frees Gawain and the *Gawain*-poet releases us; they hold the power in these godgames, and Gawain and we are at their mercy.

A crucial feature of the godgame, particularly in reference to the generic tradition of the saint's life, is the possibility of sadistic unfairness in that the god-figure wields omnipotent power, in contrast to the pawn-player, who wields no real power at all. Robert Wilson observes that literary god-figures frequently disregard the emotional repercussions of the godgame for the pawn-players, declaring that "the god of the godgame recalls the callous behavior of the gods toward human victims in certain myths."[63] Other studies of game and play likewise highlight the sadistic cruelties of some forms of play. Richard Schechner's theory of "dark play" complements the godgame's conception of cruel, sadistic, and dangerous play:

> Dark play may be conscious playing, but it can also be playing in the dark when some or even all of the players don't know they are playing. Dark play occurs when contradictory realities coexist, each seemingly capable of cancelling the other out...Dark play subverts order, dissolves frames, breaks its own rules, so that the playing itself is in danger of being destroyed....Unlike the inversions of carnivals, ritual clowns, and so on (whose agendas are public), dark play's inversions are not declared or resolved; its end is not integration but disruption, deceit, excess, and gratification.[64]

In both dark play and the godgame, the god-figure controls the pawn-player's fate, which gives the god-figure the power of sadism, should s/he choose to use it. Schechner's conception of "contradictory realities, each seemingly capable of cancelling the other out" encapsulates the conundrum of the game Gawain must play: the contradictory yet complementary realities of heaven and earth coincide, yet Gawain can only discern the earthly ramifications of the godgame—his head and his identity as the chivalric hero of a romance—rather than its spiritual ones—his soul and his identity as a Christian protagonist of an exemplum and a saint's life. The goal of dark play, in this instance, is indeed "disruption, deceit, excess, and gratification," yet these disruptive forces are paradoxically directed back toward Gawain as a means to an integrated yet suffering Christian self at the conclusion of the narrative. By reading *Sir Gawain and the Green Knight* with an eye to the sadistic edge of the godgame and the masochistic pleasures offered to but refused by Gawain, the excesses of the godgame reveal themselves as strategies to queer Gawain to God by stripping him of his sexual and Arthurian sense of self as courtly lover. Although the end result of the process—Gawain's Christian renewal—is salvifically pleasureful, the process of renewal is predicated upon confusion, cruelty, and sadomasochism.

Earlier in this chapter, I explored medieval conceptions of play and game that stress their relationship to the proper Christian life. An additional medieval view of play and game worthy of note is the hermeneutic of the *Athleticus Dei*, through which medieval exegetes interpreted spiritual tests and crises as games. Caesarius of Arles, for example, describes Job's encounters with the devil as a spiritual game: "Fortiter conluctatus est diabolus, sed athletam dei superare not potuit" ("The devil fought strongly, but he was unable to conquer the athlete of God").[65] As Alberto Ferreiro observes, "[Caesarius] described Job as a spiritual athelete, *Athleticus Dei*, in a tournament against evil whose prize is eternal life.. . .The motif of Job as *Athleticus Dei* and *Miles Christi* was widely used throughout the Middle Ages."[66] The tradition of the *Athleticus Dei* allows us to view the world of *Sir Gawain and the Green Knight* through a specifically Christian lens in which God permits his servants to be tested and condones the trials they suffer. Within this tradition, Gawain represents an Arthurian courtier unaware that he has been conscripted into God's service as an *Athleticus Dei*. Although the parallels between Gawain and Job should not be exaggerated, Gawain must similarly learn to endure hardships and to submit himself to God's plan if he is to negotiate successfully the trying and life-threatening situations he faces. The *Gawain*-poet deploys this tradition of Christian play, fraught as it is with the problematic depiction of a God who toys with his creation, within the gaming world of the Arthurian court.

Chaucer's "Friar's Tale" provides a contemporary justification for viewing the cruel game of *Sir Gawain and the Green Knight* as under the direction of the Christian deity. In the tale, the fiend who travels with the summoner of the tale reports:

"For, brother myn, thy wit is al to bare
To understonde, althogh I tolde hem thee.

> But, for thou axest why labouren we—
> For somtyme we been Goddes instrumentz
> And meenes to doon his comandementz,
> Whan that hym list, upon his creatures,
> In divers art and in diverse figures.
> Withouten hym we have no myght, certayn,
> If that hym list to stonden ther-agayn.
> And somtyme, at oure prayere, han we leve
> Oonly the body and nat the soule greve;
> Witnesse on Job, whom that we diden wo."[67]

This viewpoint suggests that God's authority can never be transgressed, and that all fiends and tormentors of Christians must have His approval before their tests unfold. As we have seen through Gawain's numerous prayers, God participates in this game, and that the game ultimately ends in Gawain's spiritual benefit indicates that his testers serve a similar narrative function as the tormentors of the Book of Job and "The Friar's Tale."

In this game in which cruelty surfaces, we see that the aggression is particularly hierarchical in that God Himself allows it. Due to the sadistic asymmetry of power between god-figure and pawn-player, godgames reinforce the patriarchal and authoritarian qualities of the god-figure. Linda Williams observes that sadism eradicates all desires except those of the father-figure:

> Sadistic pleasure and fantasy can thus be viewed as patriarchal power run rampant: the negation of the difference of the mother and the exaltation of the power of the father who is beyond all law. . . .In no way does the sadistic subject. . .solicit the pleasure of his victim. He (or she) solicits compliance to power, whether in the show of pain or the show of pleasure.[68]

This skeletal description of sadism corresponds to *Sir Gawain and the Green Knight* in that we have a Father beyond all law, since within Christianity, He is not merely the law, He is the Word that created the law. And certainly, Gawain's pleasures are never solicited, and any pleasure he inadvertently experiences in the play of the game are intended to lay the groundwork for his pain and humiliation.

The Green Knight's games, whether directly sanctioned by God or indirectly allowed in deference to Gawain's own prayers, force Gawain's identity to undergo change, whether the knight desires such change or not. As its basic impulse, sadism impels change and activity: Laura Mulvey states, "Sadism demands a story, depends on making something happen, forcing a change in another person, a battle of will and strength, victory/defeat, all occurring in a linear time with a beginning and an end."[69] This formulation highlights the sadistic qualities of *Sir Gawain and the Green Knight*, as "forcing a change in another person" structures the narrative. Gawain's spiritual growth at the conclusion of the romance, although beneficial to his soul, destroys with devastating effect his previous sense of self; further, the change is indeed forced upon him, as his actions throughout the romance attempt to stabilize and support his identity as Arthurian courtier rather than as humble Christian. The sadistic god-figure seeks compliance with His will either through the show of pain or the show of pleasure, which is evidenced both in Gawain's nascent and painful awareness of his failures as a Christian and in the Arthurian community's pleasureful assumption of the green girdle (despite Gawain's attempt to structure its semiotic valence as suffering).

Reading the godgames of *Sir Gawain and the Green Knight* sadomasochistically, we see the power dynamics at play in which God acts as sadist to Gawain's reluctant masochist. At the heart of Christianity resides a vast chasm of power between Creator and created, and in this gulf simultaneously reside pain (in separation from perfect love) and pleasure (in the promise of union in heaven). The pleasure and pain embodied in Christian suffering finds an apt metaphor in sadomasochism. As Louise Fradenburg argues,

> sadomasochism enacts itself not as a practice of masterful self-coincidence, but rather as a practice of enjoyment, in which the desires of both master and slave are at stake—no pretense of disengagement, of being beyond mortal loves—and thereby as a practice of enjoyment that calls forth the otherness within the subject, open to erogenous rezoning—with all the shattering consequences thereof for the ethical subject who would triumph over the flesh, its desires, its mortality; indeed with all the shattering consequences thereof for the sublime, militant, angelic body, shining, sempiternal, surviving, superexistent, triumphant, and thereby completely imbued with—one might almost say, made of—the power to rescue and to "correct," and to carry God's mandates to his sublunary missionaries.[70]

Fradenburg's construction of sadomasochism envisions human partners, but surely the ultimate sadomasochistic relationship can be found with the divine, in which the master is the Master. The relationship between humanity and God, which exponentially multiplies the hierarchized dynamics of solely human relationships, is rife with the possibility for sexualized fantasies, as medieval mystics frequently show us.[71] David Halperin succinctly observes that "hierarchy itself is *hot;* it is indissociably bound up with at least the potential for erotic signification."[72] As the human relationship with the Divine represents the ultimate hierarchical relationship, in which the positions of Master and servant can never be reversed, the potential for erotic signification appears latently, and sometimes blatantly, in a Christian's relationship to God.

But, like Gawain, one may not immediately see the joys of masochistically embracing martyrdom to achieve union with God in heaven because it involves so much earthly physical pain. Only Christ and martyred saints serve as such human models of blissful masochism. In regard to saints' lives, Robert Mills argues that earthly martyrdom entails a paradoxically harmonious relationship between two humans—a sadistic tormentor and a masochistic martyr: "Martyrdom, of course, entails both [sadism and masochism]: a relentless repetition of punishments dreamed up by a sadistic tyrant, and a saint who refuses to submit to his negative ambitions by asserting masochistic disavowal."[73] By participating in earthly sadomasochism with a vicious tyrant, the human saint suffers for the rewards of heaven: earthly suffering is inverted into heavenly delights.[74] In contrast, the *Gawain*-poet reconfigures the dynamics of sadomasochistic martyrdom such that God is the sadist who allows his reluctantly masochistic follower to suffer agonizing pains and to face the brink of death but then allows him to live. The *Gawain*-poet addresses these tensions between sadist and masochist within the playworld of Arthurian legend in which God's sadism, his toying with Gawain, is cloaked in the pleasures of a game and in which Gawain, though his playing of the game, attempts to refuse to accede to a masochistic position. Gawain's only hope to win the godgame is to embrace the possibility of death from the very beginning of the game rather than reluctantly (and humanly) seeking to avoid it.[75] Gawain is an excellent knight, but, as his God will teach him, no saint.

God's Sadistic Game

As has long been noted, *Sir Gawain and the Green Knight* begins and ends on New Year's Day, the Feast of Christ's Circumcision, and thus the spiritual plane and the earthly plane meet in the memory and feast of Jesus's severed foreskin. More than a mere celebration, however, the Feast of the Circumcision establishes that the godgame focuses on God's demands for painful sacrifice from both His Son and His male followers, as they lose their foreskins to mark their participation in the covenant. The human pains of the cut provide pleasure both to God (who sees His covenant fulfilled) and to the circumcised (who joins God's covenant), but these pleasures are founded upon the pains of bodily injury and the sacrifice of the foreskin.[76] Jesus's circumcised penis likewise serves as a focal point for the Arthurian community, and Gawain's journey invites him to share that identity by sharing Christ's pain through his (Gawain's) parodic circumcision ("beheading") at the hands of the Green Knight. Christ's circumcised penis serves the purpose of building a community of believers, and so too should Gawain's nicked neck.[77] As Nicholas Royle points out, "the exposure of

Christ's circumcised penis [is] a sort of phantomological revelation of the familiar-unfamiliar, an uncanny memento of the inscription of Christ's body within the logic of repetition and alterity that itself renders possible something like an ethnic or religious identity."[78] The Arthurian court builds a community of Christian believers through the celebration of Christ's circumcision, but this scene also underscores the need to reiterate circumcisions within the text. One circumcision, even Christ's, simply is not enough, although circumcision should (obviously) only be needed once.[79] The promise of "once" in circumcision, however, proves itself a lie, as Gawain relives and reincarnates Christ's circumcision through his encounter with the Green Knight's blade and thus reestablishes both his personal covenant with God and is conscripted into God's service for the entire Arthurian community. The repetition of circumcision promises pain and pleasure again within the formula of sadomasochism.

The conflation of pleasure and pain in this opening scene of revelry highlights the disjunction between earthly practice and heavenly ideal, as the Arthurian court's riotous celebration of the feast evinces their earthly pleasure as they commemorate Christ's human and salvific pain. From this foundational moment of the text, the *Gawain*-poet conflates three central themes of the romance: the Arthurian community's desire to build a functioning Christian community (despite their difficulties in this task), Gawain's growth as his community's spiritual leader through his personal reenactment of Jesus's circumcision, and the desire of the Christian deity to facilitate perversely and painfully the construction of this community, since it can occur only through the shedding of blood and the fracturing of Gawain's sense of self.[80] From the pain of Gawain's adventures bloom promised pleasures through the renewal of the Christian community.

Complementing Gawain's reluctant masochism, a range of sadists cooperate to bring him suffering: the Green Knight/Bertilak, the lady, and Morgan all orchestrate the sadistic traps that Gawain attempts to evade. Of these tormentors, Morgan appears to be the mastermind of the game, as Bertilak reports that "Ho wayned me vpon this wyse to your wynne halle / For to assay the surquidré, yif hit soth were / That rennes of the grete renoun of the Rounde Table" (2456–58). However, if Morgan's desires direct the game, these desires are left at least partially unfulfilled, as Bertilak reports that she sends him both to test the reputation of the Arthurian court and, through his shocking appearance, to kill Guinevere. Morgan succeeds in her first wish but fails in her second. That Morgan's presence is so occluded in the text, however, encourages the reader to look beyond Bertilak's surface answers.[81] Permeating the text but removed from it, Christian divinity directs and permits the action of the romance to develop, and through this occluded but active presence, divine desires surface. If Morgan's desires direct the unfolding of the plot, so too do God's. As previously mentioned, that God and other saints answer Gawain's prayers at key points in the narrative indicates that they are players in this game. When Gawain seeks to protect himself from the lady, he "sayned hym[self], as bi his saghe the saver to worthe, / with hande" (1202–03); however, God does not protect Gawain after this prayer, and the lady reports that Gawain appears before her in accordance with God's grace: "Bot I louue that ilk lorde that the lyfte haldez, / I haf hit holly in my honde that al desyres, / thurghe grace" (1256–58). Surely she is correct: God's grace precipitates these events that allow Gawain his reluctant spiritual journey. Thus, God's decisions of when and where to act highlight the *Gawain*-poet's construction of His agency and, thus, His desires. When God acts within these fictions, the poet constructs Him as a desiring agent who acts to achieve His own goals. Choosing to respond to the lady's plea rather than assisting Gawain in his struggle, God reveals that His desires are in play in this godgame in much the same way that He allows Job to be tested. As the celebration of Christ's circumcision marks the Arthurian court as a community of believers, these lines suggest that the Christian covenant is maintained both on earth and in heaven, with God harkening to the pleas of his believers when He so desires.[82]

Although Gawain cannot recognize this fact at the beginning of the narrative, his suffering emerges as the real focus of the godgame. The only way for Gawain to avoid the pain of his failure and to win the godgame is not to play it from its very beginning; as Ann Astell argues, "The Green Knight's own restrained and merciful manner of returning Gawain's stroke and his refusal 'to haf...wroght anger' (l. 2344) make it clear, in retrospect, that Arthur and Gawain could have acted differently than they did, could in fact have practiced Christian charity and the love of one's enemies that it entails rather than beheading an unarmed man."[83] If Gawain acted according to Christian precepts of charity and mercy, he would never have struck the Green Knight and, by refusing to act, would have won the game before it began. Following Arthur's advice ("'Kepe the, cosyn,' quoth the kyng, 'that thou on kyrf sette, / And if thou redez hym ryght, redly I trowe / That thou schal byden the bur that he schal bede'" [372–74]), Gawain mistakenly adheres to his secular lord's advice that he should act in violence rather than to his Christian Father's commandment that he should not kill. After the game begins, Gawain fails to realize that the only way he can win the game is not to play it.[84] Paradoxically, once the game commences, the only way for Gawain to win is to lose.

Gawain's failure, then, lies in his misreading of genre: he refuses to identify himself as the protagonist of a saint's life and to embrace masochism as the proper Christian response to the Green Knight's challenge. This refusal to embrace masochism is also a refusal to emulate Christ because Christ is the ultimate masochist.[85] Gill Saunders argues, "The central image of the Christian religion is a tortured male nude, a feminized man who has passively, even masochistically accepted humiliation, punishment, and death."[86] Rather than emulating Christ and the early Christian martyrs by accepting the potential for earthly suffering, Gawain, through his decapitating blow, attempts to refuse this identification with Christ and martyred saints that is predicated upon suffering; he insists upon remaining the ostensible hero of a romance. If *Sir Gawain and the Green Knight* were a saint's life rather than a romance, we would expect Gawain to embrace masochistic earthly suffering so that his salvation would be assured. By placing this narrative concern with masochism latently within the parameters of a romance, the *Gawain*-poet underscores that Gawain must learn to embrace such suffering rather than to live his life in courtly pleasures; to this end, the lady tricks him with her seductive pleasures, pleasures that Gawain both enjoys and enjoys denying himself.

The Sadomasochism of Queering Seductions

The sadomasochistic pleasures evident in the godgame appear prominently in the seduction scenes in which the pleasure Gawain finds in his knightly reputation traps him into highly eroticized yet somewhat uncomfortable sexual situations. Upon entering Bertilak's castle, Gawain finds a pleasureful world that first confirms his chivalric identity and solidifies his sense of his courtly reputation as a lover. In the welcoming scene at Bertilak's court, the courtiers interrogate the man before them and are delighted to learn that he is the famous Gawain:

> Thenne watz spyed and spured vpon spare wyse
> Bi preué poyntez of that prynce, put to hymseluen,
> That he beknew cortaysly of the court that he were
> That athel Arthure the hende haldez hym one,
> That is the ryche ryal kyng of the Rounde Table,
> And hit watz Wawen hymself that in that won syttez. (901–906)

The scene depicts Gawain reveling in the benefits of his status as an Arthurian celebrity. His reputation precedes him and wins him acclaim from his new companions. Before Gawain's identity is queered in subsequent scenes, before pain complements this pleasure, the courtiers fortify the knight's sense of self and lull him into a false sense of security. The courtiers convince Gawain that he still inhabits the world of romance, rather than hinting at the foreboding exemplum and latent saint's life.

As Gawain is a reluctant masochist, one who prefers simple pleasures to complex pains, it is not surprising that he seeks pleasure with the wife prior to facing the discomforts of her seductions. Indeed, Gawain and his host wife's are both such skillful players of love games that the narrator reports their playing surpasses every other princely game:

> Bot yet I wot that Wawen and the wale burde
> Such comfort of her compaynye caghten togeder
> Thurgh her dere dalyaunce of her derne wordez,
> Wyth clene cortays carp closed fro fylthe,
> That hor play watz passande vche prynce gomen,
>   in vayres. (1010–1015)

Gawain's sense of self as an Arthurian knight well versed in the play of love is not without merit, and it certainly brings him pleasure. Nevertheless, these moments that appear to confirm his sense of self belie the brewing questions of identity that the godgame will soon investigate and the torments these disruptions to his ego will catalyze. "When [his hosts] make him consciously play 'Gawain,' they make him eventually aware of the gap between the actor and his performance," concludes Arthur Lindley;[87] the play of knighthood, which the host and his wife demand, does not always accord with Gawain's actions and his sense of who he is, and this realization eventually brings with it deep suffering.

During the three days of the lady's seductions, the confusion surrounding Gawain's reputation illustrates the deep seriousness of the godgame as it questions whether Gawain will retain his previous chivalric and romantic sense of self by playing the game or whether his identity and reputation will simply fragment.[88] Gawain now denies the reputation that the lady gives him:

> "In god fayth," quoth Gawayn, "gayn hit me thynkkez
> Thagh I be not now he that ye of speken;
> To reche to such reuerence as ye reherce here
> I am wyghe vnworthy, I wot wel myseluen." (1241–44)

At this point of the text, Gawain refuses the lady's ascription of his identity but can only assert his identity negatively; rather than saying who he is, Gawain declares who he is not. The knight loses his sense of self in the bedroom scenes; as Carolyn Dinshaw explains, "The structure of identity—gender identity, sexual identity, Christian chivalric identity (which partakes of both gender and sex)—is threatened in these narrative moments. . . . Gawain's subjectivity, his identity is unfixed in the bedroom."[89] The game of courtly love loses its sense of decorous fun as Gawain faces the painful repercussions of his blindness within the godgame. Played with more than playing, Gawain's future suffering is built upon these momentary pleasures.

The lady's game depends largely upon teaching Gawain the necessity of masochism by removing his sexual agency. When she demands that Gawain respond to her mock threats of bondage (" 'I schal bynde yow in your bedde, that be ye tryst.' / Al laghande the lady lanced tho bourdez" [1211–12]), she foreshadows that, in addition to his physical body, his identity will be likewise constrained through her play, as she repeatedly fashions him to respond to her desires. Gawain fails to see this threat and responds with his mood matching her humor: " 'For I yelde me yederly, and yeghe after grace, / And that is the best, be my dome, for me byhouez nede': / And thus he bourded agayn with mony a blythe laghter" (1215–17). Gawain does not yield himself in this scene; he neither has sex with the lady nor allows himself to be physically tied by her. But as Gawain refuses to sacrifice his body to masochistic delights through death at the hands of the Green Knight, his refusal to yield himself to sexual delights with the lady bespeaks his unawareness of the ways in which both painful spiritual pleasures (masochism in a saint's life) and rejected physical pleasures (adultery in a romance) create the contours of his identity. Gawain is, in effect, paradoxically constructed by his inability to understand the ways in which pleasure should effect his identity.

In her game of love, the lady's most effective strategy is to deny that Gawain could be Gawain so that he will do as she desires. She recognizes some of his knightly qualities before shocking him with her statement that "Bot that ye be Gawan, hit gotz in mynde!" (1293). Although Gawain denies the identity that the lady assigns to him, he does not seem to know exactly who he is if he is *not* that knight. In response to the lady's pressure that humiliates Gawain into befuddlement, confusion, and psychic distress, Gawain's identity wavers: " 'Querfore?' quoth the freke, and freschly he askez, / Ferde lest he hade fayled in fourme of his castes" (1294–95). Gawain's befuddled "Querfore" suggests his bewilderment about his own sense of identity: he both resists and desires the lady's description of him, both senses the impending failure of a romantic identity yet cannot fathom another one or a different generic model for his life. He still believes in the truth of his Arthurian identity, but fails to realize that he is being reconfigured into a model of human suffering for that community.

In the godgame, the lady's strategy of denying Gawain his identity in order to reconstruct it is an effective one, and she repeats it on the second day:

> "Sir, yif ye be Wawen, wonder me thynkkez,
> Wyghe that is so wel wrast alway to god,
> And connez not of compaynye the costez vndertake,

And if mon kennes yow hom to knowe, ye kest hom of your mynde."
  (1481–84)

The lady's taunt "yif ye be Wawan" works according to her will, and, after their kiss, Gawain and she proceed to talk of love's "greme and grace" ("grief and mercy"; 1507). Gawain's kisses with the lady are as queer as his ensuing kisses with the host, as they reveal him to be stripped of his masculine agency: he kisses the lady (and then his host) because she (and then the rules of the exchange game) compel him to do so, not due to his own sexual desires. Here we see the sadomasochistic conflation of pain and pleasure common both to earthly and to heavenly love. By combining "greme and grace," love destroys as it builds, and these scenes prepare Gawain for the painful destruction of his courtly identity while simultaneously preparing him for the pleasures of his fortunate fall into salvation. Gawain, it appears, will be who he is told to be, if not told by God directly through His commandments, then by a lady whose purpose is to trap him into a suffering rebirth. Building upon her successes, the lady stresses yet again the discrepancies between Gawain's reputation and his actions:

"And ye ar knyght comlokest kyd of your elde,
Your worde and your worchip walkez ayquere,
And I haf seten by yourself here sere twyes,
Yet herde I neuer of your hed helde no wordez
That euer longed to luf, lasse ne more." (1520–24)

Once more, since Gawain's actions do not correspond to his reputation in the game of love, the lady argues that he cannot be Gawain. She is prematurely correct: Gawain must rebuild his Christian identity, but this objective can only be accomplished when he leaves the pleasures she offers behind and embraces the pains of human failure.

Why doesn't Gawain have sex with the lady? The answers to this question are many: to do so would break the codes of courtly love, would betray the honor due his host, and would force him to have sex with his host in the exchange game. In addition to these answers, however, the pleasure of *not* having sex with the lady reveals itself to be a sufficient pleasure: "Bot he defended hym so fayr that no faut semed, / Ne non euel on nawther halue, nawther thay wysten / bot blysse" (1551–53). Bliss abounds in the very location where it appears to be denied through Gawain's courtly refusal to consummate desire. Here Gawain realizes sexually what he fails to realize spiritually: denying himself the simple pleasures of sex brings him deeper pleasures through a masochistic forbearance, but he, whose only sin is that he loves life, fails to realize that denying himself the simple pleasures of earthly life, in the manner of the masochistic martyrs, would bring him the manifold pleasures of heaven.

If we see God's desires at play in this game, at least to the extent that Morgan's are, we are faced with the paradox of a God who desires His knight to flirt with queerness if he is to negotiate successfully the godgame. Carolyn Dinshaw argues, "The narrative. . .produces the possibility of homosexual relations only to—in order to—preclude it, in order to establish heterosexuality as not just the only sexual legitimacy but a principle of intelligibility itself."[90] David Lorenzo Boyd focuses on the ways in which the poem defends the chivalric ideal by burlesquing same-sex sexuality: "By shifting the focus from chivalry's internal problematics to external threat, *Sir Gawain* subtly constructs 'unnatural' sexual activity as a threat to chivalric culture's stability."[91] My interest in the queerness of *Sir Gawain and the Green Knight* builds upon Dinshaw's and Boyd's work by suggesting that the queer kisses—both with Bertilak and with the lady—should be read metonymically as the poem's defining moments. By pushing the play of the godgame to its limit and by queering Gawain from his heteronormative sexual identity, these kisses propel Gawain into a situation in which Christianity simultaneously debases and exalts, disciplines and punishes the Christian subject into spiritual acquiescence. Through this sexual play surfaces the painful pleasures and the sadomasochistic thrills of the *Gawain*-poet's relationship to his God and to his audience.

The queerness of these scenes, in which Gawain and his host exchange both kisses and the light, flirtatious banter more expressive of lovers than of combatants, is so naturalized that it occludes the fact that being queerly kissed by a woman has forced Gawain to engage in another round of amatory exchange in which normativity is under duress. The *Gawain*-poet exaggerates the queerness of these scenes, suggesting that Gawain would provide more than polite kisses exchanged with humor if the circumstances allowed: during the first exchange, Gawain tells his host that "Tas yow there my cheuicaunce, I cheued no more; / I wowche hit saf fynly, thagh feler hit were" (1390–91). How much more would Gawain give? Even if there are limits to how much he would give sexually to the Green Knight, Gawain gives the kisses with surprising enthusiasm: "Then acoles he the knyght and kysses hym thryes, / As sauerly and sadly as he hem sette couthe" (1936–37). More than merely an inadvertent and comical side-effect of the exchange game, these kisses result from a conception of a playing God who pushes his servant first into attempted murder through decapitation and then into queer flirtations with an adulterously minded woman and her homoerotically affectionate husband.[92] How is any knight, or any Christian, to act under such circumstances?

All Christians must act in response to God's will, but if circumstances are such that God's will cannot be known (as when proper conduct demands queer behavior with men and with women), the Christian is theologically queered into a position of utter powerlessness in which ostensibly simple Christian precepts no longer provide an adequate guide of conduct. In this instance, God's queering desires in the godgame push Gawain into a situation in which his agency is crippled such that he must play by kissing another man. Gawain's sexual agency is abandoned at this moment, and this sense of abandon is crucial to a reformulation of Gawain's sense of self. For sadomasochism demands abandon from the masochist, and Gawain finally offers himself in abandon to God. *Sir Gawain and the Green Knight* specifically addresses the need for Gawain's abandon when he prepares himself for what he believes is his imminent execution:

"Bi Goddez self," quoth Gawayn,
"I wyl nauther grete ne grone;
To Goddez wylle I am ful bayn,
And to hym I haf me tone." (2156–59)

Concluding his self-dedication to God's will, Gawain exclaims, "Let God worche!" (2208). This is the moment of abandon: the moment of dedication to God, and the moment when the pains of the quest and of the godgame promise to transform into the pleasures of heaven, even though this transformation can only be promised, not depicted, at the romance's conclusion. True, Gawain does not cast off the green girdle, but he nonetheless appears prepared to face his death.

After Gawain abandons himself to God, he also opens himself to masochistic pains: by submitting to the Green Knight's blade, he (still reluctantly) prepares himself to accept death. When he is spared, Gawain's reaction to the godgame shows that his humbled and penitent vision of himself is predicated upon the repetition of future pain: "And thus, quen pryde schal me pryk for prowes of armes, / The loke to this luf-lace schal lethe my hert" (2437–38). The knight who sought to avoid pain in the romance's beginning, our reluctant masochist, now accepts the benefits of seeking pain as a means to continual spiritual growth. Gawain's journey appeared to him to be a quest, like that of any other romance; the acceptance of perpetual pain as a constant reminder of his Christian failures metamorphoses the quest from one of chivalry to one of spirituality.[93]

Gawain abandons himself to God in this scene, and such abandon indicates that he casts off the reluctance guiding his accession into saintly masochism. The reader might then expect Gawain to find pleasure in his masochistic position. For sadomasochism depends on the perverse deployment of power, but not merely for the pleasure of the sadist: "Power implies the existence of inequality, subordination, humiliation, or pain, and it is primarily the concept of sado-masochism that can account for the conversion of such an experience of displeasure...into a source of pleasure," as Suzanne Gearhart explains.[94] Despite Gawain's acceptance of masochism through the love-lace, he still does not find pleasure in it. Gawain's suffering and pain dominate the romance's final fitt; if we are to find Gawain's pleasure in the sadomasochism of Christianity, it is in the text's after-life in which Gawain assumes his position in heaven.

Gawain ultimately wins the queering and sadomasochistic godgame by losing it, and the Arthurian court celebrates Gawain's return in much the same riotous manner as their celebration of Christ's circumcision. Critical responses to this scene are divided, as some scholars see this moment highlighting the courtiers' acceptance of their own individual faults (e.g., Edward Jones's argument that "each courtier, by wearing the baldric, holds himself as humorously accountable for error as Gawain seriously judges himself"),[95] whereas other scholars see the courtiers' laughter as a sign that they fail to understand the deep spiritual meaning of Gawain's journey (e.g., Peter Christmas's argument that "Gawain is right not to join in the laughter, because he understands that laughter is a fatal solvent of the chivalric code which gives meaning to his life").[96] In this contradictory signification, the courtiers' laughter denotes both their better understanding of the meaning of Gawain's journey than Gawain himself and their complete misunderstanding of its significance. Should the courtiers laugh? And what does their laughter teach us? In the concluding section of this chapter, I address how this moment traps the reader in the final gambit of the *Gawain*-poet's godgame. If the *Gawain*-poet's play with genre traps and queers Gawain, so too are we trapped and queered through the painful pleasures of narratival identification.

Gawain, the Reader, and the Sadomasochism of Signs

Reading *Sir Gawain and the Green Knight* through a sadomasochistic perspective, we see that Gawain is ensnared (and ensnares himself) through the godgame's contradictory and self-negating strategies. The trappings of romance trap Gawain in the godgame, because the many signs that the poem provides for Gawain to read are all interpreted for their secular, rather than their Christian, meanings.[97] The hazy significations of signs emerge as the godgame's chief strategy; as Robert Hanning notes, "the difficulty, perhaps impossibility of interpretation becomes not only a hallmark but a main theme of the poem."[98] The poem's manifold uncanniness—most notably the Green Knight, his hacked-off head, the contradiction of the holly branch and axe, and the magic girdle—consistently encourages Gawain to excuse himself from the rules of Christianity because he misreads the import of these signs. Monica Potkay interprets Gawain's shield as signifying that "there are no clear binary distinctions in what merely looks like a dualistic world. And [such signs] specifically insist on the complex interdependence of spirit and letter, the unity of both in an integrated textuality."[99] Such a dynamic structures the semiotic system of the text: due to the bewildering incomprehensibility of the signs, designed to fool Gawain and to mislead the reader, these signs participate in a semiotics of confusion and cruelty. Reading these signs for their secular values, Gawain interprets the Green Knight as his enemy (rather than as his benefactor) and the magic girdle as his savior (rather than as his downfall).

Beyond the indeterminacy of signs in *Sir Gawain and the Green Knight* as Christian and secular, signs can also signify both literally and parodically to further vex and confuse the protagonist's and the reader's ability to decipher a firm meaning of the text. Signs grounded in religious meaning should ostensibly symbolize clearly the salvific mission of a given sect, but these sacred signs, similar to virtually all others, become ripe for parody and miscommunication. As Hent de Vries notes, "[T]he possible success of the religious performative. . .is never guaranteed by preestablished or simply given contextual requirements. . . .Any religious utterance, act, or gesture, stands in the shadow of—more or less, but never totally avoidable—perversion, parody, and kitsch, of blasphemy and idolatry."[100] Given the circular and parodic semiotics of circumcision and beheading so central to the narrative, Gawain's humorous "beheading" at the hands of the Green Knight parodies the solemnity of Christ's circumcision, but it does so both normatively and queerly. The normative parody marks Gawain as a better Christian for renewing and reconstructing himself in light of his failures, but the queer parody depends on the fact that Gawain himself, his body and his entirety, serves as an inverted metonymic representation of himself: in the moment when he receives his gash, he is his penis—cut, bleeding, but also signifying his compact with Christ. But the penis is queer as well, as it brings to mind the kisses with his host and the homosocial bond between Gawain and Bertilak that makes possible his transformation, as well as the queering kisses with the lady that strip Gawain of his male privilege.

Similar to his shield, the Green Knight, and the green girdle, Gawain himself now serves as an inscrutable sign at the romance's end. Gawain, as newly circumcised penis reflecting his covenant with God, returns to Arthur's court, and the courtiers celebrate the return of their knight because their suffering in his absence metamorphoses into manifold pleasures through his presence. This earthly scene prefigures Gawain's entrance to heaven in death, a scene not depicted in the text but promised by Gawain's reconstituted Christian self. The rewards of Christian masochism—whether in the ready martyrdom of saints or in the reluctant masochism of Gawain—lie in the Christological vision of union in heaven with the Divine, but one must suffer on earth to get there. In the court's laughter and in the promise of Gawain's salvation, readers find a happy ending that attempts to sweep away the discomforts one might experience in realizing that God's game of salvation demands such suffering.

But can these discomforts really be forgotten at the conclusion of the narrative? The beneficial aspects of the godgame are, if not undermined, at least somewhat tempered by the method God chooses to deliver the message and Gawain's humiliated presence in which he "groned for gref and grame" (2502). We are left with a somewhat troubling vision of a God who plays with His followers to their ultimate benefit but also to their great discomfort, in a manner similar to the Book of Job.[101] Gawain's humiliation at the poem's conclusion cannot be easily reconfigured into a standard happy ending; rather, his hurt and confusion highlight his profound spiritual crisis, which can only be addressed by a blind faith in the God who tests him and a commitment never to forget his painful experience. The godgame tricks Gawain because he attempts to interpret visual signs as indicators of obvious truths, but these truths prove deceptive in the genre of romance and only enlightening when viewed with a lens of faith. In order not to be suckered by deceptive semiotic systems, Gawain needs a blind faith in God, not the visual evidence required by a doubting Thomas.

The narratival development of *Sir Gawain and the Green Knight* depends on Gawain's enforced metamorphosis into spiritual leader, but as the contradictory interpretations of the courtier's laughing response to Gawain suggests, he does not signify with absolute clarity at the romance's conclusion. The only sign that symbolizes clearly is the green girdle: when Bertilak gives Gawain the girdle, it becomes "a pure token / Of the chaunce of the grene chapel at chevalrous knyghtez" (2398–99). As the text winds down, we finally have a symbol that appears to symbolize directly and truly without any possibility of misinterpretation.[102] The pains of interpretation appear to be resolved, since the Green Knight allows this sign to mean clearly and literally. If signs have participated in the sadomasochistic play of the godgame by purposefully and sadistically misleading Gawain into pain, their sadistic valence is not eradicated at this moment; despite the fact that the girdle signifies clearly as spiritual renewal and humility, it also signifies Gawain's deep and lasting pain. Furthermore, Gawain's assumption of a symbol that appears more semiotically stable than his shield does not end the interpretive conundrums of his own personal symbolic valence. Gawain's girdle might be a "pure token" of chivalrous knights, but chivalry and the genre of romance served as the tricks that led Gawain into such a mortifying position in the first place. Why would Gawain want to symbolize chivalry, if chivalry is part of the problem?

What can Gawain and the reader do, if signs always signify in a contradictory fashion? How can one follow God's path, if that path is strewn with uninterpretable guideposts? The solution to this queer paradox in which God's will cannot be known, in which sin will lead to salvation, is self-sacrifice. By sacrificing individual desire, despite the pain of this act, the Christian achieves the pleasures of unity with the Divine as modeled by the martyrs of saints' lives. Gawain's encounter with the Green Knight transforms itself into such a self-sacrificial rite. As Kathryn Bond Stockton argues, "this break with one's individuality lies at the heart of the sacrificial urge. . .and constitutes the intimacy of sacrificial violence. . .[W]hat's at stake in religious sacrifice [is] the need to externalize the self, to throw oneself out of oneself, to disrupt the homogeneity of the self."[103] Gawain's quest to win the beheading game metamorphoses into the self-sacrifice of the godgame, but through his reluctant inculcation into the realm of saintly masochism, Gawain "wins" salvation through his loss of self.

For the reader to "win" this game as well, we must likewise sacrifice ourselves through a sense of abandon. The deconstruction of signs both between their Christian and secular meanings and between their literal and parodic meanings, as it traps Gawain, also traps the reader within a sadomasochistic semiotics. Reading *Sir Gawain and the Green Knight* is a profound literary pleasure, but if we identify with Gawain, it is a sadomasochistic (though perhaps no less pleasureful) act.[104] If we read *Sir Gawain and the Green Knight* for its full moral effect, we must suffer as painfully as Gawain, despite that we are also able to revel joyfully in narrative pleasure. By identifying with Gawain throughout his quest, the *Gawain*-poet dupes us into an acquiescent sympathy with Gawain, only to pull the rug out from under our feet. When we learn that Gawain "groned for gref and grame" (2502), his grief is our own, for we have been likewise suckered into the comforts of a romance yet confronted by the moral seriousness of an exemplum and the nearly impossible role models of the Christian martyrs found in saints' lives. If God queers Gawain into a sense of self-sacrificial abandon through the sexual play with Bertilak and his wife, so too the *Gawain*-poet queers his audience by demanding that we identify with Gawain throughout the destabilizing godgame. The sadomasochistic pleasures, then, are not contained within the text; rather, they bleed from the textual (Gawain's relationship to God) to the meta-textual (the reader's relationship both to the poet and, as allegorized through Gawain, to God).

Masochistic abandon structures not only *Sir Gawain and the Green Knight* but a range of genres and forms, and this sense of abandon constructs a readerly need for narrative. "An adult needs pornography as a child needs fairy tales," Henri Poincaré provocatively suggests.[105] Narratives are needed for the psychic release that they provide through the viewing of lives fantastically beyond our own. If, as Poincaré suggests, adults need pornography and children need fairy tales, it is for the sense of abandon that they offer. For both adult and child, escape from the quotidian and banal strictures of reality constructs an alternative to reality that nurtures fantasy. Obviously, *Sir Gawain and the Green Knight* is neither a fairy tale nor pornography (although it shares features of both, including the fantastic elements of the fairy tale and the titillating elements of pornography). More than suggesting a generic semblance between *Sir Gawain and the Green Knight* and fairy tale or pornography, however, Poincaré's words point to the necessity of narrative for making sense of the world. Fairy tales and pornography both offer narrative pleasure, but both offer these pleasures in a fashion that demands a masochistic response because, if the reader attempts to identify with the narrative's protagonist, such identification inevitably fails once the text is left behind. The child will never attain the magical capabilities of the fairy-tale protagonist, the adult will likely never live the pornographic narrative. Both genres, then, allow identifications that provide pleasure in the moment yet pain in the failure to alter reality. In similarity and in contrast, *Sir Gawain and the Green Knight* likewise offers a masochistic pleasure if one identifies with Gawain. If we do, we fail as he does. But the pleasure of failure promises success in the afterlife.

Medieval literature's licentious edge, especially in works ostensibly with an explicit moral and Christological agenda, gives further credence to reading *Sir Gawain and the Green Knight* as pornographically demanding readerly abandon. As Kathryn Gravdal observes of sexual violence and hagiography, "the representation of seduction or assault opens a licit space that permits the audience to enjoy sexual language and contemplate the naked female body. . . .Hagiography affords a sanctioned space in which eroticism can flourish and in which male voyeurism becomes licit, if not advocated."[106] The detailed seductions of *Sir Gawain and the Green Knight* provide specular pleasure that must be masochistically denied by Gawain, but they must also be denied by the reader. The sexual details of these scenes, especially the lady's seminudity ("Hir brest bare bifore, and bihinde eke" [1741]) invite the heterosexual male reader to identify with Gawain as he flirts with the lady, but these flirtations lead only to the queered fruition and repetitions of desire with the host.

To return to the question with which this section begins, Do we laugh with the courtiers at the end of the romance, or do we join Gawain in self-condemnation? How do we interpret the signs of Gawain's seriousness and the courtiers' laughter? The contradictory responses to Gawain's quest foreclose simple solutions to the question of what laughter and self-condemnation signify. As readers, we must admit that we cannot win: the excessive signs that populate *Sir Gawain and the Green Knight* prove impossible to pin down, for one meaning cannot possibly contain them. The necessary strategy, then, of reading normatively and queerly allows readers to decipher the text while still acknowledging a lack of control over it. Gawain realizes this when he abandons himself to God, and we too must abandon control. As John Clayton describes of sadomasochistic literature, "For as we submit to the ongoing process of creation, as we delight in the repeating motifs of the controlling consciousness, we find that in fact the freedom of engagement is illusory too. We *do* have to submit; the consciousness is *controlling*."[107] Resistance is futile; reading *Sir Gawain and the Green Knight* demands that readers repeatedly face the humiliations Gawain experiences, but more than that, they must accept these humiliations as their own in a similar state of abandon. And if readers choose to stake their identification with the laughing courtiers rather than with the suffering Gawain, they must nevertheless find meaning in their own laughter, a task that seeks a meaning that may not be meaningful. When we cannot know the will of God, abandon and self-sacrifice are the only solutions.

Fairy tales, pornography, and *Sir Gawain and the Green Knight*, then, share a concern with readerly and narrative abandon. These texts demand readers to give themselves entirely to their narrative pains and pleasures; anything less than a whole-hearted commitment will fail. And if we reread and continue to identify with Gawain, we do so with the knowledge that we will suffer repeatedly. As Aaron Ridley observes, readerly suffering stimulates the latent pleasures inherent in that suffering: "It is a fact that we value certain fictions, distressing fictions, for the negative emotions...which they elicit from us. We do not value such fictions *in spite* of our negative emotions, but, at least partly, *because* of our negative emotions."[108] In our repeated suffering, however, we relive and embody the Arthurian court's dualistic yet complementary reaction to Gawain's journey: we can celebrate his moral growth with laughter and joy, but his moral growth is not our own, and we must be prepared to suffer the cruelties of the Christian godgame of life, sin, death, and salvation as well. The godgame is unfair, perverse, sadistic, cruel, and queering; the genres are conflicting, negating, and impossible to reconcile; the text's semiotic system forces Gawain and the reader to misinterpret, misconstrue, and misread all possible meanings. All are cruel tricks designed to dupe Gawain and the reader, but all queerly and sadomasochistically pull the protagonist and the reader to the *Gawain*-poet's heartfelt goal of union with Christ.

CHAPTER 6

CONCLUSION: QUEERING GENRES, MEDIEVAL IDEOLOGY, AND TODAY'S READERS

In analyzing the intersection of genre and the queer in medieval literature, no simple pattern emerges. Rather, queering authors unleash the queer with specific and particular objectives in every rhetorical deployment. The range of authorial objectives examined in this monograph stresses the multiplicity of meanings of the queer during the Middle Ages, as its ideological cast as the perverse and the marginal, yet possibly the desired and the hidden, bears with it a vast range of signifying inflexions. Marbod, Baudri, and Hildebert desire the queer to lead them paradoxically to their salvation; Chaucer relies on the aggressive force of the queer to create lasting humor in *The Canterbury Tales* and to undermine easy moral and generic hermeneutics for *Troilus and Criseyde*; and the *Gawain*-poet examines humanity's fallen nature and spiritual quest for salvation through the queering intersection of romance, exemplum, saint's life, and personal identity. The disparate nature of these tactics and goals, for authors writing in different artistic and cultural milieus, reflects the power of the queer to subvert generic expectations and to force readers to consider their own relationships to cultural and religious constructions of queerness. Given the cultural construction of the perversity of the queer, it becomes a tool signifying with a taboo rhetorical valence and exposing the ways in which the forbidden inexorably acts upon identities claiming to be safely within the range of the normative.

After all of this literary queering, however, the homophobic cast of medieval ideologies still stands firm. Although the queer can certainly be used to subvert generic form and readerly expectations, it need not thus be used to subvert medieval religious ideology itself. In contrast, Marbod, Baudri, and Hildebert deploy the queer to shock their readers into a deeper understanding and more heartfelt experience of medieval Christianity; they subvert the construction of same-sex desire within Catholic ideology, and thus they expand the parameters of their religion, but they show little interest in undermining the ideological power of the religion itself. In these instances, that the queer can be used to reify rather than to subvert the prevailing ideology might appear to deny it any real destabilizing force. Queerness, from this perspective, thus appears to be yet another tool, albeit an ingeniously paradoxical one, to coerce individuals into the prevailing religious and cultural ideological systems.

Such a view, however, would undermine the complexity of the poetic strategy of queering the lyric and miss the point that these poets evince little desire to destabilize Christianity: their same-sex desires for earthly union with other males might conflict with their spiritual desire for salvation in heaven, but that they can locate the seeds of salvation in the locus of sin points to their attempts to unify earthly and spiritual desires constructed ideologically as incompatible. If we see that the queer serves rather than subverts the tenets of medieval Christianity as a sign of its co-optation, we misread the desire of these authors for a twenty-first-century identity politics rather than for a medieval Catholic union of soul with God. The power of queering genres allows the poets to speak personal desires and to create a space for queerness within medieval Christianity. Much as modern queer theory seeks to privilege the primacy of individual desires over an overarching conception of any one particular queer sense of identity, the lyrics of these poets speak a desire individual and unique in their celebration both of same-sex desire and of the ideology that constructs such desires and acts as sinful.

As Marbod, Baudri, and Hildebert subvert the ideological construction of same-sex desire yet leave the overarching ideology marginally altered yet fundamentally intact, Chaucer also expands the cultural range of queerness without seriously undermining medieval ideology. Throughout *The Canterbury Tales*, queering fabliaux and rhetorics depict the queer as a tool of antagonism and vitriol. For the male pilgrims, it is an insult with a rhetorical sting designed to ostracize enemies and to enhance the positions of the speakers through the claim to superior manhood; for the Wife of Bath, it is the destabilizing force necessary to emasculate male speech and narrative. Again, one might question the power of the queer in these instances, if it is deployed in a rhetorically aggressive, if not violent, fashion. That the queer is an insult at least partially denigrates the queer itself, as its force within the *The Canterbury Tales* derives from the fact that it represents what every man ostensibly fears—exclusion from heteronormative privilege.

Alison of Bath's reconception of sex roles subverts this paradigm, but even she fails to offer a true revisioning of heteronormative sexual politics. The recasting of a binary paradigm may in some way offer relief to those suffering in the role of the Other, but this relief then reifies the dynamics of a hierarchical ideology. By casting the men of the pilgrimage as sexually disenfranchised from heteronormative privilege, Alison finds power through the queer, but she duplicates the structure, if not the sexual politics, of the ideology that necessitated her rebellion. If such an ideological system is reinstantiated with woman on top, it nonetheless remains an authoritarian system with power failing to circulate evenly. Queerness allows a revisioning of masculine heteronormativity for Chaucer's pilgrims, and Alison's triumphant tale-telling modifies the meaning of sexual rhetoric and generic form throughout the Canterbury pilgrimage, but the ways in which sexuality is coordinated within a hierarchical system is in no way meaningfully displaced.

Of the texts examined in this monograph, *Troilus and Criseyde* most questions medieval Christian ideology through queer Pandarus's undermining of salvific teleology. In *Troilus and Criseyde*, the queer destabilizes the desire of readers for meaning and confronts them with the vast incomprehensibility of interpersonal desire, narrative form, and Christianity. At first glance, the text appears to pose such simple questions to the reader seeking to understand it: who desires whom in this narrative? What is its genre? And in what ways does Christian truth structure our understanding of the characters' fates? With queering Pandarus, however, Chaucer tacitly suggests that queer desires frustrate easy answers to ostensibly simple questions, questions that are thus revealed to be more complex than originally envisioned. Queerness forces the reader of *Troilus and Criseyde* to go beyond the limits of heteronormativity to realize the multiplicities of desire. Through Pandarus's queering tendencies, the queer powerfully expands the boundaries of human understanding through its insistent widening of romantic circles. In contrast to the antagonistic and aggressive queerness of *The Canterbury Tales*, *Troilus and Criseyde* explores the meaning of the queer in courtly love and Christian desire, as it dissolves the coherency of the courtly lovers' relationship to Christian telelogy.

The *Gawain*-poet, on the other hand, is more concerned with limning the ways in which the queer can ultimately function within Christian teleology. Despite differences in genre, both the *Gawain*-poet and Marbod, Baudri, and Hildebert share a common goal through their deployment of the queer: all four authors desire the queer to lead their readers to Christ. The primary tactical difference among the authors is that the Franco-Latin poets accomplish this goal by writing queer and anti-queer poems that confound readers' hopes for hermeneutic stability; the *Gawain*-poet achieves a similar objective through the destabilizing impetus of queering genres. Gawain, played with and eventually humiliated by the games of his quest, learns his lesson both through the sexual play of the queer and through the bewildering confusion of genres with which he attempts to interpret his adventures. Similar to the ways in which the male Canterbury pilgrims insult one another through the accusation of homosexuality, the *Gawain*-poet uses the queer and its paradoxical valence as a joke to lead his protagonist and his readers to Christ via a path of humiliation. That the queer is an insult again lessens its force as a subversive agent against medieval Christianity, but again, the *Gawain*-poet would never desire such a goal.

Thus, the necessity of a somewhat cautionary conclusion: queerness interrogates the arbitrariness of medieval constructions of same-sex desire and homosexuality, but it leaves the ideological system itself mostly unchallenged. Creating a space for same-sex desire within medieval Christianity yet preserving the hierarchical and normative functioning of religion, the queerness that these authors deploy displays limited efficacy in liberating sexually marginalized others. In these deployments of the queer, more divergence than convergence shines through. This paradigm is the strength and the liability of the queer in medieval literature: its multivalent and disparate practices construct it as a powerful authorial tool, as the reader can only conjecture at its rhetorical meaning in any given genre. It will mean *something*, but the heteronormative expectations attached to genre construct the queer as the unexpected, the forbidden, the Other. The complementary liability to this strength is that the queer does not connote in any of these medieval texts what many medieval and modern homosexual readers might most desire: the unfettered and true depiction of same-sex love as the moral, emotional, and spiritual equivalent of a heteronormative, heterosexual relationship. (Marbod, Baudri, and Hildebert come the closest to this goal with their paeans to same-sex attractions, but their homophobic lyrics, as well as their amatory verse to women, foreclose any attempt to read them as anachronistically advancing an unfettered queer identity politics.)

If the queer succeeds more in subverting generic form and in confronting readers with the limits of their own relationships to heteronormativity than in subverting medieval Christian ideology, the power of the queer should not therefore be underestimated. Given the slow pace of cultural change, it would be truly remarkable, if not secularly and theologically miraculous, if the queer succeeded fully in revising Christian doctrine. At the same time, the authorial deployments of the queer in these writings create a licit space for homosexuality in medieval Catholicism. By widening the view of the ways in which homosexuality functions within the formation of Christian spiritual identity, these authors outline a transformative feature of queer desire. Rhonda Knight details the ways in which sodomy too can be transformed within the parameters of medieval Christianity. Through the example of Gerald of Wales, who "refashions sodomy as a component of ethnic, rather than sexual, identity, challenging the medieval Christian view of sodomy," Knight argues that such a move "allow[s] us to read sodomy as a productive category of identification, rather than as an act of abjection, as medieval theologians would have it."[1] I have focused more on queerness (sexual resistance to heteronormativity) than on sodomy (sexual acts) in this monograph, but the overlap between Knight's and my analyses indicates the slipperiness of the medieval Christian construction both of queerness and of sodomy. Both are shifting signifiers of Otherness, and in this shifting cultural space, productive possibilities of expansion and resistance emerge.

Given the cultural construction of the sinfulness of homosexuality, depicting a transformative valence to the queer is itself a radical authorial move. Even the *Gawain*-poet, the most blatantly homophobic of these authors, showcases this at times paradoxical vision of literary homosexuality: it is surely difficult to imagine a pro-queer viewpoint arising from the author of *Cleanness*, but that he allows queer flirtations to elicit Gawain's eventual spiritual rebirth indicates a much more genial attitude toward sin than do the dire punishments of sodomites prayed for in *Cleanness*. As Simon Gaunt observes of the interplay of queer and straight desires in *La Vie de Sainte Euphrosine*, "the mechanisms by which homosexuality is repudiated guarantee and produce a heterosexual matrix, but they fail to occlude what they seek to repress."[2] That the queer serves a role in salvation may not subvert medieval Christianity, but it nevertheless subverts the medieval construction of homosexuality as intrinsically immoral.

In the end, though, these queering authors cannot fully control the homosexuality that they themselves unleash in their texts, especially for today's readers. If authors work as queering agents in the creation of their works, the audience serves a similar function in the reception of the literature. The author's vision of audience and the audience's reception of text may clash or coordinate in ways that spark queer readings. Recent studies in genre theory point out that genre serves a dynamic function in the role between text and audience. As Anis Bawarshi argues,

> Genres are socially constructed cognitive and rhetorical concepts—symbiotically maintained rhetorical ecosystems, if you will—within which communicants enact and reproduce specific situations, actions, relations, and identities. As individuals make their way through culture, they function within various and at times conflicting genre situations, situations that position them in specific relations to others and that contribute to the way they recognize their activities, themselves, and others.[3]

This paradigm of genre highlights the audience's power to create meaning within the ostensible confines of literary form. The audience's power to "enact and reproduce" identities gives them the authority of generic reification.

The relationships among author, genre, and audience are less a hierarchical arrangement in which the author defines the genre and the audience thus receives the text's meaning than a circular arrangement in which author and audience create complementary and/or conflicting assessments of the genre in play. As Alan Knight claims, "this question [of genre and understanding] too must follow the circular hermeneutic path. The better we understand the [texts], the more we can refine our concepts of their genres; and the more accurately we define their genres, the clearer will our understanding of the [texts] become."[4] Medieval authors, writing within traditions and in dialogue with history, authority, and scripture, participate in the construction of nascent genres, but their audiences—both medieval and modern—must be seen as also contributing to this cultural work.[5]

In the circularity of its development, genre is both a lie and a truth: it offers stability of interpretation yet often undermines this interpretative stability through the prevarications of generic interplay. Genre "promises" purity, but, as we have seen, this promise is seldom maintained. As the author uses this strategy of truth in lies, the reader employs a similar tactic that Adena Rosmarin refers to as the "edifying mistake of classification": "We are able, then, to read texts that are different as if they were similar because we are able and willing to make the edifying mistake of classification. . . . These self-conscious mistakes tend to be the most edifying, simultaneously teaching us about the text read and the procedures of that reading."[6] The paradox of a purposeful yet edifying mistake is also the paradox of a queering genre: both are purposeful misuses of a genre's meaning to find a truth hidden by the author. Queering authors, queering audiences: the possibility of singular and/or tandem approaches to queering genres suggests that we must look for the queering agent in a given rhetorical situation rather than assuming that either the author or the audience is exclusively behind the subversive play.

In addition to the gap between authors and their audiences, the centuries between the creation of the literature examined in this monograph and the analysis itself further muddy the interpretative waters. In the intervening years, cultural constructions of genre and homosexuality have changed: as modern readers, we cannot read medieval genres as medieval readers did because we can never duplicate exactly the meaning of a text in a cultural environment now centuries alien to us. Furthermore, we should not view homosexuality as medieval ideology did, lest we continue an inhumane policing of desire. These medieval authors queered their texts many years ago, but today's readers may queer them even more through their interpretative praxis. The circular model of genre construction between authors and readers must, for earlier literatures, not be viewed through a two-dimensional lens in which the interaction is limited to the authors of texts and their first generation of readers and auditors; rather, the paradigm must also include today's readers and thus metamorphose into a three-dimensional model, more like a sphere than a circle. We should not read yesteryear's literature with little concern for the ways in which the texts were appreciated and understood in their own time; on the other hand, we should not allow ourselves to be trapped by generic and sexual ideologies that no longer reflect the needs of today's readers. To this end, I offer this monograph as an attempt to make meaning of medieval literatures in some ways hostile to my own identity.[7] Genre and queerness serve not merely as strategies in the authorial game of literature; rather, readers need likewise to participate in the construction of meaning, even if we must at times read against the grain.

Queering genres, in the final analysis, empowers today's readers to assert their own rights in interpreting literature, and the political ramifications of this argument will, I hope, seep into and beyond the classroom. An awareness of genre's playful possibilities can enliven and illuminate pedagogical practice because queering is not merely a hermeneutic; it is a praxis of liberation, and queering genres allows us to practice in the classroom the very liberation we find in literature. By empowering our students to participate in the construction of generic and literary meanings, we help them to find connections between past literatures and their own lives. Certainly, if genres truly were the cut-and-dried prescriptive forces that the conservative view advances, no scholarly work in medieval genre would ever be necessary: as they were, so would they forever be. In the ongoing attempt to comprehend narratives, genre serves as one of many tools, and we—scholars and students—should always keep our tools honed through careful scrutiny of their meaning and relevance for both yesterday and today. Through the queering play of the genre contract, queer theory provides one such tool to explore the relationships among authors and readers, in which multiple and at times conflicting desires encounter one another through the intermediary position of the text.

The repercussions of this argument may well play out beyond the walls of academia, as the utility of queer genre theory in elucidating students' responses to medieval texts provides them with a theoretical framework with which to address cultural issues in their nonacademic lives. As David L. Wallace suggests, we need to help students to see the applicability of queer theory beyond the immediate environs of the literature classroom: "if we limit our uses of queer theory solely to high-culture texts, we are missing important opportunities for helping students learn to engage in and produce discursive strategies that may help bring about institutional and social change as well as transform their own lived experience."[8] Queer genre theory provides a powerful tool for analyzing literature, but its utility may be fruitfully expanded beyond academia. The parallels between actual lives and fictional narratives are too vast to count, but the ideological pressures on both demand resistance. Helping our students to comprehend the resistant strategies of queering genres will help them to see the ways in which the "genres" of real people's lives—in such terms as race, social class, age, and, of course, sexual orientation—can be overturned through the disruptive and multivalent force of queering. In so doing, professors of literature help to create a generation of queer readers—whatever their sexual orientation might be—who look between the lines for the intersections of genre, gender, and sexuality in all aspects of life.

In this manner, we renew in the modern world the medieval practice of a network of readers attuned to specific discourses through their participation in manuscript production and culture. Anna Roberts describes the possible queerness of medieval manuscript culture:

> [I]n addition to expression, coded or veiled representation, and demonstrable auctorial intent, we anticipate the production of homosexual identity in the act of reading, the commission of text or copy, manuscript ownership and lending. This, in turn, will allow us to trace the emergence and presence of queer networks among readers, patrons and owners of manuscripts.[9]

The re-creation of queer reading and writing practices from the medieval past offers a means to enact in the present the queerness of reading in the past. Finding the queer is more than pointing to a homosexual character or act; it is a practice of reading that looks to the past and to the future as it negotiates what it means to read and live in the present.

In regard to future scholarship, much more work needs to be done in analyzing the intersection of genre and the queer. I have exhausted neither the range of genres nor of authors in medieval literature, and this approach could be easily exported to literatures of other historical periods. I wonder, however, if one day this theoretical approach will be unnecessary for future critical analysis. As homosexuality continues to gain wider cultural acceptance, its subversive valence decreases as its apotheosis into banality kindly beckons and threatens: such a transition brings with it the promise of equality and the fear of the ordinary. How will the queer signify, if and when it is comfortably ensconced in the suburbs?[10] I leave this question to another writer for another day, perhaps as far in the future from me as I am from Marbod, Baudri, Hildebert, Chaucer, and the *Gawain*-poet.

NOTES

Chapter 1   Introduction: Queering Medieval Genres

1. Michel Foucault, *The History of Sexuality, Volume I: An Introduction*, trans. Robert Hurley (New York: Vintage, 1978), p. 83.
2. I began this book several years prior to the recent U.S. Supreme Court decision Lawrence v. Texas, which articulates a legal framework for dismantling the ideological construction of homosexuality as illicit and forbidden in the United States. Other such advancements in the battle for queer liberation, including the likely legalization of gay marriage in Canada, indicate that the cultural meaning of homosexuality is again shifting, as it has done throughout the centuries. These shifts, often accompanied by cultural imbroglios dedicated to the continued regulation of sexualities along the lines of the status quo, underscore the fact that queerness connotes as much as it denotes, and the connotative register of sexuality bears a heavy burden on those deemed outside the realm of the normative. Thus, while current twenty-first-century constructions of sexuality are lessening the stigma attached to certain sexual acts and actors, the historical valence of the queer as illicit and forbidden allows us to see the ways in which sexuality has participated—and continues to participate—in other discourses, including those of genre.
3. Tzvetan Todorov, *Genres in Discourse*, trans. Catherine Porter (Cambridge: Cambridge University Press, 1990), p. 19.
4. Benedetto Croce, *Aesthetic as Science of Expression and General Linguistic*, trans. Douglas Ainslie (London: Macmillan, 1922), p. 188.
5. Jacques Derrida, *Acts of Literature*, ed. Derek Attridge (London: Routledge, 1992), p. 223.
6. One "genre" that the queer community might lay almost exclusive claim to is camp. But is camp a genre in itself? It provides a paradigm for playing with and subverting traditional generic structures, but this suggests that camp acts as a praxis of parody rather than as a genre in its own right. The distinction may be critical hair-splitting, but it is vital to underscore that camping, as a tactic of parody, can (perhaps inadvertently) bolster rather than subvert heteronormative discourse. Indeed, Andrew Ross points out that camping often undermines queer political agendas: "Because of its zeal for artifice, theatricality, spectacle, and parody, camp has often been seen as pre-political, even reactionary. In its commitment to the mimicry of existing cultural forms, and its refusal to advocate wholesale breaks with these same forms, the politics of

camp fell out of step and even into disrepute (as a kind of blackface) with the dominant ethos of the women's and gay liberation movements" ("Uses of Camp," *Camp: Queer Aesthetics and the Performing Subject*, ed. Fabio Cleto [Ann Arbor: University of Michigan Press, 1999], p. 325 [308–329]). Although Ross's analysis addresses twentieth-century uses of camp, his observation that camp is essentially a discourse of mimicry accords with my argument that camp is not a genre in itself. In the ensuing analysis, I analyze authors who do not camp genres (in the sense of mimicking generic codes parodically), but who queer them (in the sense of participating in and simultaneously resisting generic expectations through the disruptive presence of same-sex desire). Both camping and queering are modes of subversion, not codes of discourse. See also David Bergman, ed., *Camp Grounds: Style and Homosexuality* (Amherst: University of Massachusetts Press, 1993).

7. Johnson locates his argument within a postmodern literary milieu, declaring that "Deconstructing genres thus becomes a means of elaborating gay culture in the post-Stonewall, AIDS-haunted present" ("Queering the Genre," *Harvard Gay and Lesbian Review* 2:2 [Spring 1995]: 21 [21–23]). My interest lies in delineating the ways in which these strategies are apparent in much earlier literatures. Our respective interests in queering genres are, of course, not mutually exclusive, and I hope that this study will stimulate expanded analysis of queering genres in other historical periods.

8. For medieval audiences and manuscript culture, we must think both of readers and of auditors. For more on medieval textual and auditory communities, see Brian Stock, *The Implications of Literacy: Written Language and Models of Interpretation in the Eleventh and Twelfth Centuries* (Princeton, NJ: Princeton University Press, 1983); M.T. Clanchy, *From Memory to Written Record: England, 1066–1307* (Cambridge, MA: Harvard University Press, 1979); and Janet Coleman, *Medieval Readers and Writers* (New York: Columbia University Press, 1981).

9. In discussing subjectivity and agency, I rely on the formulations of Paul Smith, who first defines the subject as "the complex but nonetheless unified locus of the constitution of the phenomenal world" and then demonstrates the limited viability of such an optimistically holistic definition. He concludes that the subject is "the term inaccurately used to describe what is actually the series or the conglomeration of *positions*, subject-positions, provisional and not necessarily indefeasible, into which a person is called momentarily by the discourses and the world that he/she inhabits." Smith also distinguishes the subject from the agent: "The term 'agent,' by contrast...mark[s] the idea of a form of subjectivity where, by virtue of the contradictions and disturbances in and among subject-positions, the possibility (indeed, the actuality) of resistance to ideological pressure is allowed for" (*Discerning the Subject* [Minneapolis: University of Minnesota Press, 1988], pp. xxvii and xxxv). Such a critical distinction between subject and agent, located in the gap between acquiescence with and resistance to ideological structure, underpins the ensuing analysis.

10. The French text appears in Alfred Ewert, ed., *Lais* (Oxford: Blackwell, 1965), p. 65, lines 277–86; the English translation is taken from Robert Hanning and Joan Ferrante, eds., *The Lais of Marie de France* (Durham, NC: Labyrinth, 1978), pp. 112–13.
11. For an analysis of terminology in discussing the queer Middle Ages, see Bernd-Ulrich Hergemöller, "Homosexuals in the Middle Ages?: Basic Questions on Terminology," *Sodom and Gomorrah: On the Everyday Reality and Persecution of Homosexuals in the Middle Ages*, trans. John Phillips (London: Free Association, 2001), pp. 6–25.
12. Karma Lochrie, "Presidential Improprieties and Medieval Categories: The Absurdity of Heterosexuality," *Queering the Middle Ages*, ed. Glenn Burger and Steven F. Kruger (Minneapolis: University of Minnesota Press, 2001), p. 95 [87–96].
13. For more on Greek constructions of femininity and practices of homosexuality, see Elaine Fantham, Helene Peet Foley, Natalie Boymel Kampen, Sarah B. Pomeroy, and H.A. Shapiro, *Women in the Classical World: Image and Text* (New York: Oxford University Press, 1994) and K.J. Dover, *Greek Homosexuality* (New York: Random House, 1980).
14. Allen J. Frantzen, *Before the Closet: Same-Sex Love from Beowulf to Angels in America* (Chicago: University of Chicago Press, 1998), p. 1.
15. Recent considerations of these topics are discussed in such volumes as Glenn Burger, *Chaucer's Queer Nation* (Minneapolis: University of Minnesota Press, 2003); Richard E. Zeikowitz, *Homoeroticism and Chivalry: Discourses of Male Same-Sex Desire in the Fourteenth Century* (New York: Palgrave, 2003); Burger and Kruger, eds., *Queering the Middle Ages*; Carolyn Dinshaw, *Getting Medieval: Sexualities and Communities, Pre- and Postmodern* (Durham, NC: Duke University Press, 1999); Mark Jordan, *The Invention of Sodomy in Christian Theology* (Chicago: University of Chicago Press, 1997); Karma Lochrie, Peggy McCracken, and James A. Schultz, eds., *Constructing Medieval Sexuality* (Minneapolis: University of Minnesota Press, 1997); Jeffrey Jerome Cohen and Bonnie Wheeler, eds., *Becoming Male in the Middle Ages* (New York: Garland, 1997); and Louise Fradenburg and Carla Freccero, eds., *Premodern Sexualities* (New York: Routledge, 1996).
16. In this manner, I hope to use "homosexual" and "homosexuality" to describe sexual acts rather than personal identities, and thus somewhat to alleviate the threat of anachronism in this monograph. I discuss the debate between social constructionism and essentialism subsequently in this introduction, but at this point it is necessary to underscore that I believe that "homosexual" and "homosexuality" can be used to describe accurately and neutrally sexual acts between people of the same sex in the medieval period, but the terms should only be used to describe medieval people's conceptions of themselves and others as a constituent factor of a given individual's identity with extreme care. Despite my caution here, scholarship has shown that the concept of a homosexual identity in the Middle Ages is not an impossible anachronism. See, for example Allen Frantzen, "Between the

Lines: Queer Theory, the History of Homosexuality, and Anglo-Saxon Penitentials," *Journal of Medieval and Renaissance Studies* 26:2 (1996): 255–96.

17. In a similar vein, Lochrie criticizes current scholarship on medieval same-sex desire for its almost exclusive focus on male–male sodomy. Her term "presumptive sodomy" refers to "the privileging of certain assumptions about what sodomy means without saying it—that it refers to anal sex between men, that it is primarily a masculine form of desire, and that gender exerts a negligible influence on the category" ("Presumptive Sodomy and Its Exclusions," *Textual Practice* 13 [1999]: 296 [295–310]). Both sodomy and the queer bear much wider semantic ranges than merely male homosexuality.
18. Richard Zeikowitz, "Befriending the Medieval Queer," *College English* 65:1 (2002): 67 [67–80].
19. Eve Sedgwick, *Between Men: English Literature and Male Homosocial Desire* (New York: Columbia University Press, 1985), p. 26.
20. Studies of gender and genre surface regularly in the field of literary criticism, including such volumes (listed in approximate chronological order of their subject matter) as Marshall Grossman, ed., *Aemilia Lanyer: Gender, Genre, and the Canon* (Lexington: University Press of Kentucky, 1998); Karen Raber, *Dramatic Difference: Gender, Class, and Genre in the Early Modern Closet Drama* (Newark: University of Delaware Press, 2001); Philip Cox, *Gender, Genre, and the Romantic Poets* (Manchester: Manchester University Press, 1996); Rohan Amanda Maitzen, *Gender, Genre, and Victorian Historical Writing* (New York: Garland, 1998); Darby Lewes, *Dream Revisionaries: Gender and Genre in Women's Utopian Fiction, 1870–1920* (Tuscaloosa: University of Alabama Press, 1995); Franziska Gygax, *Gender and Genre in Gertrude Stein* (Westport, CT: Greenwood, 1998); Lynette Felber, *Gender and Genre in Novels Without End: The British Roman-fleuve* (Gainesville: University Press of Florida, 1995); and Linda S. Kauffman, *Discourses of Desire: Gender, Genre, and Epistolary Fictions* (Ithaca: Cornell University Press, 1986). This brief bibliography concentrates on texts of literary criticism, but film criticism frequently addresses the interrelationship of gender and genre as well (such as Kathleen Rowe, *The Unruly Woman: Gender and the Genres of Laughter* [Austin: University of Texas Press, 1995]). Queer studies of genre are noticeably less common. The critical bibliography consists of such articles as Christopher Gittings, "Zero Patience: Genre, Difference, and Ideology: Singing and Dancing Queer Nation," *Cinema Journal* 41:1 (2001): 28–39; Lawrence Schehr, "A Queer Theory Approach: Gender and Genre in *Old Goriot*," *Approaches to Teaching Balzac's Old Goriot*, ed. Michal Peled Ginsburg (New York: MLA, 2000), pp. 118–25; Thomas Spear, ed., "Autobiographical Que(e)ries," *Auto/biography Studies* 15:1 (2000): 1–165; and Glen Johnson, "Queering the Genre," *Harvard Gay and Lesbian Review* 2:2 (Spring 1995): 21–23.
21. Susan Crane, *Gender and Romance in Chaucer's Canterbury Tales* (Princeton, NJ: Princeton University Press, 1994), p. 3.
22. Simon Gaunt, *Gender and Genre in Medieval French Literature* (Cambridge: Cambridge University Press, 1995), p. 1.

23. This argument expands on Crane's and Gaunt's seminal works by considering the queer as a similar tactic of narrative subversion but also by exploring the ways in which the queer affects the audience of a given text. Additional sources on gender and genre in medieval literature include Margaret Brabant, ed., *Politics, Gender, and Genre: The Political Thought of Christine de Pizan* (Boulder, CO: Westview, 1992) and Angela Jane Weisl, *Conquering the Reign of Femeny: Gender and Genre in Chaucer's Romance* (Suffolk, UK: D.S. Brewer, 1995). Lynn Tarte Ramey studies medieval genre, religion, and otherness in *Christian, Saracen and Genre in Medieval French Literature* (New York: Routledge, 2001).
24. Mary Eagleton outlines the dual objectives of feminist criticism in analyzing gender and genre together: "Feminist criticism's primary response to genre has been to look at it in terms of sexual difference, to try to account for the presence or absence of women in the major genres of the novel, poetry, and drama, and to explore further those forms in which women writers are highly represented....The second major way in which feminist criticism has approached the gender/genre debate has been in relating to genre what it sees as the subversive potential of women's writing" ("Genre and Gender," *Re-Reading the Short Story*, ed. Clare Hanson [Basingstoke: Macmillan, 1989], pp. 56–58 [56–68]). The dual functionality of feminist criticism exposes the historical conditions in which women are depicted or effaced and questions the ways in which female characters undermine or reify male privilege. Queer criticism has likewise shown an interest in both of these hermeneutic tasks in regard to narrative constructions of sexualities.
25. Eve Sedgwick, *Epistemology of the Closet* (Berkeley: University of California Press, 1990), p. 32.
26. Judith Butler, "Against Proper Objects," *Feminism Meets Queer Theory*, ed. Elizabeth Weed and Naomi Schor (Bloomington: Indiana University Press, 1997), p. 7 [1–30]. For more on the relationship between feminist and queer theories, see the essays in Weed and Schor, ed. *Feminism Meets Queer Theory*.
27. Sue-Ellen Case, "Tracking the Vampire," *differences* 3:2 (1991): 3 [1–20].
28. Feminist theory is often (although not always) concerned with the communal: as Patrocinio Schweikart declares, "Feminist reading and writing alike are grounded in the interest of producing a community of feminist readers and writers, and in the hope that ultimately this community will expand to include everyone" ("Reading Ourselves: Toward a Feminist Theory of Reading," *Gender and Reading: Essay on Readers, Texts, and Contexts*, ed. Elizabeth Flynn and Patrocinio Schweickart [Baltimore, MD: Johns Hopkins University Press, 1986], p. 56 [31–62]). Similar to my observation that queer theory is typically aligned with the sexual and feminist theory is typically aligned with gender, however, I do not wish for these overarching observations to construct either theory in absolute terms. Feminism and queer theory, despite some differences in focus, share many of the same agendas and are more complementary than divergent.
29. Lee Edelman, "Queer Theory: Unstating Desire," *GLQ: A Journal of Lesbian and Gay Studies* 2:4 (1995): 346 [343–46].

30. Ibid., p. 346.
31. Judith Butler, *Gender Trouble: Feminism and the Subversion of Identity* (New York: Routledge, 1990), p. 136; her italics.
32. Judith Butler, *Bodies That Matter: On the Discursive Limits of "Sex"* (New York: Routledge, 1993), p. 15.
33. Elizabeth B. Keiser, *Courtly Desire and Medieval Homophobia* (New Haven: Yale University Press, 1997), p. 14.
34. Peter Damian, *The Book of Gomorrah: An Eleventh-Century Treatise Against Clerical Homosexual Practices*, trans. Pierre Payer (Waterloo, Ontario: Wilfrid Laurier University Press, 1982), p. 60.
35. Alain de Lille, *The Plaint of Nature*, trans. James Sheridan (Toronto: Pontifical Institute of Mediaeval Studies, 1980), p. 157.
36. *The Poems of the Pearl Manuscript*, ed. Malcolm Andrew and Ronald Waldron (Exeter: University of Exeter Press, 1978), p. 141, lines 693–96.
37. A thorough analysis of this debate appears in Edward Stein, ed., *Forms of Desire: Sexual Orientation and the Social Constructionist Controversy* (New York: Routledge, 1992). For pro-essentialist positions, see also Rictor Norton, *The Myth of the Modern Homosexual* (London: Cassell, 1997) and Richard Mohr, "The Thing of It Is: Some Problems with Models for the Social Construction of Homosexuality," *Gay Ideas: Outing and Other Controversies* (Boston: Beacon, 1992), pp. 221–42; for a pro-social-constructionist view, see David M. Halperin, *One Hundred Years of Homosexuality and Other Essays on Greek Love* (New York: Routledge, 1990).
38. For example, obese people have been culturally constructed as beautiful (e.g., in the paintings of Rubens in the seventeenth century) and as unattractive (e.g., the current emphasis on emaciated fashion models). Regardless of how they are viewed, larger people have existed in the past and continue to exist in the present. Furthermore, scientific research points toward a genetic predisposition toward fatness, and so the cultural constructions of obese people may be founded upon an innate fact of their biological make-up. (For an analysis of the biological and genetic roots of obesity accessible to the nonspecialist, see W. Wayt Gibbs, "Gaining on Fat," *Scientific American* 275:2 [1996]: 88–94.) The same paradigm could well be true for the people we recognize as homosexuals today: various cultures construct both homosexual people and societal reactions to homosexuality in myriad ways, but the culture is responding to a core truth of these individuals' biological identity that leads to homosexual activities.
39. Claude Summers, "Homosexuality and Renaissance Literature, or the Anxieties of Anachronism," *South Central Review* 9:1 (1992): 3 [2–23].
40. Jonathan Dollimore, *Sexual Dissidence: Augustine to Wilde, Freud to Foucault* (Oxford: Clarendon, 1991), p. 33; his italics.
41. Frederic Jameson, *The Political Unconscious: Narrative as a Socially Symbolic Act* (Ithaca, NY: Cornell University Press, 1981), p. 106; his italics.
42. Thomas Beebee, *The Ideology of Genre: A Comparative Study of Generic Instability* (University Park: Pennsylvania State University Press, 1994), pp. 249–50.

43. Alastair Fowler provides a litany of such modes of generic interplay, including *topical invention, combination, aggregation, change of scale, change of function, counterstatement,* and *inclusion* (*Kinds of Literature: An Introduction to the Theory of Genres and Modes* [Oxford: Oxford University Press, 1982], pp. 170–83. For analyses of intergenres and intertexts in, medieval literature, see Sara Sturm-Maddox and Donald Maddox, "Intergenres: Intergeneric Perspectives on Medieval French Literature," *L'Esprit Créateur* 33:4 (1993): 1–100 and Norris Lacy, ed., *Text and Intertext in Medieval Arthurian Literature* (New York: Garland, 1996).
44. Quintilian likewise identifies the three primary genres as *fabula, argumentum,* and *historiam:* "Et quia narrationum. . .tres accepimus species, fabulam, quae versatur in tragoediis atque carminibus, non a veritate modo sed etiam a form veritatis remota; argumentum, quod falsum sed vero simile comoediae fingunt; historiam, in qua est gestae rei expositio" [Now there are three forms of narrative. First there is the fictitious narrative as we get it in tragedies and poems, which is not merely not true but has little resemblance to truth. Second, there is the realistic narrative as presented by comedies, which, though not true, has yet a certain verisimilitude. Third there is the historical narrative, which is an exposition of actual fact] (*Institutio Oratoria*, bk. II, chap. IV, pp. 224–25 ed. and trans. H.E. Butler [Cambridge, MA: Loeb, 1958]).
45. Päivi Mehtonen, *Old Concepts and New Poetics: Historia, Argumentum, and Fabula in the Twelfth- and Early-Thirteenth-Century Latim Poetics of Fiction* (Helsinki, Finland: Societas Scientiarum Fennica, 1996), p. 13.
46. The classical models of genre provided one schema of generic forms; additionally, medieval writers of the twelfth and thirteenth centuries were trained in such genres as philosophical maxims, eclogues, fables, elegies, and epics, as Paul Clogan explores in "Literary Genres in a Medieval Textbook," *Medievalia et Humanistica* 11 (1982): 199–209. Hans-Robert Jauss offers extensive bibliographies of literary genre theories and medieval genre studies in "Littérature médiévale et théorie des genres," *Poetique* 1 (1970): 79–101.
47. Ernst Robert Curtius, *European Literature and the Latin Middle Ages* (Princeton, NJ: Princeton University Press, 1953), p. 358.
48. Erich Auerbach, *Mimesis: The Representation of Reality in Western Literature*, trans. Willard Trask (Princeton, NJ: Princeton University Press, 1953), p. 133.
49. Kathryn Gravdal, "Poem Unlimited: Medieval Genre Theory and the Fabliau," *L'Esprit Créateur* 33:4 (1993): 10 [10–17].
50. Labeling *Troilus and Criseyde* with any genre invites a critical fracas to erupt, as its generic identity continues to perplex and intrigue. I consider the text a tragedy on the surface alone, and I address the conflicting levels of generic interplay and their queering repercussions in the chapter.
51. The argument that Marbod, Baudri, and Hildebert might have been sexually queer (as opposed to Chaucer and the *Gawain*-poet, who are authorially queer but who leave no autobiographical record of sexual queerness) arises from the disjunction between the desires expressed in their poetry for both men and women and the sexually normative goal of chastity in a

monastic setting. Obviously, I cannot prove that these authors themselves experienced the desires expressed in their poetry, and other scholars have claimed that their lyrics participate within normative social codes of the time (e.g., Stephen Jaeger, *Ennobling Love: In Search of a Lost Sensibility* [Philadelphia: University of Pennsylvania Press, 1999], pp. 71–73). Nonetheless, in terms of the structure of this book, I thought it necessary to include at least one chapter on authors who likely experienced queer sexual desire and who depicted it in unapologetically praiseful terms in some of their verse. In writing a book on queer theory, I did not want to occlude sexual queers struggling with ideological constructions of same-sex sexuality and focus only on authors who deploy the queer but who did not personally experience queer sexual desires. Finding authors as blatantly homoerotic in their poetry as Marbod, Baudri, and Hildebert necessitated casting a wider net across the field of medieval literature than focusing solely on fourteenth-century England. At the very least, Marbod, Baudri, and Hildebert express a necessary balancing view of queerness in contrast to Chaucer and the *Gawain*-poet.

52. The chronological gap of approximately 200 years between the Franco-Latin poets and Chaucer and the *Gawain*-poet occludes to some degree the cultural gaps between these two fourteenth-century English writers. Chaucer lived and wrote in an increasingly cosmopolitan, courtly, and continentally influenced London, whereas the *Gawain*-poet is generally assumed to have lived in the North-West Midlands and may have been a chaplain by profession. Again, this book focuses on the ways in which the queer is deployed to subvert readerly expectations in a sampling of medieval genres; it does not attempt to circumscribe a universal cultural meaning to the queer either within all of Western medieval Europe or within a particular geographical setting of the medieval world.

53. That some of Chaucer's fabliaux include religious characters does not seem to me to indicate any deep engagement with matters of Christian theology or spirituality. Religious figures in fabliaux, although often hilariously lampooning abuses of the Church, are primarily stock figures who invite laughter through the disconnection between religious ideals and earthly humor. I do not wish to obscure the ways in which Chaucerian fabliaux comment on religious failures to reach spiritual ideals, but I do not think it the primary goal of these texts. The primary goal of fabliaux is always humor—raunchy, rude, and outrageous.

54. For a theoretical model of the medieval self, I rely upon Paul Smith's discussion of the subject and agent (quoted previously). To align this conception of the subject within the medieval period, due attention must be paid to the disjunction between self and society inherent to medieval Christianity, in which individuals focused simultaneously on the call for spiritual community and on the attention required to one's personal salvation. Useful studies of medieval subjectivity that inform this monograph include Colin Morris, *The Discovery of the Individual, 1050–1200* (New York: Harper and Row, 1972); H. Marshall Leicester, *The Disenchanted Self: Representing the*

Subject in the Canterbury Tales (Berkeley: University of California Press, 1990); and Lee Patterson, *Chaucer and the Subject of History* (Madison: University of Wisconsin Press, 1991).
55. Burger, *Chaucer's Queer Nation*, p. x.
56. While formulating the structure of this book, I considered two additional chapters addressing postmedieval literature—one on Mark Twain's *A Connecticut Yankee in King Arthur's Court* and another on Truman Capote's *Other Voices, Other Rooms*. (In my articles on these texts, I do not specifically address the issue of queering genres, but the issue is latent within the analyses. See "Dialectical History, White Indians, and Queer Anxiety in Mark Twain's *A Connecticut Yankee in King Arthur's Court*," *Essays in Arts and Sciences* 31 [2002]: 83–102 and "Boundless Hearts in a Nightmare World: Queer Sentimentalism and Southern Gothicism in Truman Capote's *Other Voices, Other Rooms*," *Mississippi Quarterly* 51:4 [1998]: 663–82.) Obviously, such chapters would have necessitated envisioning a book much broader in historical scope than the Middle Ages. The appeal of writing such a diachronic book arose in its potential depiction of queering genres as a largely transhistorical phenomenon, along the lines of Sedgwick's *Between Men*, which ranges from Shakespeare to Dickens. Similar to the manner in which her book offers scholars a supple hermeneutic tool for the analysis of a wide range of texts, I hope that the hermeneutic of queering genres will likewise be of use to scholars of other historical periods. Other scholars will determine the relative utility of queering genres as a diachronic hermeneutic; in this monograph, I concentrate on the ways in which queering genres function within the particular religious, yet disparate cultural, worlds of medieval Western Europe. In this regard, I focus my analysis on medieval texts that appeared particularly apt for this hermeneutic, paying more attention to the ways in which genres function queerly than for developing an analysis of queer genres across either the historical and chronological range of the Middle Ages or the geographical range of Western Europe.
57. Heather Dubrow, *Genre* (London: Methuen, 1982), p. 39.

Chapter 2   Queering the Lyric: Personae, Same-Sex Desire, and Salvation in the Poetry of Marbod of Rennes, Baudri of Bourgueil, and Hildebert of Lavardin

1. For recent scholarship on the generic characteristics of the medieval lyric, see Peter Dronke, *The Medieval Lyric*, 3rd ed. (Cambridge, UK: D.S. Brewer, 1996) and William D. Paden, ed., *Medieval Lyric: Genres in Historical Context* (Urbana: University of Illinois Press, 2000).
2. Dronke, *The Medieval Lyric*, p. 207.
3. It would be anachronistic to argue that the three poets addressed in this chapter were men who would today identify themselves as homosexuals, especially since they also write amatory verse addressed to women. Their passionate lyrics and spirited defenses of same-sex relationships nevertheless hint strongly

that they experienced homoerotic desire; furthermore, the lyrics of these men at times indicate that they are writing to an audience of like-minded men, which might suggest that they perceived their nonnormative desires as constructing themselves in contradistinction to normative society. We can certainly view these men as queer in their resistance to societal normativity, although it would be imprudent to label them as homosexuals and as participating with a modern sense of sexual identity. See the introduction for a discussion of queerness, homosexuality, social constructionism, essentialism, and personal identity in the Middle Ages.

4. Scholarship on twelfth-century individuality and subjectivity demonstrates the vast array of possibilities for the human subject to negotiate the boundaries between group and self-identity. See Walter Ullman, *The Individual and Society in the Middle Ages* (Baltimore: Johns Hopkins University Press, 1966); Peter Dronke, *Poetic Individuality in the Middle Ages: New Departures in Poetry, 1000–1150* (Oxford: Oxford University Press, 1970); Colin Morris, *The Discovery of the Individual, 1050–1200* (New York: Harper and Row, 1972); John F. Benton, "Consciousness of Self and Perceptions of Individuality," *Renaissance and Renewal in the Twelfth Century*, ed. Robert L. Benson and Giles Constable (Cambridge, MA: Harvard University Press, 1982), pp. 263–95; Sarah Kay, *Subjectivity in Troubadour Poetry* (Cambridge: Cambridge University Press, 1990); Steven Shurtleff, "The Archpoet as Poet, Persona and Self: The Problem of Individuality in the Confession," *Philological Quarterly* 73 (1994): 373–84; and Gerald Bond, *The Loving Subject: Desire, Eloquence, and Power in Romanesque France* (Philadelphia: University of Pennsylvania Press, 1995). For opposing viewpoints, see Caroline Walker Bynum, "Did the Twelfth Century Discover the Individual?" *Jesus as Mother: Studies in the Spirituality of the High Middle Ages* (Berkeley: University of California Press, 1982), pp. 82–109; Judson Boyce Allen, "Grammar, Poetic Form, and the Lyric Ego," *Vernacular Poetics in the Middle Ages*, ed. Lois Ebin (Kalamazoo, MI: Medieval Institute Publications, 1984), pp. 199–226; and C. Stephen Jaeger, "Pessimism in the Twelfth-Century 'Renaissance,'" *Speculum* 78:4 (2003): 1151–83.

5. Burt Kimmelman, *The Poetics of Authorship in the Later Middle Ages* (New York: Peter Lang, 1996), p. 37.

6. Scholarship has demonstrated that twelfth-century clerics and their literature may have been known to troubadours and their audiences. R.N.B. Goddard traces connections between Marbod's lyrics and those of Marcabru and provocatively concludes that "If Marcabru was not simply borrowing—which already implies a clerical education on his part—but actually alluding to these mediaeval Latin poems [of Marbod of Rennes and Eugenius of Toledo], then this would have several interesting possible implications: first, clerks were perhaps also present in troubadour audiences; secondly, certain contemporary noblemen and their wives may have been so educated in the learned language that they could pick up allusions to specific Latin poems; and, thirdly, mediaeval Latin lyrics, often dismissed as 'school exercises' by modern scholars, were probably often widely circulated as works of art in their day" ("Eugenius of Toledo and Marbod of Rennes

in Marcabru's 'Pois la fuoilla revirola,' " *Medium Aevum* 57 [1988]: 34–35 [27–37]. Thus, Marbod's, Baudri's, and Hildebert's lyrics could well have been available to a much wider readership than their fellow monks, although it is unclear exactly which verses were known by which audiences.
7. Morris, *The Discovery of the Individual, 1050–1200*, p. 45.
8. V.A. Kolve, "Ganymede/*Son of Getron:* Medieval Monasticism and the Drama of Same-Sex Desire," *Speculum* 73 (1998): 1041 [1014–67].
9. Ernst Robert Curtius, *European Literature and the Latin Middle Ages*, trans. Willard R. Trask (Princeton, NJ: Princeton University Press, 1953), p. 115.
10. Arno Karlen, "The Homosexual Heresy," *Chaucer Review* 6 (1971): 45 [44–63].
11. John Boswell, *Christianity, Social Tolerance, and Homosexuality* (Chicago: University of Chicago Press, 1980), p. 237.
12. Thomas Stehling, trans., *Medieval Poems of Male Love and Friendship* (New York: Garland, 1984), p. xxiv.
13. The texts of Marbod's lyrics are found in *Patrologia Latina*, ed. J.-P. Migne (Paris, 1844–1904), vol. 171, cols. 1458–1782. These lines appear in the poem "Poenitudo lascivi amoris," *PL* 171, col. 1655. Translations are my own. I have striven for accurate and literal translations beyond all other objectives, and thus I have not attempted to convey from Latin to English certain poetic devices the authors use that might obscure their meaning. For a more poetic translation of some of the poems in question, see Stehling, trans., *Medieval Poems of Male Love and Friendship*.
14. C. Stephen Jaeger, *Ennobling Love: In Search of a Lost Sensibility* (Philadelphia: University of Pennsylvania Press, 1999), p. 26.
15. In his book, Jaeger analyzes several poems by Marbod, Baudri, and Hildebert (*Ennobling Love*, pp. 71–73, 84–86, 91–101). Complementary views on the platonic nature of such male–male relationships can be found in the articles by Elizabeth A.R. Brown, Claudia Rapp, and Brent D. Shaw in "Ritual Brotherhood in Ancient and Medieval Europe: A Symposium," *Traditio* 52 (1997): 259–381.
16. Latin biblical quotations are taken from the Vulgate, *Biblia Sacra Iuxta Vulgatam Versionem* (Stuttgart: Deutsche Bibelgesellschaft, 1969). Translations of the Bible are taken from the Douay Rheims (Rockford, IL: Tan, 1971), and I have modernized archaic verb forms. Other passages of biblical inversion include: Job 5:11 ("[H]e sets up the humble on high, and comforts with health those that mourn"); Isaiah 66:5 ("Hear the word of the Lord, you that tremble at his word: Your brethren that hate you, and cast you out for my name's sake, have said, 'Let the Lord be glorified, and we shall see in you joy: but they shall be confounded' "); Lamentations 4:5 ("They that were fed delicately have died in the streets; they that were brought up in scarlet have embraced the dung"); Baruch 5:7 ("For God has appointed to bring down every high mountain, and the everlasting rocks, and to fill up the valleys to make them even with the ground: that Israel may walk diligently to the honour of God"); Daniel 5:19 ("and whom he would, he set up: and whom he would, he brought down"); Matthew 10:39 ("He that finds his life, shall

lose it: and he that shall lose his life for me, shall find it"); Matthew 23:11–12 ("He that is the greatest among you shall be your servant. And whoever shall exalt himself shall be humbled: and he that shall humble himself shall be exalted"); Luke 1:53 ("He has filled the hungry with good things: and the rich he has sent empty away"); Luke 22:26 ("But you not so: but he that is the greater among you, let him become as the younger; and he that is the leader, as he that serves"); I Corinthians 1:20 ("Has not God made foolish the wisdom of this world?"); and I Corinthians 9:19 ("For whereas I was free as to all, I made myself the servant of all, that I might gain the more"). This list is intended to be indicative—not exhaustive—of the range of biblical teachings on inversion. As is well known, the primary text on inversion as medieval social practice is Mikhail Bakhtin, *Rabelais and His World* (Bloomington: Indiana University Press, 1984), as well as Natalie Zemon Davis, "Women on Top," *Society and Culture in Early Modern France* (Stanford, CA: Stanford University Press, 1975), pp. 124–51.

17. Caroline Walker Bynum, *Fragmentation and Redemption* (New York: Zone, 1991), p. 166.
18. Bond, *The Loving Subject*, p. 9.
19. The references to a community of readers suggest a common readership of these lyrics and epistles in which sexual desire—whether heteronormative or not—could be expressed in an acceptable fashion. Such a readership appears congruous to Joan Ferrante's description of the concurrent writing communities—often addressing sexual topics—between men and women: "In the late eleventh and early twelfth centuries, there seems to have been a whole circle of poets, men and women, who played an elaborate literary game, exchanging rhetorical elegance and literary flirtation, such desire as may have been felt sublimated through the poetry" (*To the Glory of Her Sex* [Bloomington: Indiana University Press, 1997], p. 31). Ferrante includes Marbod and Hildebert in her descriptions of this literary play; as mentioned earlier, the two poets engaged in the composition of verses for both male/female and exclusively male audiences.
20. Marbod of Rennes, "Ad amicum absentem," *PL* 171, col. 1717.
21. Marbod of Rennes, *PL* 171, col. 1718. The final line of this passage does not appear in the *Patrologia Latina*; J. Werner includes it in his edition of the poem in *Beiträge zur Kunde der lateinischen Literatur des Mittelalters* (Hildesheim: Georg Olms, 1979), p. 6.
22. Norman Roth, " 'Deal Gently with the Young Man': Love of Boys in Medieval Hebrew Poetry of Spain," *Speculum* 57 (1982): 39 [20–51].
23. Marbod of Rennes, *PL* 171, cols. 1717–18.
24. For analysis of the Song of Songs in the Middle Ages, see Ann W. Astell, *The Song of Songs in the Middle Ages* (Ithaca: Cornell University Press, 1990) and E. Ann Matter, *The Voice of My Beloved: The Song of Songs in Western Medieval Christianity* (Philadelphia: University of Pennsylvania Press, 1990).
25. Marbod of Rennes, *PL* 171, col. 1655.
26. This poem appears in *PL* 171, col. 1669 and Werner, *Beiträge zur Kunde der lateinischen Literatur des Mittelalters*, pp. 4 and 89. The final two lines quoted

do not appear in the *Patrologia Latina*, but they are included in Werner's edition. The poem is also titled "De multiplicibus damnatorum poenis" ("On the Manifold Pains of the Damned Ones").

27. The texts of Baudri's lyrics are found in *Les Oeuvres poétiques de Baudri de Bourgueil*, ed. Phyllis Abrahams (Paris: Champion, 1926). "Ad juvenem nimis elatum" appears on pages 23–26.
28. Bond, *The Loving Subject*, p. 50.
29. For analysis of Baudri's amorous epistolary verse to women, see Peter Dronke, *Women Writers of the Middle Ages* (Cambridge: Cambridge University Press, 1984), pp. 84–90 and Ferrante, *To the Glory of Her Sex*, pp. 31–35. Although my argument focuses on Baudri's same-sex lyrics, I believe that the thesis of this chapter—that these poets find redemptive possibilities through the assumption of sinful personae that allow them to speak taboo desires—would equally apply to Baudri's suggestive letters to women. Indeed, such letters to women queer monasterial normativity as much as the homoerotic lyrics queer cultural normativity.
30. Baudri of Bourgueil, *Les Oeuvres poétiques de Baudri de Bourgueil*, p. 163.
31. Ibid., p. 25; emphasis added.
32. Ibid., p. 333.
33. Kolve, "Ganymede/*Son of Getron*," p. 1048.
34. Hildebert's lyrics are found in *Les Mélanges poétiques d'Hildebert de Lavardin*, ed. Barthélemy Hauréau (Paris: Pedone-Lauriel, 1882). "Cum peteret puerum" appears on page 177.
35. In the beginning of the chapter, I situated the three poets' lyrics within the genre of "lyrics of realism," but Hildebert's classically influenced lyrics leave the realm of realism in their use of mythological characters and subject matter. Nonetheless, the resulting tensions between his classically influenced lyrics sympathetic to same-sex desire and his realistic lyrics condemning such desires create a disjunction in authorial stance similar to the poetic strategies of Marbod and Baudri.
36. Stehling sees "an attempt to place homosexual love in a respectable context" in the references to classical literature in medieval homoerotic poetry ("To Love a Medieval Boy," *Journal of Homosexuality* 8 [1983]: 167 [151–70]). Certainly, I agree with his assessment, but I think that the nexus between the classical past and the author's present needs to be probed further. Gerhart B. Ladner observes in the writings of Marbod, Baudri, Hildebert, and their contemporaries "a greatly increased receptivity of the late eleventh and twelfth centuries toward the ancients in many diverse fields of human endeavor"; he proceeds to argue that in this time period "the *antiqui*, whether long known or recently rediscovered, were often thought of as still alive rather than as reborn" ("Terms and Ideas of Renewals," *Renaissance and Renewal in the Twelfth Century*, ed. Robert Benson and Giles Constable [Cambridge, MA: Harvard University Press, 1982], p. 9 [1–33]). Thus, although Hildebert's classically influenced homoerotic poems are set in the past, their use of such ancient models would not in itself be sufficient evidence to distance the author from a cultural influence still very much alive.

37. Hildebert of Lavardin, *Les Mélanges poétiques d'Hildebert de Lavardin*, p. 192.
38. Ibid., pp. 68–69.
39. Ibid., pp. 68–69.
40. The ultimate eschatological reversal is embodied in the Antichrist, which underscores the potential fears generated by the world turned upside-down. Joachim of Fiore (ca. 1135–202) argues that, as Jesus came to save the world through truth, the Antichrist will come to spread falseness: "Ut ergo Christus Iesus venit in signis veris et tamen palliatus et occultus ob similitudinem carnis peccati, ita ut vix a paucis agnosceretur quod ipse esset Christus: ita rex iste septimus venturus est in signis mendacibus et tamen occultus et palliatus ob similitudinem spiritualis iustitie, adeo ut vix pauci sint qui possint illum agnoscere quod ipse sit Antichristus: propter quod si fieri possit in errorem etiam ducentur electi" [So, therefore, as Jesus Christ came in true signs, even though cloaked and hidden on account of the similitude of sinful flesh, so that it was scarcely acknowledged by a few that he was the Christ, so too that seventh king will come in false signs and will be hidden and cloaked on account of the similitude of spiritual justice, so that there are scarcely a few who will be able to recognize that he is the Antichrist. On account of this, even the elect will be led into error, if it is able to be done] (*Il Libro delle figure dell'abate Gioachino da Fiore*, ed. Leone Tondelli, Marjorie Reeves, and Beatrice Hirsch-Reich, 2nd ed. [Turin: Società Editrice Internazionale, 1953] 2, tavola XIV). The reversals that we see in Marbod's, Baudri's, and Hildebert's poetry appear to be part of widespread cultural anxieties based upon the world's impending judgment. As the poets use personae and reversals to position themselves as saved, they also see threats in reversals that they do not control. For scholarship on eschatology and the apocalypse in the Middle Ages, see Richard K. Emmerson and Ronald B. Herzman, *The Apocalyptic Imagination in Medieval Literature* (Philadelphia: University of Philadelphia Press, 1992).
41. Hildebert of Lavardin, *Les Mélanges poétiques d'Hildebert de Lavardin*, pp. 68–69.
42. Baudri of Bourgueil, *Les Oeuvres poétiques de Baudri de Bourgueil*, p. 89.
43. Ibid., p. 90.
44. Marbod of Rennes, *PL* 171: 1655.
45. Ibid., 1655–56.
46. Ibid., 1656.
47. Ibid., 1655.
48. One must note, however, a significant difference between Bernard's assumption of female traits and Marbod's, Baudri's, and Hildebert's relationships to same-sex desire: Bernard was not a woman, whereas Marbod, Baudri, and Hildebert may or may not have been those whom we recognize today as homosexuals. In line with the distinction between homosexuality and queerness established in the introduction, we can conclude that Marbod, Baudri, and Hildebert are queering authors who were possibly homosexual. Again, though, their amatory verse to women makes any putative claims about their possible homosexuality difficult to defend.

49. Steven Shurtleff, "The Archpoet as Poet, Persona and Self," p. 374.
50. Such a posture requires Marbod to visualize homoerotic sin as repentable, although Mark Jordan has demonstrated how Peter Damian's construction of sodomy renders it "as a sin that cannot be repented. [Damian's] conception violates the fundamental Christian teaching about sins of the flesh, namely, that they are always repentable. To conceive of a fleshly sin that cannot be repented is to set in motion an interminable dialectic. The dialectic can be stopped only by admitting that what has been categorized as an unrepentable fleshly sin is either not a sin or not fleshly" (*The Invention of Sodomy in Christian Theology* [Chicago: University of Chicago Press, 1997], p. 66). Marbod's poetry removes the fleshliness of the sin by delineating his rejection of the male body.
51. F.J.E. Raby, *A History of Christian-Latin Poetry*, 2nd ed. (Oxford: Clarendon, 1953), p. 279.
52. *Anthologia Latina*, ed. Alexander Riese (Leipzig: Teubner, 1894–1921), p. 261, no. 795.
53. Eugene Vance, "Augustine's *Confessions* and the Grammar of Selfhood," *Genre* 6.1 (1973): 3 [1–28].
54. Judson Boyce Allen, "Grammar, Poetic Form, and the Lyric Ego," p. 205.
55. Martin Stevens, "The Performing Self in Twelfth-Century Culture," *Viator* 9 (1978): 199 [193–212].
56. Leo Spitzer, "Note on the Poetic and the Empirical 'I' in Medieval Authors," *Traditio* 4 (1946): 419 [414–22].

Chapter 3   Chaucer's Queering Fabliaux

1. Recent scholarship on the Old French fabliaux includes B.J. Levy, *The Comic Text: Patterns and Images in the Old French Fabliaux* (Amsterdam: Rodopi, 2000); Norris Lacy, *Reading Fabliaux* (New York: Garland, 1993); E. Jane Burns, "A Close Look at Female Orifices in Farce and Fabliau," *Bodytalk: When Women Speak in Old French Literature* (Philadelphia: University of Pennsylvania Press, 1993), pp. 31–70; Mary Jane Stearns Schenck, *The Fabliaux: Tales of Wit and Deception* (Amsterdam: Benjamins, 1987); Charles Muscatine, *The Old French Fabliaux* (New Haven: Yale University Press, 1986); and R. Howard Bloch, *The Scandal of the Fabliaux* (Chicago: University of Chicago Press, 1986). Monographs addressing Chaucerian fabliaux include John Hines, *The Fabliaux in English* (London: Longman, 1993); Thomas D. Cooke, *The Old French and Chaucerian Fabliaux: A Study of Their Comic Climax* (Columbia: University of Missouri Press, 1978); and Janette Richardson, *"Blameth Nat Me": A Study of Imagery in Chaucer's Fabliaux* (The Hague: Mouton, 1970).
2. See the introduction for a discussion of homosexuality and queerness and the ways in which these terms are constructed for the subsequent analysis. Briefly, "homosexuality" is used as a neutral term to describe same-sex acts and desires, but without imputing a modern sense of homosexual identity

to a medieval character or text. "Queer" refers to the disruptions to cultural and sexual ideology occasioned by those acts and actors deemed beyond the parameters of the normative.

3. Should all of these tales be considered fabliaux, however? Robert Lewis warns that "Like all genres, the fabliau is impossible to define" ("The English Fabliau Tradition and Chaucer's 'Miller's Tale,' " *Modern Philology* 79 [1982]: 242 [241–55]). Nevertheless, fabliaux share certain recognizable features. Joseph Bédier's succinct summary of the genre as "contes à rire en vers" ("laughable tales in verse") establishes an excellent starting point for a definition (*Les Fabliaux*, Bibl. de l'école des hautes études, fasc. 98. Paris: Emile Bouillon, 1893), and Beryl Rowland elaborates that "[t]he plot is single and clear-cut with a dénouement that seems inevitable; it makes a steady progression usually involving some kind of sexual conflict whereby one character or group of characters is outwitted by another" ("What Chaucer Did to the Fabliau," *Studia Neophilologica* 51 [1979]: 205 [205–13]). "The Miller's Tale," "The Reeve's Tale," "The Summoner's Tale," "The Merchant's Tale," and "The Shipman's Tale" have been identified as fabliaux by critical consensus. John Hines addresses each in his study *The Fabliau in English*, as do other scholars in their respective works, notably Beryl Rowland, "What Chaucer Did to the Fabliau"; D.S. Brewer, "The Fabliaux," *Companion to Chaucer Studies*, ed. Beryl Rowland (New York: Oxford University Press, 1979), pp. 296–325; and J.A. Burrow, *Medieval Writers and Their Work* (Oxford: Oxford University Press, 1982), pp. 77–85.

Some scholars question whether "The Friar's Tale" and "The Cook's Tale" are fabliaux. Rowland considers "The Friar's Tale" a fabliau ("What Chaucer Did to the Fabliau," p. 206); Hines does not include a chapter on it in *The Fabliau in English*. Brewer outlines the haziness of the relationship between the "The Friar's Tale" and the fabliau tradition by conceding that it fits only loosely within his definition of the term, yet he includes it in his list of Chaucer's fabliaux because it is "more or less close in form and spirit" ("The Fabliaux," p. 297). Larry Scanlon locates the tale within the exemplum tradition (*Narrative, Authority, and Power: The Medieval Exemplum and the Chaucerian Tradition* [Cambridge: Cambridge University Press, 1994], pp. 147 ff.). Although the exemplum is typically a moral genre, more predicated upon seriousness than laughter, exempla share with fabliaux a basic structure of a tale with a moral (although the morals of fabliaux, if they appear at all, often reveal themselves to be excessively tendentious, if not altogether arbitrarily attached to the narratives that precede them). Still, as John Hines observes, "the basic tales that could be recomposed as fabliuax could circulate as *exempla*" (*The Fabliau in English*, p. 213). I address "The Friar's Tale" as a fabliau because it fits within the skeletal definitions offered by Bédier, Rowland, and Brewer and because I believe that the antagonism between the Friar and the Summoner plays out by telling tales of the same genre. Certainly, the tale ends with the "punchline" of the summoner's damnation, and the humor of the conclusion suggests that the tale is indeed a fabliau. "The Cook's Tale," in its fragmented form, appears to be developing as a

fabliau, and I address it as such; however, V.A. Kolve points out that we have insufficient evidence to draw such a conclusion definitively and suggests the possibility of other narrative forms developing (*Chaucer and Imagery of Narrative* [Stanford, CA: Stanford University Press, 1984], pp. 257–85).
4. Labeling "The Cook's Tale" as one of the female queer fabliau may appear incongruous, as the tale's teller, Roger, and its protagonist, Perkyn Revelour, are both men; however, as I will address subsequently, the character of Perkyn Revelour's friend's wife, who is a prostitute, destabilizes masculine aggression and heteronormativity and, through this gendered dialectic, asserts a claim for female sexual agency. This argument is expanded in the section of this chapter entitled. "When Women Queer, or How Heteronormative Is Female Desire? The Fabliaux of the Cook, the Merchant, and the Shipman."
5. I use the term "queer anxiety" to identify the fears generated by the presence of the homosexual in medieval culture. See Elizabeth Keiser, *Courtly Desire and Medieval Homophobia* (New Haven: Yale University Press, 1997), pp. 14 ff., as well as the discussion in the introduction.
6. Eve Sedgwick, "The Beast in the Closet: James and the Writing of Homosexual Panic," *Sex, Politics, and Science in the Nineteenth-Century Novel*, ed. Ruth Bernard Yeazell (Baltimore, MD: Johns Hopkins University Press, 1986), p. 151 [148–86]. Although Sedgwick establishes the eighteenth century in England and America as a possible starting point for this dynamic, she also suggests that it may well have developed earlier. Its relevance to Chaucer lies in the battleground of masculine identity in which sexual acts serve as identifying markers. The limits of Sedgwick's analysis to the medieval world emerge in its vision of a post–eighteenth-century homosexuality, limits that Sedgwick herself highlights as she points out the need to examine homosexuality's "predecessor terms." The social constructionist camp of queer inquiry would suggest that homosexuality, as we recognize it today, did not exist in the medieval period. As important a point as this criticism makes, the benefits of proceeding with this analysis outweigh its liabilities, as the queer anxieties of these fabliaux function with a remarkably similar dynamic to the one that Sedgwick describes. With due deference to the multiple and variant responses to same-sex sexuality throughout the centuries, this chapter examines a polymorphous vision of queer sexuality under Sedgwick's rubric by delineating the fears and anxieties evoked by social and sexual interactions among men.
7. Glenn Burger, "Queer Chaucer," *English Studies in Canada* 20 (1994): 161 [153–70].
8. Sigmund Freud, *Wit and Its Relation to the Unconscious* (London: Routledge, 1999), pp. 127–74.
9. Per Nykrog was the first to locate the origins of the fabliau within an aristocratic milieu (*Les Fabliaux: étude d'histoire littéraire et de stylistique médiévale* [1957. New ed. Genève: Librairie Drox, 1973]), in response to J. Bédier's hypothesis that the genre flowered in the middle class. John Hines addresses the connections among French, Anglo-Norman, and English fabliau (*The Fabliau in English*, pp. 1–42).

10. Charles Muscatine, *Chaucer and the French Tradition* (Berkeley: University of California Press, 1957), p. 58.
11. Brewer, "The Fabliaux," p. 299.
12. Ross Arthur, " 'Why Artow Angry': The Malice of Chaucer's Reeve," *English Studies in Canada* 13 (1987): 6 [1–11].
13. David Wallace, *Chaucerian Polity: Absolutist Lineages and Associational Forms in England and Italty* (Stanford, CA: Stanford University Press, 1997), pp. 125–81.
14. Glending Olson, " 'The Reeve's Tale' as a Fabliau," *Modern Language Quarterly* 35 (1974): 228–29 [219–30].
15. Indeed, such authorial innovation appears consistent with the "improvements" certain critics observe in Chaucer's reworkings of his source tales, improvements that lead Roy Pearcy to describe Chaucer's tales as " 'fabliaux-with-a-difference'. . .resulting from some process of accretion, expansion, or elaboration, whereby the tales in question have taken on the qualities of 'enriched' fabliaux" ("The Genre of Chaucer's Fabliau-Tales," *Chaucer and the Craft of Fiction*, ed. Leigh A. Arrathoon [Rochester, MI: Solaris, 1986], p. 329 [329–84]). Rossell Robbins sees such artistic innovations in Chaucer's fabliaux that, he argues, they "go so far beyond the traditional genre, in fact, to cease being fabliaux at all" ("The English Fabliau: Before and After Chaucer," *Moderna Sprak* 64 [1970]: 235 [231–44]).
16. In regard to Chaucer and class conflict, historian Christopher Dyer observes: "Chaucer. . .acknowledged the existence of the three orders idea by depicting a model knight, parson and ploughman. Their virtues shone out from a much more numerous group of characters who did not accord with the ideal because they pursued a variety of (mainly urban) trades and professions. . .From the vantage point of a sophisticated London civil servant, having close connections with aristocratic, mercantile and clerical society, Chaucer was gently criticizing this simple notion, and demonstrating that it was an unworkable model in a complex and sinful world" (*Standards of Living in the Later Middle Ages: Social Change in England c. 1200–1520* [Cambridge: Cambridge University Press, 1989], p. 17). For scholarship on Chaucer and estates satire, the definitive work remains Jill Mann, *Chaucer and Medieval Estates Satire: The Literature of Social Classes and the General Prologue to the Canterbury Tales* (Cambridge: Cambridge University Press, 1973); for analysis of class tensions among members of Chaucer's bourgeois, see Carl Lindahl, "Conventions of a Narrative War," *Earnest Games: Folkloric Patterns in the Canterbury Tales* (Bloomington: Indiana University Press, 1987), pp. 73–155.
17. All citations of Chaucer refer to *The Riverside Chaucer*, ed. Larry D. Benson, 3rd ed. (Boston: Houghton Mifflin, 1987) and are noted parenthetically.
18. Although "male" means "bag" or "pouch" in a medieval lexicon, the *Oxford English Dictionary* attests that its meaning as "masculine" was developing in the 1380s, which makes possible a bawdy yet typically Chaucerian pun. Such a sexual interpretation of the phrase "unbokeled is the male" gains further credence when compared with the Pardoner's more openly suggestive

pun in his request to Harry Bailly: "Com forth, sire Hoost, and offre first anon, / And thou shalt kisse the relikes everychon, / Ye, for a grote! Unbokele anon thy purs" (943–45). For further discussion of this passage, see Robert Sturges, *Chaucer's Pardoner and Gender Theory: Bodies of Discourse* (New York: St. Martin's, 2000), pp. 74–76. The interpretation of "unbokeled is the male" as meaning "the game is well begun" belongs to the editors of *The Riverside Chaucer*, p. 66.

19. Looking outside Chaucer's fabliaux at the tellers of these tales, we see a world of masculine rivalry, but we see a similar male orientation in the tales themselves. One need only scan the cast of characters of Chaucer's fabliaux to ascertain that a primarily male society populates them. In "The Miller's Tale," three men (John, Nicholas, and Absolon) struggle over sexual control of one woman (Alison), and in "The Reeve's Tale" the rivalry between the clerks John and Aleyn and the crooked miller Symkyn resolves itself through the sexual conquest of Symkyn's wife and daughter. (If we add to the cast of characters of this fabliau Symkyn's infant son, who inadvertently assists John's "seduction" of his mother, the count of males increases.) "The Friar's Tale" depicts only one female in its predominantly masculine world, and the female characters of "The Summoner's Tale" play little part in the plot at all, as the story concerns itself primarily with the adversarial relationship between Friar John and Thomas. In these male queer fabliaux, female presence is marginalized, and female sexuality, if it appears at all, serves as a conduit for male sexual satisfaction and the expression of homosocial aggression. The three female queer fabliaux, despite the fact that the female protagonists of "The Merchant's Tale" and "The Shipman's Tale" stand at the center of their narratives, likewise depict a predominantly masculine world: "The Merchant's Tale" involves five men (January, Damian, Pluto, Placebo, and Justinus) and two women (May and Proserpina), whereas "The Shipman's Tale" unfolds with two men (Daun John and the Merchant) and one woman (the merchant's wife). Even these female characters with much greater control of their sexuality must negotiate the overwhelmingly masculine world of Chaucerian fabliaux. "The Cook's Tale" likewise depicts more male than female characters.

20. Emily Jensen, "Male Competition as a Unifying Motif in Fragment A of the *Canterbury Tales*," *Chaucer Review* 24 (1990): 327 [320–28]. See also Anne Laskaya, "Men in Love and Competition: 'The Miller's Tale' and 'The Merchant's Tale,' " *Chaucer's Approach to Gender in the Canterbury Tales* (Suffolk, UK: D.S. Brewer, 1995), pp. 78–98.

21. Scott Vaszily offers a structural analysis of fabliau elements in "The Knight's Tale" in "Fabliau Plotting Against Romance in Chaucer's 'Knight's Tale,' " *Style* 31 (1997): 523–42.

22. Chaucer's description of the Miller's propensity for "wrastlynge" further establishes the connection between physical and rhetorical violence in the tales; Gregory Semenza argues that this detail "level[s] the playing field in the discursive contest between two seemingly unequal contestants, the Miller and the Knight" ("Historicizing 'Wrastlynge' in the 'Miller's Tale,' " *Chaucer Review* 38 [2003]: 66 [66–82]).

23. Karma Lochrie, "Women's 'Pryvetees' and Fabliau Politics in the 'Miller's Tale,'" *Exemplaria* 6 (1994): 288–89 [287–304]. Derek Brewer outlines a similar connection between the theme of sexual honor and the bourgeois social setting of the tales in "The Couple in Chaucer's Fabliaux," *The Making of the Couple: The Social Function of Short-Form Medieval Narrative*, ed. Flemming Andersen and Morten Nojgaard (Odense: Odense University Press, 1991), p. 137 [129–43].
24. Linda Lomperis comments on this gender reversal, noting that it contributes to a deconstruction of sexual normativity in the tale: "Heterosexuality, it seems, is a troubled category in the 'Miller's Tale.' Expectations of heterosexual activity seem to loom larger than actual instances of it, leaving us to wonder about the precise erotic basis of this ostensibly heterosexual, theologically-based narrative about a carpenter and his wife" ("Bodies That Matter in the Court of Late Medieval England and in Chaucer's 'Miller's Tale,'" *Romanic Review* 86:2 [1995]: 253 [243–64]).
25. Glenn Burger, "Erotic Discipline...Or 'Tee Hee, I Like My Boys To Be Girls': Inventing with the Body in Chaucer's 'Miller's Tale,'" *Becoming Male in the Middle Ages*, ed. Jeffrey Jerome Cohen and Bonnie Wheeler (New York: Garland, 1997), p. 225 [245–60].
26. Roy Peter Clark, "Christmas Games in Chaucer's 'The Miller's Tale,'" *Studies in Short Fiction* 13 (1976): 284 [277–87]. Clark also links Absolon's symbolic sodomy of Nicholas to Jacobus de Voraigne's *Legenda Aurea* (p. 283).
27. Tracey Jordan, "Fairy Tale and Fabliau: Chaucer's 'The Miller's Tale,'" *Studies in Short Fiction* 21 (1984): 88 [87–93].
28. Reading this line, Ross Arthur notes the double valence of the Reeve's revenge both against the Miller as pilgrim and against his miller as fictional character (" 'Why Artow Angry': The Malice of Chaucer's Reeve," p. 8).
29. Paul Olson, *The Canterbury Tales and the Good Society* (Princeton, NJ: Princeton University Press, 1986), p. 184. Jean Jost suggests that the aggression between the Friar and Summoner may be the result of a latent sexual attraction for each other: "the Friar and the Summoner, despite their apparent antagonism, may simultaneously feel more than a fraternal attraction, in fact a sexual attraction to each other, with which neither is comfortable" ("Ambiguous Brotherhood in the 'Friar's Tale' and 'Summoner's Tale,'" *Masculinities in Chaucer*, ed. Peter Beidler [Cambridge: D.S. Brewer, 1998], p. 77 [77–90]). For further analysis of the Summoner, see Catherine Cox, *Gender and Language in Chaucer* (Gainseville: University Press of Florida, 1997), pp. 115–18 and Laurel Braswell-Means, "A New Look at an Old Patient: Chaucer's Summoner and Medieval Physiognomia," *Chaucer Review* 25:3 (1991): 266–75. Penn R. Szittya explores Chaucer's depiction of the Friar in *The Anti-Fraternal Tradition in Medieval Literature* (Princeton, NJ: Princeton University Press, 1986), pp. 231–46.
30. Mary Godfrey, "Only Words: Cursing and the Authority of Language in Chaucer's 'Friar's Tale,'" *Exemplaria* 10 (1998): 327 [307–28].
31. See *A Glossarial Concordance to the Riverside Chaucer*, ed. Larry D. Benson (New York: Garland, 1993).

32. Britton Harwood supports an interpretation of "The Friar's Tale" as a fabliau with his observation that this moment "is the joke that the tale is organized to tell" ("Chaucer on 'Speche': *House of Fame*, the 'Friar's Tale,' and the 'Summoner's Tale,'" *Chaucer Review* 26 [1992]: 346 [343–49]).
33. It may be worth reiterating the distinction between homosexuality and queerness at this point, in that "homosexual queerness" adumbrates the disruptions to heteronormativity specifically occasioned by same-sex acts, desires, and depictions, whereas "heterosexual queerness" delineates disruptions to ideologically constructed sexual normativity occasioned by heterosexual acts, desires, and depictions.
34. The Shipman's words appear in the Epilogue to "The Man of Law's Tale" rather than as a "Prologue" to his own tale. Still, these lines indicate that Chaucer did not intend for the Shipman to be fighting with another pilgrim.
35. I do not wish to occlude the ways in which some of Chaucer's fabliaux depict scenes of sexual violence against women and the proximity of this violence to rape. "The Miller's Tale" and "The Reeve's Tale" depict an aggressive male sexuality in a manner which, as Jill Mann describes, "female acquiescence retrospectively sanctions male coercion, and reveals reluctance to have been a merely ritual female role" (*Feminizing Chaucer* [Cambridge: D.S. Brewer, 2002], p. 79). At the same time, genre somewhat mitigates the shock of this sexual violence. Chaucer is certainly capable of stirring up his audience's outrage at female violation, as in "The Physician's Tale." The focus of "The Miller's Tale" and "The Reeve's Tale" is the humor of cuckoldry and masculine hostility, not the female characters who in essence become little more than conduits of male aggression.
36. Is "The Wife of Bath's Tale" truly a romance? Critical consensus suggests that it is, but the overarching frame of romance should not occlude the possibility of intergeneric play. The primary sources and analogues of "The Wife of Bath's Tale" offered Chaucer a mix of generic options, as "The Marriage of Sir Gawaine" is a ballad, "The Weddynge of Sir Gawen and Dame Ragnell" is a burlesque, and John Gower's "The Tale of Florent" is a romance. The crucial distinction between "The Wife of Bath's Tale" and its sources and analogues, however, is not in the narrative details that are shifted in the retelling, but in the aggressive narrative frame of *The Canterbury Tales*. For instance, that "The Weddynge of Sir Gawen and Dame Ragnell" offers a burlesque model of romance is less important, I think, than the ways in which Alison rhetorically positions her genre as a queering weapon. Meredith Cary notes that "The striking similarity of plot between the Wife of Bath's Tale and its English analogues is deceptive, however, for Chaucer used this common material to a new end. One aspect of his different purpose is the consistency with which he shifted the focus of the tale away from the traditional suggestion of a masculine system of values emphasized by scenes of battle and revenge and by discussion of, and fidelity to, abstract notions of honor. Signaling his intentions by providing a woman as narrator for his tale, Chaucer recast each episode in such a way as to reconstitute the traditional

plot with a feminine protagonist and to redefine such central concepts as 'honor' and 'sovereignty' in feminine terms" ("Sovereignty and Old Wife," *Papers on Language and Literature* 5 [1969]: 376 [375–88]. Cary's observations encourage the reader to analyze "The Wife of Bath's Tale" for such a move from a masculine genre to one reformulated to reflect queering female desires.

37. The Friar and the Summoner offer the primary exceptions to this rule with their fabliaux, but in these instances, Chaucer satirizes the disjunction between the religious ideals they ostensibly represent and their dissolute lifestyles. As discussed earlier in the chapter, the majority of Chaucer's fabliau-tellers are members of the bourgeoisie.

38. The correct order of *The Canterbury Tales* and the order in which Chaucer wrote them are subjects of great debate; still, that the Wife of Bath appears so connected to other fabliau-tellers, both in social class and in the generally accepted order of the tales, suggests that she would also tell a bawdy tale.

39. Chaucer's preference for the fabliau over other genres also makes it more likely that Alison would tell a fabliau. Thomas Cooke observes that of "the twenty-one completed stories in *The Canterbury Tales* there are six fabliaux, more than a quarter of the total number. . . .No other genre is as frequently represented in Geoffrey Chaucer's major work" (*The Old French and Chaucerian Fabliaux*, p. 170).

40. Robert A. Pratt, "The Development of the Wife of Bath," *Studies in Medieval Literature in Honor of Professor Albert Croll Baugh*, ed. MacEdward Leach (Philadelphia: University of Pennsylvania Press, 1961), p. 47 [45–79].

41. Helen Cooper, *Oxford Guides to Chaucer: The Canterbury Tales* (Oxford: Oxford University Press, 1989), p. 156.

42. Walter Long, "The Wife as Moral Revolutionary," *Chaucer Review* 20 (1986): 282 [273–84].

43. Louise Fradenburg suggests that "Chaucer chose to give the Wife a romance rather than a fabliau because he found that by doing so he could explore in a more complex way the crisis in desire brought on by the end of the feudal order"; she proceeds to argue that Alison's "*Prologue* relates to her tale, her fabliau to her romance, through a structure which presents fabliau as having interiorized and privatized romance in the form of a wish-fulfillment fantasy" ("The Wife of Bath's Passing Fancy," *Studies in the Age of Chaucer* 8 [1986]: 46 [31–58]). Fradenburg's subtle and powerful analysis of the ways in which Alison's desires are constructed in the passing genre of romance offers an intriguing understanding of her character and her resistance to hegemonic narratives; I differ from her interpretation by focusing on the ways that Alison reconfigures and queers both genres to subvert male privilege.

44. Laura Kendrick, *Chaucerian Play: Comedy and Control in The Canterbury Tales* (Berkeley: University of California Press, 1988), p. 125.

45. Melissa Furrow, "Middle English Fabliaux and Modern Myth," *English Literary History* 56 (1989): 7 [1–18].

46. Keith Busby concludes that the artistic achievement of Chaucerian fabliaux emerges most clearly through such a comparative lens, that the genre

necessitates a reflexive analysis: "[The] true richness [of Chaucer's fabliaux] is only revealed once they are compared with each other and with the romances of *The Canterbury Tales*" ("Conspicuous by Its Absence: The English Fabliau," *Dutch Quarterly Review of Anglo-American Letters* 12 [1982]: 32 [30–41]).

47. Much work has been done on Alison's speech and its relationship to male language structures. Some recent articles that address Alison's rhetorical strategies include: Warren Smith, "The Wife of Bath Debates Jerome," *Chaucer Review* 32 (1997): 129–45; Susan Signe Morrison, "Don't Ask, Don't Tell: The Wife of Bath and Vernacular Translations," *Exemplaria* 8 (1996): 97–123; Jerry Root " 'Space To Speke': The Wife of Bath and the Discourse of Confession," *Chaucer Review* 28 (1994): 252–74; and R.W. Hanning, "Roasting a Friar, Mis-Taking a Wife, and Other Acts of Textual Harassment in Chaucer's *Canterbury Tales*," *Studies in the Age of Chaucer* 7 (1985): 3–20.

48. Barrie Ruth Straus, "The Subversive Discourse of the Wife of Bath," *English Literary History* 55 (1988): 527 [527–54].

49. Angela Jane Weisl, *Conquering the Reign of Femeny: Gender and Genre in Chaucer's Romance* (Suffolk, UK: D.S. Brewer, 1995), p. 14.

50. Lacy, *Reading Fabliaux*, p. 76.

51. David Reid argues that "The romance is under Venus but Mars spoils it, as fits the teller. This is not tragedy but bathos" ("Crocodilian Humor: A Discussion of Chaucer's Wife of Bath," *Chaucer Review* 4 [1970]: 77 [73–89]). I disagree with Reid in his ascription of Alison's romance to Venus, since Alison consistently aligns the goddess with the unruly world of sexuality rather than with the decorous realm of romance, as when she declares that "Venus loveth ryot and dispence" (700) and proceeds to disparage old clerks for failing to perform "Venus werkes" (708). Despite this interpretive quibble with Reid, I am indebted to his observation that the "equivocal nature of the 'Tale' is apt for burlesque and, as the Wife tells it, one senses that she is in ambush behind the beautiful impossibilities of romance" ("Crocodilian Humor: A Discussion of Chaucer's Wife of Bath," p. 82). This comment stoked my curiosity to the ways in which Alison deploys queering genres to pursue her sexual agendas. As discussed previously, the burlesqueing of the tale disrupts the promise of romance.

52. Mary Carruthers, "The Wife of Bath and the Painting of Lions," *PMLA* 94 (1979): 214 [209–22].

53. Cox, *Gender and Language in Chaucer*, p. 22.

54. James Winny, ed., *The Wife of Bath's Prologue and Tale* (Cambridge: Cambridge University Press, 1965), p. 13.

55. Discussing Alison in terms of feminism or feminist sensibilities brings up similar critical difficulties as those of discussing homosexuality in the Middle Ages, in that "feminism" and "homosexuality" are both historically bounded terms that can only be applied to the Middle Ages with sufficient contextualization. In using the term "proto-feminism," I refer to Alison's resistance to medieval patriarchy rather than to a nascent sense of feminist identity politics.

56. Identifying "The Man of Law's Tale" as a romance summons up a critical debate in itself; Helen Cooper, for one, notes that " 'The Man of Law's Tale' inhabits the undefined border between romance and saint's life" (*Oxford Guides to Chaucer: The Canterbury Tales*, p. 126). Although the generic hybridization of the tale obscures firm conclusions about its construction of gender in relation to genre, Custance certainly represents yet another restrained female agency against which the Wife of Bath rebels.
57. Alison's comprehension of the commercial aspects of sexuality is reinforced when she remarks upon the possibility of selling both her "*bele chose*" (447) and herself, metaphorically embodied as "bren" (478). See Stewart Justman on the nexus of consumerism and sexuality in the tale, in "Trade as Pudendum: Chaucer's Wife of Bath," *Chaucer Review* 28 (1994): 344–52.
58. See Bernard Levy's analysis of Alison's focus on genitalia in "The Wife of Bath's Queynte Fantasy," *Chaucer Review* 4 (1970): 106–122.
59. See note 18 for the connection between purses, money, and sexuality.
60. Conventional modern distinctions among love, sex, and sexuality were not as clearly demarcated in the medieval period, so an imprecise lexicon is inevitable. (See, e.g., Stephen Jaeger, *Ennobling Love: In Search of a Lost Sensibility* [Philadelphia: University of Pennsylvania Press, 1999]). Nonetheless, Alison distinguishes between the emotional involvement of love and the physical carnality of sex throughout her "Prologue" and "Tale," in which the former is consistently connected to the masculine whereas the latter is consistently connected to the feminine.
61. Even Christ's love for humanity receives a ribald sexual turn when Alison compares wives with "barly-breed" (144) and then claims "And yet with barly-breed, Mark telle kan, / Oure Lord Jhesu refresshed many a man" (145–46). R.W. Hanning describes this moment—"when the Wife imposes a delightfully bawdy meaning upon Christ's feeding the multitude with barley bread"—as an example of Alison's self-serving textual glossing ("Roasting a Friar, Mis-Taking a Wife," p. 9).
62. For the sources of Jankyn's misogyny, see Ralph Hanna III and Traugott Lawler, eds., *Jankyn's Book of Wikked Wyves: The Primary Texts* (Athens: University of Georgia Press, 1997).
63. This passage is often linked to the *Roman de la Rose*; see B.J. and H.W. Whiting, *Proverbs, Sentences and Proverbial Phrases* (Cambridge, MA: Harvard University Press, 1968), p. 68. John Finlayson traces the passage to the Sixth Day, Seventh Story of Boccaccio's *Decameron* in "The Wife of Bath's 'Prologue,' LL. 328–36, and Boccaccio's *Decameron*," *Neophilologus* 83 (1999): 313–16.
64. Certainly, the narrator's statement that "[Alison] coude muchel of wandrynge by the weye" ("The General Prologue," line 467) indicates her own propensity for adultery. Martin Puhvel notes that "one may recall this phrase when she mentions her walking from 'hous' to 'hous' (D 640), another questionable type of wandering" ("The Wife of Bath's 'Remedies of Love,' " *Chaucer Review* 20 [1986]: 311 [307–12]). Jerry Root, on the other hand, connects Alison's "wandrynge by the weye" to her confessional discourse (" 'Space To Speke': The Wife of Bath and the Discourse of Confession," p. 267).

65. For the sources of "The Wife of Bath's Tale," see W.F. Bryan and Germaine Dempster, eds., *Sources and Analogues of Chaucer's Canterbury Tales* (Chicago: University of Chicago Press, 1941; New York: Humanities, 1958); Sigmund Eisner, *A Tale of Wonder: A Source Study of "The Wife of Bath's Tale"* (New York: Burt Franklin, 1957); and G.H. Maynadier, "*The Wife of Bath's Tale*": *Its Sources and Analogues* (London: D. Nutt, 1901). Eisner's collection addresses the connections between Chaucer's tale and its Irish sources, but Patricia Clare Ingham suggests that criticism of the tale has overlooked its Welsh roots and concludes that "in 'The Wife of Bath's Tale' Chaucer uses traditions of pastoral history important to Welsh fantasies of rule, traditions that offer us trace evidence of an alternative insular past" ("Pastoral Histories: Utopia, Conquest, and 'The Wife of Bath's Tale,'" *Texas Studies in Literature and Language* 44 [2002]: 44 [34–46]).
66. Dorothy Yamamoto asserts that incubi were associated not only with impregnating their victims but of committing acts of horrendous violence as well. These friars, in contrast, only impregnate. See "'Noon Oother Incubus But He': Lines 878–81 in the 'Wife of Bath's Tale,'" *Chaucer Review* 28 (1994): 275–78.
67. Alison's digression into the story of Midas (951–82) also hints that she would prefer to tell a story other than a romance, as she breaks off from her narrative to ask "wol ye here the tale?" (951); it seems almost as if she hopes that one of her fellow Pilgrims will ask her to switch stories.
68. Marc Glasser, "'He nedes moste hire wedde': The Forced Marriage in 'The Wife of Bath's Tale' and Its Middle English Analogues," *Neuphilologische Mitteilungen* 85:2 (1984): 239 [239–41].
69. For the sources and analogues of the marital dilemma, see Margaret Schlauch, "The Marital Dilemma in 'The Wife of Bath's Tale,'" *PMLA* 61 (1946): 416–30; Richard Firth Green, "An Analogue to the 'Marital Dilemma' in 'The Wife of Bath's Tale,'" *English Language Notes* 38 (1991): 9–12; and Glending Olson, "The Marital Dilemma in 'The Wife of Bath's Tale': An Unnoticed Analogue and Its Chaucerian Court Context," *English Language Notes* 33 (1995): 1–7.
70. Louise Fradenburg, "The Wife of Bath's Passing Fancy," p. 55.
71. Alison's skills as a reader and glosser of textual authority are well established. Recent criticism on Alison's glossing includes Cox, *Gender and Language in Chaucer*; Thomas Van, "False Texts and Disappearing Women in the Wife of Bath's Prologue and Tale," *Chaucer Review* 29 (1994): 179–93; Richard Neuse, "'Alisoun Still Lives Here': Provocations, Politics, and Pedagogy in 'The Wife of Bath's Tale,' *Hamlet*, and *Paradise Lost*," *Exemplaria* 4 (1992): 469–80; Carolyn Dinshaw, *Chaucer's Sexual Poetics* (Madison: University of Wisconsin Press, 1989); and Peggy Knapp, "Alisoun of Bathe and the Reappropriation of Tradition," *Chaucer Review* 24 (1989): 45–52. On Chaucer and medieval interpretation more generally, see Judith Ferster, *Chaucer on Interpretation* (Cambridge: Cambridge University Press, 1985) and Robert Sturges, *Medieval Interpretation: Models of Reading in Literary Narrative, 1100–1500* (Carbondale: Southern Illinois University Press, 1991). Sturges

addresses the Wife of Bath specifically on pages 160–75, concluding that, for Alison, "writing, though it preserves speech and gives it an aura of authority, also opens it to interpretation and subversion" (p. 166).
72. Peggy Knapp, *Chaucer and the Social Contest* (New York: Routledge, 1990), p. 116.
73. Susan Crane, *Gender and Romance in Chaucer's Canterbury Tales* (Princeton, NJ: Princeton University Press, 1994), pp. 130–31.
74. Hanning, "Roasting a Friar, Mis-Taking a Wife," p. 20.
75. Robert Meyer, "Chaucer's Tandem Romances," *Chaucer Review* 18 (1984): 235–36 [221–38].
76. I think it nearly impossible to exaggerate the rhetorical force of the Wife of Bath's curse predicated upon the plague. As is well known, the Black Death was commonly viewed as God's punishment for humanity's sinfulness, as the words of the Prior of Christchurch, Canterbury, in 1348 attest: "[God] often allows plagues, miserable famines, conflicts, wars and other forms of suffering to arise, and uses them to terrify and torment men and so drive out their sins" (Rosemary Horrox, ed. and trans., *The Black Death* [Manchester: Manchester University Press, 1994], p. 113). In her curse, the Wife of Bath includes male patriarchal privilege as such a necessitating cause for God's revenge. For additional scholarship on the Black Death, see Mavis Mate, *Daughters, Wives, and Widows after the Black Death: Women in Sussex, 1350–1535* (Woodbridge, Suffolk: Boydell, 1998); David Herlihy, *The Black Death and the Transformation of the West* (Cambridge, MA: Harvard University Press, 1997); Robert S. Gottfried, *The Black Death: Natural and Human Disaster in Medieval Europe* (New York: Free Press, 1983); and Daniel Williman, ed., *The Black Death: The Impact of the Fourteenth-Century Plague* (Binghampton, NY: Medieval and Renaissance Texts and Studies, 1982).
77. D.S. Brewer, "Chaucer and Chrétien and Arthurian Romance," *Chaucer and Middle English Studies in Honour of Rossell Hope Robbins*, ed. Beryl Rowland (Kent, OH: Kent State University Press, 1974), p. 258 [255–59].
78. Sarah Disbrow, "The Wife of Bath's Old Wives' Tale," *Studies in the Age of Chaucer* 8 (1986): 70 [59–71].

Chapter 4 Queering Tragedy: Queer Desires and Queering Genres in Chaucer's *Troilus and Criseyde*

1. See the introduction for a discussion of the ways in which "queer" and "homosexual" are distinguished in this monograph. In brief, "queer" suggests a disruptive agency working, at least implicitly, to undermine heteronormativity; "homosexual" refers to same-sex sexuality.
2. C. Stephen Jaeger demonstrates that many medieval same-sex relationships that appear homosexual are actually heteronormative relationships based upon the medieval belief in the ennobling qualities of love. See *Ennobling Love: In Search of a Lost Sensibility* (Philadelphia: University of Pennsylvania Press, 1999).

3. Beryl Rowland, "Pandarus and the Fate of Tantalus," *Orbis Litterarum* 24 (1969): 3–15.
4. Carolyn Dinshaw, "Reading Like a Man: The Critics, the Narrator, Troilus, and Pandarus," *Chaucer's Troilus and Criseyde: "Subgit to Alle Poesye"—Essays in Criticism*, ed. R.A. Shoaf (Binghamton, NY: Center for Medieval and Early Renaissance Studies, 1992), p. 65 [47–73].
5. For more on Richard's affinity, see Paul Strohm, *Social Chaucer* (Cambridge, MA: Harvard University Press, 1989), pp. 25–34.
6. Michael Hanrahan, "Seduction and Betrayal: Treason in the Prologue to the *Legend of Good Women*," *Chaucer Review* 30 (1996): 235 [229–40].
7. Strohm documents that Chaucer had at least a passing acquaintanceship with Robert de Vere: "Robert de Vere served as King's Chamberlain (hence Chaucer's superior in the household), and in that category endorsed and possibly personally signed Chaucer's 1385 petition for a permanent deputy in the office of controller. While the connection may have been nothing more than official business, and Vere himself was more often than not absent from his post, he and Chaucer must have had some direct contact" (*Social Chaucer*, pp. 27–28). Chaucer composed *Troilus and Criseyde* during the middle years of the 1380s, finishing it in 1387. Thus, during the time of the romance's authorship, Chaucer was at least professionally, if not personally, acquainted with Robert de Vere. The queer possibilities of Robert de Vere and Richard II's friendship are also discussed by Elizabeth Keiser, *Courtly Desire and Medieval Homophobia* (New Haven, CT: Yale University Press, 1997), pp. 149–51 and Richard Zeikowitz, *Homoeroticism and Chivalry: Discourses of Male Same-Sex Desire in the Fourteenth Century* (New York: Palgrave, 2003), pp. 120–26.
8. For more on royal household politics, see Chris Given-Wilson, *The English Nobility in the Late Middle Ages: The Fourteenth-Century Political Community* (London: Routledge and Kegan Paul, 1987) and *The Royal Household and the King's Affinity: Service, Politics and Finance in England 1360–1413* (New Haven, CT: Yale University Press, 1986). Henry Kelly traces further connections between Pandarus and contemporary English politics in "Shades of Incest and Cuckoldry: Pandarus and John of Gaunt," *Studies in the Age of Chaucer* 13 (1991): 121–40.
9. Strohm discusses Chaucer's contemporary audience of *Troilus and Criseyde*, describing it as "an audience of some literary sophistication, which shares literary expectations formed not only by the experience of the work at hand but also by acquaintance with other major texts and genres of antiquity and the newly flourishing vernaculars." He concludes that "[c]ommon sense supports the likelihood that this Westminster-London audience of gentlepersons and clerks was at the heart of Chaucer's public" (*Social Chaucer*, p. 63).
10. John Boswell, K.J. Dover, and Richard Zeikowitz address the ways in which same-sex activities are discursively constructed in affirmative and condemnatory valences. Boswell's analysis bridges the classical and medieval worlds, whereas Dover and Zeikowitz focus respectively on the classical Greek and fourteenth-century English milieus. See John Boswell, *Christianity, Social Tolerance, and Homosexuality* (Chicago: University of Chicago Press, 1980);

K.J. Dover, *Greek Homosexuality* (New York: Random House, 1980); and Richard Zeikowitz, *Homoeroticism and Chivalry: Discourses of Male Same-Sex Desire in the Fourteenth Century*. The chapter "Queering the Lyric: Personae, Same-Sex Desire, and Salvation in the Poetry of Marbod of Rennes, Baudri of Bourgueil, and Hildebert of Lavardin" also addresses such a tension between praising and condemning same-sex relationships.

11. C. Stephen Jaeger, *Ennobling Love: In Search of a Lost Sensibility*, p. 26.
12. Robert Levine, "Pandarus as Davus," *Neuphilologische Mitteilungen* 92 (1991): 464 [463–68].
13. All quotations of Chaucer are from *The Riverside Chaucer*, ed. Larry Benson, 3rd ed. (Boston: Houghton Mifflin, 1987).
14. Pierre Macherey, *A Theory of Literary Production*, trans. Geoffrey Wall (London: Routledge, 1978), p. 86.
15. Roman Ingarden, *The Literary Work of Art: An Investigation on the Borderlines of Ontology, Logic, and Theory of Literature*, trans. George G. Grabowicz (Evanston, IL: Northwestern University Press, 1973), p. 249.
16. See also Wolfgang Iser, *The Act of Reading: A Theory of Aesthetic Response* (Baltimore, MD: Johns Hopkins University Press, 1978), pp. 163–231. Iser implicitly compares the search for literary meaning to a medieval romance: "the reader will only begin to search for (and so actualize) the meaning if he does not *know* it, and so it is the unknown factors in the text that set him off on his quest" (p. 43).
17. Pandarus's silence could be viewed as within the rules of courtly love, as Andreas Capellanus admonishes that "When made public love rarely endures" (*The Art of Courtly Love*, trans. John Jay Parry [New York: Columbia University Press, 1990], p. 185). However, that Pandarus desires Troilus to break this rule yet refuses to break it himself results in, at the least, a hypocritical form of obfuscation.
18. Richard Green, "Troilus and the Game of Love," *Chaucer Review* 13 (1979): 208 [201–20].
19. For the medieval implications of secrecy and the open secret, see Karma Lochrie, *Covert Operations: The Medieval Uses of Secrecy* (Philadelphia: University of Pennsylvania Press, 1999), pp. 1–11. The introduction of Lochrie's book provides an excellent overview of medieval and modern uses of secrecy.
20. Although Stephen Barney writes in *The Riverside Chaucer* that "The now widespread view that Pandarus here seduces or rapes Criseyde, or that Chaucer hints at such an action, is baseless and absurd" (p. 1043), a number of critics disagree with his reading, many noting that the ambiguity of the scene at least makes possible such an interpretation. Beryl Rowland and Haldeen Braddy were among the first to discuss the incestuous implications of the passage (Beryl Rowland, "Pandarus and the Fate of Tantalus," *Orbis Litterarum* 24 [1969]: 3–15; Haldeen Braddy, "Chaucer's Playful Pandarus," *Southern Folklore Quarterly* 34 [1970]: 71–81). H. Ansgar Kelly analyzes the contemporary parallels to Chaucer of such a coupling ("Shades of Incest and Cuckoldry: Pandarus and John of Gaunt"); Evan Carton argues that

such obfuscated scenes contribute to "the evolution of sexual and linguistic relationships [that mark] the way to the palinode's repudiation of all things earthly" ("Complicity and Responsibility in Pandarus' Bed and Chaucer's Art," *PMLA* 94 [1979]: 60 [47–61]). Richard Fehrenbacher provides an excellent summary of critical responses to this scene, as well as a thorough investigation into other moments of incestuous desire and its relationship to the theme of Troy's origins (" 'Al that which chargeth nought to seye': The Theme of Incest in *Troilus and Criseyde*," *Exemplaria* 9 [1997]: 341–69).

21. Louise Fradenburg, " 'Our owen wo to drynke': Loss, Gender, and Chivalry in *Troilus and Criseyde*," *Chaucer's Troilus and Criseyde: "Subgit to Alle Poesye"—Essays in Criticism*, ed. R.A. Shoaf (Binghamton, NY: Center for Medieval and Early Renaissance Studies, 1992), pp. 101–102 [88–106].
22. For more on Chaucerian contraries, see Donald Rowe, *"O Love, O Charite!" Contraries Harmonized in Chaucer's Troilus* (Carbondale: Southern Illinois University Press, 1976) and Peter Elbow, *Oppositions in Chaucer* (Middletown, CT: Wesleyan University Press, 1973), pp. 49–72.
23. Elaine Tuttle Hansen, *Chaucer and the Fictions of Gender* (Berkeley: University of California Press, 1992), p. 154.
24. Eve Sedgwick, "Gender Asymmetry and Erotic Triangles," *Between Men: English Literature and Male Homosocial Desire* (New York: Columbia University Press, 1985), pp. 21–27.
25. Sarah Stanbury, "The Voyeur and the Private Life in *Troilus and Criseyde*," *Studies in the Age of Chaucer* 13 (1991): 153 [141–58].
26. A possible link between iron rods and sodomy lies in the legendary accounts surrounding Edward II's and Piers Gaveston's executions that suggest the two men were murdered by iron rods inserted in their anuses. J.S. Hamilton traces this legend to "Geoffrey le Baker's grisly report of Edward II's murder with a red-hot poker"; he discredits this claim, as it "is founded on anachronistic literary evidence, especially in Gaveston's case" (*Piers Gaveston, Earl of Cornwall, 1307–1312: Politics and Patronage in the Reign of Edward II* [Detroit, MI: Wayne State University Press, 1988], p. 17). John Boswell also discusses the legend of the iron rod (*Christianity, Social Tolerance, and Homosexuality*, pp. 299–301). I can find no conclusive evidence that Chaucer knew of this legend; until such evidence emerges, this connection must remain merely an intriguing possibility.
27. Leah Rieber Freiwald, " 'Swych Love of Frendes': Pandarus and Troilus," *Chaucer Review* 6 (1971): 129 [120–29].
28. Steven F. Kruger, "Claiming the Pardoner: Toward a Gay Reading of Chaucer's 'Pardoner's Tale,' " *Exemplaria* 6 (1994): 139 [115–39].
29. Alice Kaminsky summarizes critical stances on the genre of *Troilus and Criseyde* in *Chaucer's Troilus and Criseyde and the Critics* (Athens: Ohio University Press, 1980), pp. 74–83.
30. Barry Windeatt, *Oxford Guides to Chaucer: Troilus and Criseyde* (Oxford: Oxford University Press, 1992), pp. 138–79.
31. Individual tales of the Canterbury pilgrimage often play with generic paradigms (e.g., the play between romance and saint's life in "The Man of Law's

Tale"), but many tales clearly, if not exclusively, belong to a single generic tradition (e.g., "The Miller's Tale" is inarguably a fabliau). The narrative arc of *The Canterbury Tales* showcases a more coherent presentation of generic form than does the insistent generic hybridity of *Troilus and Criseyde*.

32. The opening stanza of "The Monk's Tale" aligns its treatment of tragedy with Boethian conceptions of Fortune:

> I wol biwaille in manere of tragedie
> The harm of hem that stoode in heigh degree,
> And fillen so that ther nas no remedie
> To brynge hem out of hir adversitee.
> For certein, what that Fortune list to flee,
> Ther may no man the cours of hire withholde.
> Lat no man truste on blynd prosperitee;
> Be war by thise ensamples trewe and olde. (VII: 1991–98)

The sententious nature of the Monk's litany of tragedies does little to convey the vast complexity of the form for Chaucer, as evidenced by *Troilus and Criseyde*.

33. Henry Kelly, *Chaucerian Tragedy* (Suffolk, UK: D.S. Brewer, 1997), p. 1.
34. Kelly includes Chaucer's own translation of these lines: "What other thynge bywaylen the cryinges of tragedyes but oonly the dedes of Fortune, that with an unwar strook overturneth the realmes of greet nobleye?" (*Chaucerian Tragedy*, p. 50; see also *The Riverside Chaucer*, p. 409). Kelly also cites Nicholas Trevet's glosses in his translation of *The Consolation of Philosophy* as influencing Chaucer; he notes that, for Trevet, "tragedies were doleful poems that contained nothing but the uncertain mutability of Fortune; they were recited in the theater by the poets themselves in front of spectators, as pointed out by Isidore of Seville when defining the *ludus scenicus*. The poets sang of the ancient deeds and misdeeds of wicked kings. Tragedy therefore is a poem about great iniquities beginning in prosperity and ending in adversity" (*Chaucerian Tragedy*, p. 51). Kelly amply addresses Chaucer's understanding of tragedy (pp. 39–91) and the tragic cast of *Troilus and Criseyde* (pp. 92–148); in the ensuing analysis, I build upon his work by considering the queering effects of Pandarus and generic instability on Chaucerian tragedy.
35. Gayle Margherita, *The Romance of Origins: Language and Sexual Difference in Middle English Literature* (Philadelphia: University of Pennsylvania Press, 1994), p. 111.
36. Andrea Clough, "Medieval Tragedy and the Genre of *Troilus and Criseyde*," *Medievalia et Humanistica* 11 (1982): 213 [211–27].
37. Monica McAlpine, "The Boethian Comedy of Troilus" and "The Boethian Tragedy of Criseyde," *The Genre of Troilus and Criseyde* (Ithaca, NY: Cornell University Press, 1978), pp. 148–217.
38. Despite his increased understanding of human affairs when he ascends to the eighth sphere, Troilus does not reside eternally there; rather, Mercury appoints him to his final resting place: "And forth he wente, shortly for to telle, / Ther as Mercurye sorted hym to dwelle" (V: 1826–27). Both

Boccaccio and Chaucer are vague about the ultimate location of Troilus's shade, but it seems likely that, despite the anachronistic Christianity of *Troilus and Criseyde*, it would be the Elysian Fields of Greek mythology or a location similar to the first circle of Dante's *Inferno*. As a pagan god, Mercury surely takes Troilus away from any further experience of Christian revelation, but that Troilus takes with him his increased understanding of human affairs would nonetheless offer some degree of comic solace as he awaits the salvific destiny of righteous pagans.

39. Stanbury, "The Voyeur and the Private Life in *Troilus and Criseyde*," p. 157.
40. As is well known, although Chaucer does not depict her ultimate fate, Robert Henryson's *Testament of Cresseid* imaginatively supplies a narrative revenge and ignoble end for Criseyde, as a result of her desertion of Troilus. See also Gayle Margherita, "Criseyde's Remains: Romance and the Question of Justice," *Exemplaria* 12:2 (2000): 257–92.
41. Hansen, *Chaucer and the Fictions of Gender*, p. 148.
42. Clare Kinney, *Strategies of Poetic Narrative: Chaucer, Spenser, Milton, Eliot* (Cambridge: Cambridge University Press, 1992), p. 21.
43. Nancy Reale, " 'Bitwixen Game and Ernest': *Troilus and Criseyde* as a Post-Boccaccian Response to the *Commedia*," *Philological Quarterly* 71 (1992): 157 [155–71].
44. Pandarus orchestrates virtually all of Troilus's actions, and even Troilus's death and apotheosis are, in some way, a response to Pandarus's directives. When Troilus laments the loss of Criseyde, Pandarus advises him that

    "Forthi tak herte, and thynk right as a knyght:
    Thorugh love is broken al day every lawe.
    Kith now somwhat thi corage and thi myght;
    Have mercy on thiself for any awe.
    Lat nat this wrecched wo thyn herte gnawe,
    But manly sette the world on six and sevene;
    And if thow deye a martyr, go to hevene!" (IV: 617–23)

    Obviously, Chaucer does not give Pandarus the power to grant Troilus his comic salvation, but the panderer does set in motion the events that lead to Troilus's apotheosis through the queer game of love.
45. Claudia Rattazzi Papka, "Transgression, the End of Troilus, and the Ending of Chaucer's *Troilus and Criseyde*," *Chaucer Review* 32 (1998): 279 [267–81]. Michaela Grudin's analysis of Chaucer's discourse also accentuates the openness of the conclusion: "In his ending, as in [*Troilus and Criseyde*] generally, Chaucer seems to be showing us that speech can show us numerous (and often necessarily conflicting) realities. . .By refusing finally to let discourse wrap up the experience of the poem conclusively, Chaucer points to that newly discovered potentiality of speech" (*Chaucer and the Politics of Discourse* [Columbia: University of South Carolina Press, 1996], pp. 82–83).
46. McAlpine, *The Genre of Troilus and Criseyde*, p. 240.
47. Does "Withouten wordes mo" refer to Pandarus's or to Troilus's speech? The ambiguous phrasing of the passages makes either interpretation possible.

Regardless of which character's language is specifically envisioned as muted, Troilus foresees that silence will characterize his death.
48. Jennifer Goodman, "Nature as Destiny in *Troilus and Criseyde*," *Style* 31 (1997): 419 [413–27].

Chapter 5 Queering Arthurian Romance: Genres, Godgames, and Sadomasochism in *Sir Gawain and the Green Knight*

1. Peggy Knapp, "*Gawain* and the Middle Ages: Teaching History, Teaching Genre," *Approaches to Teaching Sir Gawain and the Green Knight*, ed. Miriam Youngerman Miller and Jane Chance (New York: MLA, 1986), p. 138 [138–42].
2. For brief and useful discussions of romance as a genre, see Simon Gaunt, "Romance and Other Genres," *Cambridge Companion to Medieval Romance*, ed. Roberta Krueger (Cambridge: Cambridge University Press, 2000), pp. 45–59 and Cesare Segre, "What Bakhtin Left Unsaid: The Case of Medieval Romance," *Romance: Generic Transformation from Chrétien de Troyes to Cervantes*, ed. Kevin Brownlee and Marina Brownlee (Hanover and London: University Press of New England, 1985), pp. 23–46. The exemplum is typically defined as a short narrative illustrating a moral. In his study of Chaucer and the exemplum tradition, Larry Scanlon redefines the term as "a narrative enactment of cultural authority" (*Narrative, Authority, and Power: The Medieval Exemplum and the Chaucerian Tradition* [Cambridge: Cambridge University Press, 1994], p. 34), which well applies to the nexus between narrative and Christian ideology as constructed in *Sir Gawain and the Green Knight*.
3. A reader interested primarily in the ways in which genre intersects with sexuality in *Sir Gawain and the Green Knight* might well question the utility of spending half a chapter on an admittedly normative interpretation of the text. Through this analysis, however, I hope to demonstrate the necessity of reading *Sir Gawain and the Green Knight* simultaneously through somewhat conflicting, yet also complementary, hermeneutics. *Sir Gawain and the Green Knight* demands "both/and" rather than "either/or" analyses, and in order to do justice to its complexity, this chapter must address the ways in which a normative interpretation inspires the conditions necessary for a nonnormative one. This process is also instructive for understanding the very praxis of queering genres, as it uncovers in depth the necessary and enabling tensions between normative and nonnormative readings.
4. For a generic model of the saint's life, I rely on Thomas Heffernan's succinct formulation: "The lives of the saints were sacred stories designed to teach the faithful to imitate actions which the community had decided were paradigmatic. Christ's behavior in the Gospels was the single authenticating norm for all action. For actions (*res*) narrated in the lives of the saints to be binding for the community, they had to be an *imitatio Christi*" (*Sacred Biography: Saints and Their Biographers in the Middle Ages* [New York: Oxford University Press, 1988], p. 5). As I will show, *Sir Gawain and the Green Knight*

concerns itself with Gawain's failure to imitate Christ as he identifies his experience under the rubric of a secular romance rather than that of a Christian saint's life. Other recent scholarship on hagiography includes Jocelyn Wogan-Browne, *Saints' Lives and Women's Literary Culture, ca. 1150–1300: Virginity and Its Authorizations* (New York: Oxford University Press, 2001); Catherine Mooney, ed., *Gendered Voices: Medieval Saints and Their Interpreters* (Philadelphia: University of Pennsylvania Press, 1999); Lynda Coon, *Sacred Fictions: Holy Women and Hagiography in Late Antiquity* (Philadelphia: University of Pennsylvania Press, 1997); Paul Szarmach, ed., *Holy Men and Holy Women: Old English Prose Saints' Lives and Their Contexts* (Albany: State University of New York Press, 1996); Sandro Sticca, *Saints: Studies in Hagiography* (Binghamton, NY: Medieval and Renaissance Texts and Studies, 1996); and Renate Blumenfeld-Kosinski and Timea Szell, eds., *Images of Sainthood in Medieval Europe* (Ithaca, NY: Cornell University Press, 1991).

5. For analyses of Gawain and games, see Setsuko Haruta, "Sir Gawain and the Grisly Game," *Medieval Heritage: Essays in Honour of Tadahiro Ikegami*, ed. Masahiko Kanno, Hiroshi Yamashita, Matatoshi Kawasaki, Junko Asakawa, and Naoko Shirai (Tokyo: Yushodo Press, 1997), pp. 283–96; Victoria Weiss, "The Playworld and the Real World: Chivalry in *Sir Gawain and the Green Knight*," *Philological Quarterly* 72 (1993): 403–18; Thomas Rendall, "*Gawain* and the Game of Chess," *Chaucer Review* 27 (1992): 186–99; Henk Aertsen, "Game and Earnest in *Sir Gawain and the Green Knight*," *Companion to Middle English Romance*, ed. Henk Aertsen and Alasdair A. MacDonald (Amsterdam: Vrije University Press, 1990), pp. 83–100; John Leyerle, "The Game and Play of Hero," *Concepts of the Hero in the Middle Ages and the Renaissance*, ed. Norman Burns and Christopher Reagan (Albany: State University of New York Press, 1975), pp. 49–82; Peter Christmas, "A Reading of *Sir Gawain and the Green Knight*," *Neophilologus* 58 (1974): 238–47; Martin Stevens, "Laughter and Game in *Sir Gawain and the Green Knight*," *Speculum* 47 (1972): 65–78; Edward Trostle Jones, "The Sound of Laughter in *Sir Gawain and the Green Knight*," *Mediaeval Studies* 31 (1969): 343–45; R.H. Bowers, "*Gawain and the Green Knight* as Entertainment," *Modern Language Quarterly* 24 (1963): 333–41; and Robert G. Cook, "The Play-Element in *Sir Gawain and the Green Knight*," *Tulane Studies in English* 13 (1963): 5–31.
6. Bernard Suits, *The Grasshopper: Games, Life, and Utopia* (Toronto: University of Toronto Press, 1978), p. 41.
7. Robert Rawdon Wilson, "Rules/Conventions: Three Paradoxes in the Game/Text Analogy," *South Central Review* 3 (1986): 23 [15–27].
8. Johan Huizinga, *Homo Ludens: A Study of the Play-Element in Culture* (Boston: Beacon, 1950), p. 13.
9. Roger Caillois criticizes Huizinga's definition for its focus on the agonistic mode of play and for its failure to establish boundaries between the domains of play and of the sacred; Caillois then expands the concept of play in directions not considered by Huizinga (*Man, Play, and Games* [New York: Free Press of Glencoe, 1961], pp. 9–10). I quibble with Huizinga's declaration

that play "proceeds...according to fixed rules and in an orderly manner," as these characteristics are more clearly linked to games than to play.
10. Brad Lowell Stone, "The Self and the Play-Element in Culture," *Play and Culture* 2 (1989): 68 [64–79].
11. Robert Rawdon Wilson, "Godgames and Labyrinths," *Mosaic* 15:4 (1982): 6–7 [1–22].
12. One question that must be asked about the godgame is how much power it accords the god character. Some critics contend that, if the god is omnipotent, the game would lose its exciting tension since its end is preordained. Thus, contrary to Jewish and Christian belief, Steven Brams does not assume that the Judeo-Christian God is omnipotent in the biblical games He plays because of human free will: "Since God does not always get His way, He can properly be viewed as a participant, or *player*, in a game. This is so because a *game*...is an interdependent decision situation whose outcome depends on the choices of *all* players" (*Biblical Games* [Cambridge, MA: MIT Press, 1980], p. 5). Other critics posit that one cannot play a godgame with abstract forces such as chance or fate because they receive no benefit from the game. Anatol Rapoport argues that "[a] bona fide player is one who (1) makes choices and (2) receives payoffs. Thus, although we called Chance a player in a card game (because she 'chose' the arrangement of the cards), we cannot call her a bona fide player, because she gets no payoffs" (*Two-Person Game Theory* [Ann Arbor: University of Michigan Press, 1966], p. 20).
13. John Fowles, *The Magus*, rev. ed. (London: Jonathan Cape, 1977), p. 10.
14. All references to and quotations of the text are taken from the second edition, edited by Norman Davis, of *Sir Gawain and the Green Knight*, ed. J.R.R. Tolkien and E.V. Gordon (Oxford: Clarendon, 1967). I have modernized thorn and yogh.
15. Considering that virtually all literature can be construed as a godgame, with the author as a god-figure and the reader as a pawn-player, surprisingly little criticism employs it as a hermeneutic. Examples include Ellen McDaniel, "Games and Godgames in *The Magus* and *The French Lieutenant's Woman*," *MFS: Modern Fiction Studies* 31:1 (1985): 31–42 and Martin Kuester, "Godgames in Paradise: Educational Strategies in Milton and Fowles," *Anglia: Zeitschrift für Englische Philologie* 115:1 (1997): 29–43.
16. The ensuing brief discussion of medieval play is meant to be indicative, not exhaustive, though many more such examples spring to mind. Chaucer's "The Parson's Tale" as the conclusion of the storytelling game in *The Canterbury Tales*, Langland's Christ Knight traveling to a tournament in *Piers Plowman*, Jesus's childhood play in the *Vita Christi*, Augustine's autobiographically sinful play in the *Confessions*, the ubiquitous play of chivalry in medieval romance: these examples testify to the widely disparate views of play and its theological and spiritual ramifications in the medieval world. Critical texts that address the range of cultural responses to play, games, jokes, and fun in the Middle Ages include Hugo Rahner, *Man at Play* (New York: Herder & Herder, 1972); Joachim Suchomski, *Delectatio und Utilitas* (Bern: Francke, 1975); Carl Lindahl, *Earnest Games: Folkloric Patters in the*

Canterbury Tales (Bloomington: Indiana University Press, 1987); Laura Kendrick, *Chaucerian Play: Comedy and Control in the Canterbury Tales* (Berkeley: University of California Press, 1988) and *The Game of Love: Troubadour Wordplay* (Berkeley: University of California Press, 1988); *Le rire au Moyen Age dans la litterature et dans les arts*, ed. Thérèse Bouché and Hélène Charpentier (Bordeaux: Presses Universitaires de Bordeaux, 1990); and Martha Bayless, *Parody in the Middle Ages* (Ann Arbor: University of Michigan Press, 1996).

17. Thomas of Aquinas, *Summa Theologiae* (Madrid: Biblioteca de Autores Cristianos, 1956), 1039 (2-2 q. 168,a.3).
18. Ibid., 1040–1041 (2-2 q. 168, a.4).
19. The Italian text is taken from Dante, *Convivio*, ed. Franca Brambilla Ageno (Florence: Casa Editrice Le Lettere, 1995), p. 199; the translation is from Philip H. Wicksteed, *The Convivio of Dante Alighieri* (London: Dent, 1903), p. 181.
20. *The Towneley Plays*, ed. Martin Stevens and A.C. Cawley (Oxford: Early English Text Society, 1994), p. 323, lines 13–20.
21. *The Middle English Dictionary* defines "game" in myriad ways, including "joy, happiness, pleasure"; "festivity, revelry"; "an athletic contest. . .behavior or success in a contest"; "a joke, jest"; and "an action, proceeding; happening, occurrence." As modern usages of play and game confuse the semantic borders between the two, so too does the medieval range of "game" slip beyond the parameters of agonistic contests. The importance of the passage cited is not that it constructs salvation itself as a game with rules, winners, and losers, but that Jesus imbues salvation with a sense of playful mirth and festivity.
22. Scott D. Troyan, "True Tokens: Of Signs and Words and Other Things Bespeaking Truth in *Sir Gawain and the Green Knight*," *The Arthurian Yearbook III*, ed. Keith Busby (New York: Garland, 1993), p. 165 [141–70].
23. Mikhail Bakhtin, *Rabelais and His World*, trans. Hélène Iswolsky (Bloomington: Indiana University Press, 1984), p. 79. Bakhtin's words here describe humorous Christmas songs, but his point holds in reference to *Sir Gawain and the Green Knight*, as the *Gawain*-poet similarly reconfigures a secular form to a moral lesson. Certainly, few phrases sum up the meaning of *Sir Gawain and the Green Knight* better than "Christmas laughter," with its almost oxymoronic conflation of the spiritual significance of celebrating Christ's birth and circumcision with the levity of laughter.
24. Morton W. Bloomfield, "*Sir Gawain and the Green Knight*: An Appraisal," *Critical Studies of Sir Gawain and the Green Knight*, ed. Donald Howard and Christian Zacher (South Bend, IN: University of Notre Dame Press, 1968), p. 47 [24–55].
25. Sheri Ann Strite argues that to label the contest between Gawain and the Green Knight a "beheading game" is somewhat inaccurate because the Green Knight never mentions the possibility of decapitation in the initial terms of his game; rather, Gawain's mighty blow raises the possibility of dying due to the exchange of blows ("*Sir Gawain and the Green Knight*: To Behead or Not To Behead—That *Is* a Question," *Philological Quarterly* 70 [1991]: 1–12).

26. The game, of course, is not as simple as these initial rules imply; Gawain nevertheless attempts to end the game by appealing to this first set of rules after receiving his cut from the Green Knight:

> "Bot on stroke here me fallez—
> The couenaunt schop ryght so,
> Fermed in Arthurez hallez—
> And therfore, hende, now hoo!" (2327–30)

Clinging to these rules, Gawain ignores the possibility that other sets of rules have been in play throughout the game, including the rules of the exchange game and the spiritual claims of the pentangle.
27. J.A. Burrow, *A Reading of Sir Gawain and the Green Knight* (New York: Barnes and Noble, 1966), p. 66.
28. Although the pentangle shield is also a statement of knightly identity, as I discuss subsequently, it establishes certain guidelines for Gawain's actions, albeit ones that he himself chooses, within the parameters of the godgame. The shield represents rules imposed both internally and externally, and this confusion thus lays the groundwork for Gawain's fortunate fall.
29. The one escape possible is to refuse to play the game, which should be considered a real option for Gawain. I do not want to occlude that Gawain has real choices to make at the beginning of the game and that Christian humility demands more than Gawain's subsequent recognition of his inability to achieve human perfection. Once Gawain enters the game, however, he is trapped inside its multiple layers and escape becomes impossible. I discuss this point in greater detail in the section "God's Sadistic Game."
30. Indeed, this scene contains such abundance of entertainment that the narrator confesses that to describe it fully would require too great an effort: "There watz mete, ther watz myrthe, ther watz much ioye, / That for to telle therof hit me tene were, / And to poynte hit yet I pyned me parauenture" (1007–1009).
31. The psychology of identification between reader and character is a dense and complex topic. In the ensuing descriptions of narratival and readerly identifications, I rely on Diana Fuss's analysis of the paradoxical maneuvers necessitated in attempts to establish personal identity: "Identification is a process that keeps identity at a distance, that prevents identity from ever approximating the status of an ontological given, even as it makes possible the formulation of an *illusion* of identity as immediate, secure, totalizible" (*Identification Papers* [New York: Routledge, 1995], p. 2). In just this manner, *Sir Gawain and the Green Knight* explores the tremulous and hesitant nature of identity, in which Gawain and the reader must constantly face the precariousness of their own self-identifications. Of course, resistant readers may stake their identification with characters other than Gawain, or refuse to identify with any character at all, but surely the *Gawain*-poet intends for his audience to identify with Gawain and to take his moral lesson as their own. He carefully constructs a narrative that meta-textually forces the reader to confront the same moral dilemma as the protagonist, which creates an ideal

reader who enjoys a romance in the same manner that Gawain attempts to enjoy his adventure. In the end, however, both character and reader are surprised with the moral force of an exemplum and the latent sadomasochistic tensions of a saint's life.

32. In a game, the strategy of the sacrifice may appear counterproductive, yet it can be used effectively. John Harsanyi points out that if players could rely on their opponents always to act rationally, strategies would devolve into obvious ploys, and, hence, games would lose their appealing uncertainty: "If a given player could regard his opponents' strategies as *given*, the problem of rational behavior for him would reduce to the selection of a strategy that maximizes his expected utility...But the point is precisely that in general he cannot regard his opponent's strategies as given independently of his own. For, if his opponents behave rationally, then their strategies will depend on the strategy they expect *him* to follow, in the same way as his own strategy depends on the strategies he expects *them* to follow" (*Papers in Game Theory* [Dordrecht, Holland: Reidel, 1982], p. 20).

33. For explications of the occluded sexuality of these daily exchanges, see Carolyn Dinshaw, "A Kiss Is Just a Kiss: Heterosexuality and Its Consolations in *Sir Gawain and the Green Knight*," Diacritics 24 (1994): 205–226 and David Boyd, "Sodomy, Misogyny, and Displacement: Occluding Queer Desire in *Sir Gawain and the Green Knight*," Arthuriana 8 (1998): 77–113. For analysis of the cultural meanings of kissing in the Middle Ages, see Yannick Carré, *Le Baiser sur la bouche au moyen age: rites, symboles, mentalités, à travers les texts et les images, XIe–XVe siècles* (Paris: Le Léopard d'Or, 1992).

34. The passages that depict the playfulness of their subsequent daily meetings include: "And efte in her bourdyng thay baythen in the morn / To fylle the same forwardez that thay byfore maden" (1404–1405); and "Quen thay hade played in halle / As longe as hor wylle hom last, / To chambre he con hym calle, / And to the chemné thay past" (1664–67).

35. The *Gawain*-poet suggests in the beginning of the second fitt that alcohol causes Gawain's troubles ("For thagh men ben mery in mynde quen thay han mayn drynk" [497]). Gawain's inebriation in this scene is thus an ironic reminder of the trouble that festive drinking and game playing brought him one year earlier and a foreshadowing of the new game he is about to begin with his host. Throughout his stay at Bertilak's court, drinking obscures the full repercussions of the game to Gawain; see lines 1112–15, 1409, 1668–69, 1934–35, and 1955–56.

36. Thomas Rendall sees a similar strategy in the beheading scene when the Green Knight gives Gawain the advantage of the first blow ("*Gawain* and the Game of Chess," Chaucer Review 27 [1992]: 186–99).

37. I further address the implications of the seduction scenes in the section "The Sado-masochism of Queering Seductions"; at this moment, it is important to recognize the playful strategy of the lady's game within the larger structure of the godgame of romance.

38. The only moment when the Green Knight refrains from telling Gawain the complete truth is when he does not tell Gawain his real name, even though

he promises to do so. In their initial agreement, the Green Knight avers: "Yif I the telle trwly, quen I the tape haue / And thou me smothely hatz smyten, smartly I the teche / Of my hous and my home and myn owen nome" (406–08). The Green Knight comes close to cheating here, although he does answer in half-truths when the time arrives.

39. Gawain's prayers are numerous; at this key point of the narrative, he also prays in lines 548–49, 736–39, and 759–64.
40. Stephanie J. Hollis, "The Pentangle Knight: *Sir Gawain and the Green Knight*," *Chaucer Review* 15 (1981): 272–73 [267–81].
41. Weiss, "The Playworld and the Real World," p. 416.
42. All returns to normal in Arthur's playful court after the Green Knight departs, but the *Gawain*-poet hints that changes will arise in the court as he describes the passage of time and the effects it bears: "A yere yernes ful yerne, and yeldez neuer lyke, / The forme to the fynisment foldez ful selden" (498–99). These words foreshadow the end of the poem in which the courtiers adopt the green girdle and articulate a new self-identity.
43. The only exception to the Arthurian court's outright embrace of play is depicted immediately before Gawain departs on his quest. The *Gawain*-poet describes the courtiers hiding their fears with jokes and merriment: "Knyghtez ful cortays and comlych ladies / Al for luf of that lede in longynge thay were, / Bot neuer the lece ne the later thay neuened bot merthe" (539–41). The jokes, however, give way to sorrow and a sense that the game could lead to grief:

> Alle this compayny of court com the kyng nerre
> For to counseyl the knyght, with care at her hert.
> There watz much derue doel driuen in the sale
> That so worthé as Wawan schulde wende on that ernde,
> To dryghe a delful dynt, and dele no more
>   wyth bronde. (556–61)

The sorrow of the court, anticipating Gawain's certain demise, then develops into resentment toward Arthur ("Who knew euer any kyng such counsel to take / As knyghtez in cauelaciounz on Crystmasse gomnez!" [682–83]).

44. Leyerle, "The Game and Play of Hero," p. 70.
45. As Simon Gaunt notes in his analysis of the *Roman de Silence*, "clothes are a metaphor of representation" ("The Significance of Silence," *Paragraph* 13 [1990]: 206 [202–16]; this observation is certainly true of Gawain as he asserts his identity through his armor and shield.
46. If clothes speak the man, the reference to the "silk sayn vmbe his syde" (589) foreshadows the new accessory Gawain will adopt after his adventures in the Green Knight's court.
47. Would the Green Knight have killed Gawain if Gawain had slept with his wife? It is an intriguing question, but one that I do not believe the *Gawain*-poet considers as an option. If Gawain sleeps with the lady, he would be compelled by the game's rules to sleep with Bertilak as well. As Carolyn

Dinshaw points out, the text allows this possibility only to shut it down; it is a "forbidden end. . .*unintelligible* within the heterosexual world of this poem" ("A Kiss Is Just a Kiss," p. 206).

48. As John Kitely observes, "Gawain, ironically, fails when he tries to combat what to him is a malignant magic with magic: when he places reliance on the magical qualities of the girdle rather than on the integration of moral virtue signified by the Pentangle" (" 'The Endless Knot': Magical Aspects of the Pentangle in *Sir Gawain and the Green Knight*," *Studies in the Literary Imagination* 4 [1971]: 48 [41–50]). Had Gawain ignored the magical elements of the game, he would have nonetheless survived, but without having learned his moral lesson.

49. One could see at stake in the game Morgan's desire to kill Guinevere, as the Green Knight reports that Morgan bewitched him "For to haf greued Gaynour and gart hir to dyghe" (2460). Moreover, her actions are consistent with her history of antagonism to the Arthurian court. Her presence is so occluded in the text, however, that it is difficult to ascertain what, if anything, is truly at stake for her in the game. We do not read, for example, of any disappointment at her failure to kill Guinevere. Elizabeth Scala interprets Morgan as "a figure of the text's unconscious itself" ("The Wanting Words of *Sir Gawain and the Green Knight*," *Exemplaria* 6 [1994]: 334 [305–38].

50. Derek Pearsall, "Courtesy and Chivalry in *Sir Gawain and the Green Knight*: The Order of Shame and the Invention of Embarrassment," *A Companion to the Gawain-Poet*, ed. Derek Brewer and Jonathan Gibson (Suffolk, UK: D.S. Brewer, 1997), p. 361 [351–62].

51. Ad Putter, *An Introduction to the Gawain-Poet* (London: Longman, 1996), p. 94.

52. Ibid., p. 95.

53. W.R.J. Barron believes that Gawain's assumption of the green girdle bespeaks a self-condemnation as excessive as his earlier self-definition through the pentangle: "The superimposition of the symbol of *untrawthe* upon the pentangle shows the same absolutism in self-degradation as in his former idealism." Barron then somewhat tempers his own view when he declares that "Gawain's intemperance under failure is gradually mastered by penitence, his reputation voluntarily exposed to public censure, his fault self-defined in both chivalric and spiritual terms; signs of contrition which give hope for the future" (*Trawthe and Treason: The Sin of Gawain Reconsidered* [Manchester: Manchester University Press, 1980], pp. 143–44). Gawain's newly constructed livery suggests that he sees himself in new terms, certainly, and he states that he will maintain this sign of spiritual defeat for his entire life; he now sees himself as a fallible human, not as a perfectly virtuous knight.

54. Lynn Johnson, *The Voice of the Gawain-Poet* (Madison: University of Wisconsin Press, 1984), pp. 89–90.

55. R.H. Bowers refers to the Green Knight as a "practical joker" ("*Gawain and the Green Knight* as Entertainment," *Modern Language Quarterly* 24 [1963]: 339 [333–41]).

56. A.C. Spearing, *The Gawain-Poet* (Cambridge: Cambridge University Press, 1970), p. 230.
57. Gerald Morgan, "The Significance of the Pentangle Symbolism in *Sir Gawain and the Green Knight*," *Modern Language Review* 74 (1979): 788 [769–90].
58. The "tulk that the trammes of tresoun ther wrought" (3) is generally identified as Aeneas, although Israel Gollancz identifies him as Antenor in his edition of the poem (*Sir Gawain and the Green Knight* [London: Early English Text Society, 1940], p. 95, n. 3).
59. Ann Astell, "*Sir Gawain and the Green Knight*: A Study in the Rhetoric of Romance," *Journal of English and Germanic Philology* 84 (1985): 190 [188–202].
60. Gilles Deleuze, *Sacher-Masoch: An Interpretation* (London: Faber and Faber, 1971), p. 16.
61. See Robert Mills, " 'Whatever you do is a delight to me!': Masculinity, Masochism, and Queer Play in Representations of Male Martyrdom," *Exemplaria* 13 (2001): 1–37; Louise Fradenburg, "Sacrificial Desire in Chaucer's 'Knight's Tale,' " *Journal of Medieval and Early Modern Studies* 27:1 (1997): 47–75 and *Sacrifice Your Love: Psychoanalysis, Historicism, Chaucer* (Minneapolis: University of Minnesota Press, 2002); Jeffrey Jerome Cohen, "Masoch/Lancelotism," *New Literary History* 28 (1997): 231–60; and Kathryn Gravdal, *Ravishing Maidens: Writing Rape in Medieval French Literature and Law* (Philadelphia: University of Pennsylvania Press, 1991).
62. Leopold Sacher-Masoch, *Venus in Furs*, trans. Jean McNeil, ed. Gilles Deleuze, *Sacher-Masoch: An Interpretation*, p. 144 [117–248].
63. Wilson, "Godgames and Labyrinths," p. 7.
64. Richard Schechner, "Playing," *Play and Culture* 1 (1988): 12–13 [3–19].
65. Caesarius of Arles, *Sermones*, ed. D. Germani Morin, 2 vols. *Corpus Christianorum, Series latina*, 1953. Vols. 103–104. (Sermon 131, vol. 103, p. 539).
66. Alberto Ferreiro, "Job in the Sermons of Caesarius of Arles," *Recherches de thâeologie ancienne et, medievale* 54 (1987): 17 [13–26].
67. Geoffrey Chaucer, "The Friar's Tale," *The Canterbury Tales*, ed. Larry D. Benson, 3rd ed. (Boston: Houghton Mifflin, 1987), pp. 123–28, lines 1480–1491.
68. Linda Williams, *Hard Core: Power, Pleasure, and the "Frenzy of the Visible"* (Berkeley: University of California Press, 1989), p. 212.
69. Laura Mulvey, "Visual Pleasure and Narrative Cinema," *A Critical and Cultural Studies Reader*, ed. Antony Easthope and Kate McGowan (Toronto: University of Toronto Press, 1994), p. 165 [158–66].
70. Fradenburg, "Sacrificial Desire in Chaucer's 'Knight's Tale,' " p. 52.
71. Sadism and masochism, however, need not always be intertwined within a singular relationship or exchange. Gilles Deleuze notes that the "etiological fallacy of the unity of sadism and masochism may perhaps be due to an erroneous interpretation of the nature of the ego and the superego and of their interrelations" (*Sacher-Masoch: An Interpretation*, p. 111). Of course, that sadism and masochism need not be so intertwined does not preclude their paradoxically harmonious union in some relationships.

72. David Halperin, "How To Do the History of Male Homosexuality," *GLQ* 6:1 (2000): 99 [87–123].
73. Mills, " 'Whatever you do is a delight to me!' " p. 35.
74. See note 16 of chapter 2 for an exploration of biblical passages of inversion. The idea is explored in relation to *Sir Gawain and the Green Knight* by Victor Yelverton Haines, *The Fortunate Fall of Sir Gawain* (Washington, DC: University Press of America, 1982).
75. In describing Gawain's relationship with God as one that stresses his reluctant masochism, the agency latent in masochism may be marginalized. Despite the apparent sacrifice of their desires to those of their sadists, masochists possess and express agency. Linda Williams points out that the agency of masochists surfaces despite its apparent disavowal: "What is tricky about masochism, however, is that this search for recognition through apparent passivity is a ruse intended to disavow what the masochist actually knows to exist but plays the game of denying: his (or her) very real sexual agency and pleasure" (*Hard Core: Power, Pleasure, and the "Frenzy of the Visible*," p. 212). This paradigm is not true for Gawain, however: beyond his position as a reluctant masochist, he also does not understand the ramifications of the game that he is playing. Within the confused and confusing parameters of the godgame, Gawain's agency is crippled to uselessness.
76. Circumcision marks God's covenant with Jews, not with Christians, as Paul and early Church fathers replaced the rite of circumcision with that of baptism (Philippians 3:3; Colossians 2:11–12). This conflation of Jewish ritual and Christian celebration blurs the borders between the two communities. The *Gawain*-poet explores here the tensions inherent in the Feast of the Circumcision, which, beyond its association with Judaism, also bore traces of pagan celebrations because it was celebrated on the same day as festivals of the new year: "[The Feast of the Circumcision] did not become established at Rome till the eleventh century. Its relatively late introduction into the Christian calendar has been connected with the unwillingness of the Church to introduce a festival on New Year's Day, which had been kept with great riot and license by the pagans" (F.L. Cross, *The Oxford Dictionary of the Christian Church*, 3rd ed., ed. E.A. Livingstone [Oxford: Oxford University Press, 1997], p. 354). The ambiguity of the Feast of the Circumcision itself heightens the ambiguity of the Arthurian court's celebration of it, and thus many scholars ponder whether the riotous celebration represents appropriate behavior for a Christian feast. As I demonstrate, this ambiguity serves as yet another mechanism through which to trap Gawain and the reader.
77. Despite the connection between decapitation and castration latent in the Green Knight's beheading game, along the lines of Freud's famous formulation "To decapitate = to castrate," circumcision provides a stronger interpretive structure to the narrative ("Medusa's Head," *The Standard Edition of the Complete Psychological Works of Sigmund Freud*, ed. and trans. James Strachey. [London: Hogarth, 1991], vol. 18, p. 273). Within *Sir Gawain and the Green Knight*, the interrelationships of the Green Knight's false decapitation, Gawain's cut neck, and Jesus's circumcision suggest that we inhabit a narrative

world more concerned with marking the Christian community through renewed circumcisions rather than with symbolic castrations, as the Green Knight's decapitation might suggest. For a critique of Freud's equation of decapitation with castration in relation to medieval literature, see H. Marshall Leicester, "New Currents in Psychoanalytic Criticism, and the Difference 'IT' Makes: Gender and Desire in 'The Miller's Tale,' " *ELH* 61 (1994): 473–99.

78. Nicholas Royle, "The Private Parts of Jesus Christ," *Writing the Bodies of Christ*, ed. John Schad (Aldershot, England: Ashgate, 2001), p. 172 [159–76].

79. Despite the promise of "once," the repetition of religious rites inevitably inscribes itself back on the body. As Jacques Derrida observes, "One time alone: circumcision takes place but once. Such, at least, is the appearance we receive, and the tradition of the appearance, we do not say of the semblance...We will have to circle around this appearance. Not so much in order to circumscribe or circumvent the truth of circumcision....But rather to let ourselves be approached by the resistance which 'once' may offer to thought" (*Acts of Literature*, ed. Derek Attridge [London: Routledge, 1992], p. 373). Thus, in the construction of a human's religious body, that body may need to be repeatedly reinscribed within the religion's semiotic system: the Word must be on the body.

80. The five works attributed to the *Gawain*-poet by critical consensus—*Sir Gawain and the Green Knight*, *Pearl*, *Patience*, *Cleanness*, and *St. Erkenwald*—share a thematic interest in human suffering and the pleasures latent within that suffering through Christian revelation. The conclusion of *St. Erkenwald* highlights this paradox: "Then wos louynge oure Lorde wyt love vp-halden, / Meche mournynge and myrthe was mellyd to-geder; / Thai passyed forthe in processioun and alle the pepulle folowid / And alle the belles in the burghe beryd at ones" (*The Complete Works of the Pearl-Poet*, trans. Casey Finch, facing-page Middle English texts by Clifford Peterson, Malcolm Andrew, and Ronald Waldron [Berkeley: University of California Press, 1993], p. 339, lines 349–52). Mourning mixed with mirth may appear paradoxical, but it is, of course, a commonplace in Christianity that earthly suffering leads to heavenly rewards. Within *Sir Gawain and the Green Knight*, this dynamic is revealed in the wheel of the first stanza in the description of the joys and pains residing in Britain: "Where werre and wrake and wonder / By sythez hatz wont therinne, / And oft bothe blysse and blunder / Ful skete hatz skyfted synne" (16–19). The alternations between "blysse and blunder" accord with the sadomasochistic tensions crucial to the romance. This doubled interest in the pleasures and pains of Christianity reveals an edge to the poet's works in which pleasures are revealed only after suffering.

81. Morgan's supernatural abilities link her with the text's pagan elements, but she nonetheless attends a Christian mass (928–69). Are Morgan and her court Christian? The text never provides evidence to suggest that the masses that Gawain attends throughout his stay at Bertilak's castle are anything but true Christian celebrations, and Gawain's subsequent confession to this court's priest is seen as evidence of his failure to maintain his Christian fidelity to truth. Surely this point can only be granted if he is indeed

confessing to a Christian priest, not a pagan frontman. As Helen Cooper explains, "the poet insists that the supernatural is not finally 'other,' alien or exotic, but rather stands for something within the protagonist of [the] poem, and therefore, given the poet's insistent moral concern, within the reader, too" ("The Supernatural," *A Companion to the Gawain-Poet*, ed. Derek Brewer and Jonathan Gibson [Cambridge: D.S. Brewer, 1997], p. 277 [277–91]). Again we see the ways in which the text demands a both/and rather than an either/or approach: Morgan is a supernatural pagan witch, yet one who paradoxically presides over a devout Christian court. In the end, all is subsumed within an overarching Christian mythology, and the text's ostensibly evil characters, in a similar manner to Satan in the Book of Job and the demon of Chaucer's "Friar's Tale," are revealed to be, if not themselves good, nonetheless part of a divine master plan.

82. Game theory posits that games are played for their possible pay-offs, and this also encourages the reader to see God as the mastermind of the game because He too "wins" the game as Gawain assumes a new, stronger Christian identity. The Green Knight/Bertilak, the Lady, and Morgan all participate in the game, but their pay-offs are less than God's. They may enjoy the play and fun of the game, and Morgan may revel in the humiliations enacted upon the Arthurian court, but certainly God and Gawain win more than anyone else.

83. Ann Astell, *Political Allegory in Late Medieval England* (Ithaca: Cornell University Press, 1999), pp. 131–32.

84. Of course, the romance is constructed upon this necessary failure. The narrative would end prematurely if Gawain displayed sufficient awareness that the game need not be played at all.

85. Despite their unity within the Trinity, God the Heavenly Sadistic Father and Christ the Earthly Masochistic Son act separately within the poem, as the former acts as the poem's sadist while the latter, through his crucifixion and suffering, serves as a model of masochism.

86. Gill Saunders, *The Nude: A New Perspective* (London: Herbert Press, 1989), p. 27 (qtd. in Mills, " 'Whatever you do is a delight to me!' " p. 36, n. 86).

87. Arthur Lindley, " 'Ther he watz dispoyled, with spechez of myerthe': Carnival and the Undoing of Sir Gawain," *Exemplaria* 6 (1994): 83 [67–86].

88. Geraldine Heng suggests that the seduction scenes address female desire and proposes that the woman wants to express her desire: "To the vexed question of the Lady's desire, then, the spectacle of her performance returns only the impressively enigmatic legacy of a boundless desire" ("A Woman Wants: The Lady, Gawain, and the Forms of Seduction," *Yale Journal of Criticism* 5 [1992]: 124 [101–34]. However, the lady's desire, if indeed it exists as an expression of her individual will, finds its expression through the godgame: her desires are in the service of desires beyond her own. At the very least, she knows that the conflict between the game of courtly love and the ideals of knightly virtue prohibit Gawain from acting upon her demands, regardless of whether they express her own personal desires or merely desires she must simulate in service of a deeper spiritual purpose. See also Heng,

"Feminine Knots and the Other *Sir Gawain and the Green Knight*," *PMLA* 106 (1991): 500–514.
89. Dinshaw, "A Kiss Is Just a Kiss," p. 211.
90. Ibid., p. 206.
91. Boyd, "Sodomy, Misogyny, and Displacement," p. 78.
92. When viewed in light of the *Gawain*-poet's graphic homophobia in *Cleanness*, these scenes of same-sex flirtation are especially startling. Although the generic differences between a poetic sermon and a romance explain some of their divergence, the harsh condemnation of homosexuality in *Cleanness* clashes with the light-hearted queerness of *Sir Gawain and the Green Knight*. This conflict between the two visions of queerness suggests that the queer undermines the *Gawain*-poet's understanding of his religion and of his God because he cannot formulate a consistent theological response to the ostensible sin. Who is the *Gawain*-poet's God, and what does He think of homosexuality? Is He the mostly unforgiving and excessively wrathful deity of *Cleanness*, or the forgiving and playfully sadistic God who creates a labyrinthine yet pedagogically beneficial game for Gawain? Dinshaw suggests that the sexual themes of *Cleanness* provide a backdrop for *Sir Gawain and the Green Knight*, in which heteronormativity ultimately contains the queer play of the romance ("A Kiss Is Just a Kiss," pp. 216–20). See also Elizabeth Keiser, *Courtly Desire and Medieval Homophobia* (New Haven: Yale University Press, 1997), pp. 9–10, 194.
93. The *Gawain*-poet provides the reader with little reason to surmise the spiritual nature of Gawain's quest prior to the protagonist's realization of its true meaning, except that the narrator reports that he will gloss over the traditional material of romance, including fights with dragons, wolves, wild men, bulls, bears, boars, and giants (713–25). This moment provides the primary clue to the reader that Gawain's quest is not the typical plot structure of romance.
94. Suzanne Gearhart, "Foucault's Response to Freud: Sado-Masochism and the Aestheticization of Power," *Style* 29 (1995): 391 [389–403].
95. Edward Trostle Jones, "The Sound of Laughter in *Sir Gawain and the Green Knight*, *Mediaeval Studies* 31 (1969): 344 [343–45]; see also Larry D. Benson, *Art and Tradition in Sir Gawain and the Green Knight* (New Brunswick, NJ: Rutgers University Press, 1965), p. 241.
96. Peter Christmas, "A Reading of *Sir Gawain and the Green Knight*": 243 [238–47].
97. Signs structure the *Gawain*-poet's works, and he specifically addresses the importance of interpreting signs in *Cleanness*: "Alle thyse ar teches and tokenes to trow vpon yet, / And wittnesse of that wykked werk, and the wrake after / That oure Fader forthrede for fylthe of those ledes. / Thenne ych wyghe may wel wyt that He the wlonk louies" (The Poems of the *Pearl Manuscript*, ed. Malcolm Andrew and Ronald Waldron, p. 155, lines 1049–52). The call to "trow vpon" signs suggests that, for the *Gawain*-poet, signs must be analyzed carefully if one is to discern their semiotic sense.
98. Robert W. Hanning, "Sir Gawain and the Red Herring: The Perils of Interpretation," *Acts of Interpretation*, ed. Mary Carruthers and Elizabeth Kirk (Norman, OK: Pilgrim, 1982), p. 5 [5–23].

99. Monica Potkay, "The Violence of Courtly Exegesis in *Sir Gawain and the Green Knight*," *Representing Rape in Medieval and Early Modern Literature*, ed. Elizabeth Robertson and Christine Rose (New York: Palgrave, 2001), p. 111 [97–124].
100. Hent de Vries, *Philosophy and the Turn to Religion* (Baltimore, MD: Johns Hopkins University Press, 1999), p. 11.
101. Such a lesson is similar to the lesson of the Book of Job's godgame in its "denial of the assumption that the universe is explicable in human terms; it is a corrective to the presumption of human beings in applying their standards of value to the cosmos" (James Conant, "Job: The Twofold Answer," *Dimensions of Job*, ed. Nahum Glatzer [New York: Schocken, 1969], p. 247). Again, we see a point of connection with the godgame of the Book of Job, as it is easy to imagine Job's closing words to God spoken by Gawain: "I know that thou canst do all things, and that no purpose of thine can be thwarted. Who is this that hides counsel without knowledge? Therefore I have uttered what I did not understand, things too wonderful for me, which I did not know" (42:2–3).
102. For more on the semiotic play in *Sir Gawain and the Green Knight*, see Scott D. Troyan, "True Tokens," pp. 141–70; R.A. Shoaf, "The 'Syngne of Surfet' and the Surfeit of Signs in *Sir Gawain and the Green Knight*," *The Passing of Arthur: New Essays in Arthurian Traditions*, ed. Christopher Baswell and William Sharpe (New York: Garland, 1988), pp. 152–691; and Ross Arthur, "Gawain's Shield as Signum," *Text and Matter: New Critical Perspectives of the Pearl-Poet*, ed. Robert Blanch, Miriam Youngerman Miller, Ross Arthur, and Julian Wasserman (Troy, NY: Whitson, 1991), pp. 221–26 and *Medieval Sign Theory and Sir Gawain and the Green Knight* (Toronto: University of Toronto Press, 1987). David Boyd comments directly on the queer and normative vacillations of the girdle's meaning, declaring that "While the laughing redeployment of the girdle from token of feminizing shame and lack to one of homosocial triumph might seem a peculiar move, it is nonetheless a powerful one. Disarmed through laughter and assigned another signified, the Lady's gift becomes a sign illustrating the power of a homosocial hegemony to recuperate—and use to its advancement—those very threats to its existence" ("Sodomy, Misogyny, and Displacement," p. 104).
103. Kathryn Bond Stockton, "Christ's Queer Wound, or Divine Humiliation Among the Unchurched," *Writing the Bodies of Christ*, ed. John Schad (Aldershot, England: Ashgate, 2001), p. 132 [127–44].
104. As previously mentioned, the reader may resist identifying with Gawain, but the text encourages us to share his fortunate fall into grace.
105. Alain Robbe-Grillet quotes Poincaré in "For a Voluptuous Tomorrow" (*Saturday Review*, May 20, 1972), p. 46. I have been unable to find the original source of the quotation.
106. Kathryn Gravdal, *Ravishing Maidens*, p. 24.
107. John Clayton, "Alain Robbe-Grillet: The Aesthetics of Sado-Masochism," *Massachusetts Review* 18 (1977): 117 [106–119].

108. Aaron Ridley, "Desire in the Experience of Fiction," *Philosophy and Literature* 16:2 (1992): 285 [279–91].

Chapter 6   Conclusion: Queering Genres, Medieval Ideology, and Today's Readers

1. Rhonda Knight, "Procreative Sodomy: Textuality and the Construction of Ethnicities in Gerald of Wales's *Descriptio Cambriae*," *Exemplaria* 14 (2002): 77 [47–77].
2. Simon Gaunt, "Straight Minds/'Queer' Wishes in Old French Hagiography: *La Vie de Sainte Euphrosine*," *Premodern Sexualities*, ed. Louise Fradenburg and Carla Freccero (New York: Routledge, 1996), p. 169 [155–73].
3. Anis Bawarshi, "The Genre Function," *College English* 62 (2000): 352 [335–60].
4. Alan E. Knight, *Aspects of Genre in Late Medieval French Drama* (Manchester: Manchester University Press, 1983), p. 14.
5. Robert Sturges notes that the reading culture of the Middle Ages accorded itself a role in the construction of meaning of secular texts: "The intellectual conditions of the high Middle Ages would now seem to be prepared for a literature of indeterminate meanings: Abelard's bracketing of the traditional divine guarantees of signification releases language from the signified and opens it to the hearer's interpretation, while rhetoricians, classical scholars, and theologians recognize a secular literature existing on the purely literal level, the level characterized by ambiguity and undecidability" (*Medieval Interpretation* [Carbondale: Southern Illinois University Press, 1991], p. 19).
6. Adena Rosmarin, *The Power of Genre* (Minneapolis: University of Minnesota Press, 1985), pp. 21–22.
7. As recent critical discussions suggest, scholars often accord a place for the personal in their own scholarship. See, for example, Michael Bérubé, Cathy Davidson, Sylvia Molloy, and David Palumbo-Liu, "Four Views on the Place of the Personal in Scholarship," *PMLA* 11:5 (1996): 1063–79 (as well as the "Forum" section of this issue, pp. 1146–69) and a recent special issue of *College English* (66:1 [September 2003]: 9–104) on "The Personal in Academic Writing," edited by Jane Hindman. Hindman proposes that literature professors work toward "developing embodied professional reading practices that sanction a critical, self-reflective awareness of the emotional and ideological origins of our textual interpretations" (15).
8. David L. Wallace, "Out in the Academy: Heterosexism, Invisibility, and Double Consciousness," *College English* 65:1 (2002): 66 [53–66].
9. Anna Roberts, "Queer Fisher King: Castration as a Site of Queer Representation (*Perceval*, *Stabat Mater*, *The City of God*)," *Arthuriana* 11:3 (2001): 82 [49–88].
10. For a screed against the integration of queer sexuality within mainstream culture, see Daniel Harris, *The Rise and Fall of Gay Culture* (New York: Hyperion, 1997).

WORKS CITED

Aertsen, Henk. "Game and Earnest in *Sir Gawain and the Green Knight*." *Companion to Middle English Romance*. Ed. Henk Aertsen and Alasdair A. MacDonald. Amsterdam: Vrije University Press, 1990. 83–100.
Alain de Lille. *The Plaint of Nature*. Trans. James Sheridan. Toronto: Pontifical Institute of Mediaeval Studies, 1980.
Allen, Judson Boyce. "Grammar, Poetic Form, and the Lyric Ego." *Vernacular Poetics in the Middle Ages*. Ed. Lois Ebin. Kalamazoo, MI: Medieval Institute Publications, 1984. 199–226.
Andreas Capellanus. *The Art of Courtly Love*. Trans. John Jay Parry. New York: Columbia University Press, 1990.
Aquinas, Thomas. *Summa Theologiae*. Madrid: Biblioteca de Autores Cristianos, 1956.
Arthur, Ross. "Gawain's Shield as Signum." *Text and Matter: New Critical Perspectives of the Pearl-Poet*. Ed. Robert Blanch, Miriam Youngerman Miller, and Julian Wasserman. Troy, NY: Whitson, 1991. 221–26.
———. *Medieval Sign Theory and Sir Gawain and the Green Knight*. Toronto: University of Toronto Press, 1987.
———. " 'Why Artow Angry': The Malice of Chaucer's Reeve." *English Studies in Canada* 13 (1987): 1–11.
Astell, Ann. *Political Allegory in Late Medieval England*. Ithaca: Cornell University Press, 1999.
———. *The Song of Songs in the Middle Ages*. Ithaca: Cornell University Press, 1990.
———. "*Sir Gawain and the Green Knight*: A Study in the Rhetoric of Romance." *Journal of English and Germanic Philology* 84 (1985): 188–202.
Auerbach, Erich. *Mimesis: The Representation of Reality in Western Literature*. Trans. Willard Trask. Princeton: Princeton University Press, 1953.
Augustine. *Confessions*. Trans. Maria Boulding. Hyde Park, NY: New City, 1997.
Bakhtin, Mikhail. *Rabelais and His World*. Trans. Hélène Iswolsky. Bloomington: Indiana University Press, 1984.
Barr, Marleen. *Genre Fission: A New Discourse Practice for Cultural Studies*. Iowa City: University of Iowa Press, 2000.
Barron, W.R.J. *Trawthe and Treason: The Sin of Gawain Reconsidered*. Manchester: Manchester University Press, 1980.
Baudri of Bourgueil. *Les Oeuvres poétiques de Baudri de Bourgueil*. Ed. Phyllis Abrahams. Paris: Champion, 1926.
Bawarshi, Anis. "The Genre Function." *College English* 62 (2000): 335–60.

Bayless, Martha. *Parody in the Middle Ages.* Ann Arbor: University of Michigan Press, 1996.

Bédier, J. *Les Fabliaux.* Bibl. de l'école des hautes études, fasc. 98. Paris: Emile Bouillon, 1893.

Beebee, Thomas. *The Ideology of Genre: A Comparative Study of Generic Instability.* University Park: Pennsylvania State University Press, 1994.

Beidler, Peter, ed. *Masculinities in Chaucer.* Cambridge: D.S. Brewer, 1998.

Benson, Larry D., ed. *A Glossarial Concordance to the Riverside Chaucer.* New York: Garland, 1993.

———. *Art and Tradition in* Sir Gawain and the Green Knight. New Brunswick, NJ: Rutgers University Press, 1965.

Benson, Robert and Giles Constable, eds. *Renaissance and Renewal in the Twelfth Century.* Cambridge: Harvard University Press, 1982.

Benton, John F. "Consciousness of Self and Perceptions of Individuality." Benson and Constable 263–95.

Bergman, David, ed. *Camp Grounds: Style and Homosexuality.* Amherst: University of Massachusetts Press, 1993.

Bérubé, Michael, Cathy Davidson, Sylvia Molloy, and David Palumbo-Liu. "Four Views on the Place of the Personal in Scholarship." *PMLA* 11:5 (1996): 1063–1079.

Biblia Sacra Iuxta Vulgatam Versionem. Stuttgart: Deutsche Bibelgesellschaft, 1969.

Bloch, R. Howard. *The Scandal of the Fabliaux.* Chicago: University of Chicago Press, 1986.

Bloomfield, Morton W. "*Sir Gawain and the Green Knight*: An Appraisal." Howard and Zacher 24–55.

Blumenfeld-Kosinski, Renate and Timea Szell, eds. *Images of Sainthood in Medieval Europe.* Ithaca, NY: Cornell University Press, 1991.

Bond, Gerald. *The Loving Subject: Desire, Eloquence, and Power in Romanesque France.* Philadelphia: University of Pennsylvania Press, 1995.

Boswell, John. *Christianity, Social Tolerance, and Homosexuality.* Chicago: University of Chicago Press, 1980.

Bouché, Thérèse and Hélène Charpentier, eds. *Le rire au Moyen Age dans la litterature et dans les arts.* Bordeaux: Presses Universitaires de Bordeaux, 1990.

Bowers, R.H. "*Gawain and the Green Knight* as Entertainment." *Modern Language Quarterly* 24 (1963): 333–41.

Boyd, David. "Sodomy, Misogyny, and Displacement: Occluding Queer Desire in *Sir Gawain and the Green Knight.*" *Arthuriana* 8 (1998): 77–113.

Brabant, Margaret, ed. *Politics, Gender, and Genre: The Political Thought of Christine de Pizan.* Boulder, CO: Westview, 1992.

Braddy, Haldeen. "Chaucer's Playful Pandarus." *Southern Folklore Quarterly* 34 (1970): 71–81.

Brams, Steven J. *Biblical Games.* Cambridge, MA: MIT Press, 1980.

Braswell-Means, Laurel. "A New Look at an Old Patient: Chaucer's Summoner and Medieval Physiognomia." *Chaucer Review* 25:3 (1991): 266–75.

Brewer, D.S. and Jonathan Gibson, eds. *A Companion to the Gawain-Poet*. Suffolk, UK: D.S. Brewer, 1997.

———. "The Couple in Chaucer's Fabliaux." *The Making of the Couple: The Social Function of Short-Form Medieval Narrative*. Ed. Flemming Andersen and Morten Nojgaard. Odense: Odense University Press, 1991. 129–43.

———. "The Fabliaux." *Companion to Chaucer Studies*. Ed. Beryl Rowland. New York: Oxford University Press, 1979. 296–325.

———. "Chaucer and Chrétien and Arthurian Romance." *Chaucer and Middle English Studies in Honour of Rossell Hope Robbins*. Ed. Beryl Rowland. Kent, OH: Kent State University Press, 1974. 255–59.

Brown, Elizabeth A.R., Claudia Rapp, and Brent D. Shaw. "Ritual Brotherhood in Ancient and Medieval Europe: A Symposium." *Traditio* 52 (1997): 259–381.

Bryan, W.F. and Germaine Dempster, eds. *Sources and Analogues of Chaucer's Canterbury Tales*. Chicago: University of Chicago Press, 1941; New York: Humanities, 1958.

Burger, Glenn. *Chaucer's Queer Nation*. Minneapolis: University of Minnesota Press, 2003.

———. "Erotic Discipline. . .or 'Tee Hee, I Like My Boys To Be Girls': Inventing with the Body in Chaucer's 'Miller's Tale.' " Cohen and Wheeler 245–60.

———. "Queer Chaucer." *English Studies in Canada* 20 (1994): 153–70.

Burger, Glenn and Steven F. Krueger, eds. *Queering the Middle Ages*. Minneapolis: University of Minnesota Press, 2001.

Burns, E. Jane. *Bodytalk: When Women Speak in Old French Literature*. Philadelphia: University of Pennsylvania Press, 1993.

Burrow, J.A. *Medieval Writers and Their Work*. Oxford: Oxford University Press, 1982.

———. *A Reading of Sir Gawain and the Green Knight*. New York: Barnes and Noble, 1966.

Busby, Keith. "Conspicuous by Its Absence: The English Fabliau." *Dutch Quarterly Review of Anglo-American Letters* 12 (1982): 30–41.

Butler, Judith. "Against Proper Objects." Weed and Schor 1–30.

———. *Bodies That Matter: On the Discursive Limits of "Sex."* New York: Routledge, 1993.

———. *Gender Trouble: Feminism and the Subversion of Identity*. New York: Routledge, 1990.

Bynum, Caroline Walker. *Fragmentation and Redemption*. New York: Zone, 1991.

———. *Jesus as Mother*. Berkeley: University of California Press, 1982.

Caesarius of Arles. *Sermones*. Ed. D. Germani Morin. 2 vols. *Corpus Christianorum, Series latina*, 1953. Vols. 103–104.

Caillois, Roger. *Man, Play, and Games*. Trans. Meyer Barash. New York: Free Press of Glencoe, 1961.

Carré, Yannick. *Le Baiser sur la bouche au moyen age: rites, symboles, mentalités, à travers les texts et les images, XIe-XVe siècles*. Paris: Léopard d'Or, 1992.

Carruthers, Mary. "The Wife of Bath and the Painting of Lions." *PMLA* 94 (1979): 209–222.

Carton, Evan. "Complicity and Responsibility in Pandarus' Bed and Chaucer's Art." *PMLA* 94 (1979): 47–61.
Cary, Meredith. "Sovereignty and Old Wife." *Papers on Language and Literature* 5 (1969): 375–88.
Case, Sue-Ellen. "Tracking the Vampire." *differences* 3:2 (1991): 1–20.
Chaucer, Geoffrey. *The Riverside Chaucer*. Ed. Larry D. Benson. 3rd ed. Boston: Houghton Mifflin, 1987.
Christmas, Peter. "A Reading of *Sir Gawain and the Green Knight*." *Neophilologus* 58 (1974): 238–47.
Clanchy, M.T. *From Memory to Written Record: England, 1066–1307*. Cambridge, MA: Harvard University Press, 1979.
Clark, Roy Peter. "Christmas Games in Chaucer's 'The Miller's Tale.' " *Studies in Short Fiction* 13 (1976): 277–87.
Clayton, John. "Alain Robbe-Grillet: The Aesthetics of Sado-Masochism." *Massachusetts Review* 18 (1977): 106–119.
Cleto, Fabio, ed. *Camp: Queer Aesthetics and the Performing Subject*. Ann Arbor: University of Michigan Press, 1999.
Clogan, Paul. "Literary Genres in a Medieval Textbook." *Medievalia et Humanistica* 11 (1982): 199–209.
Clough, Andrea. "Medieval Tragedy and the Genre of *Troilus and Criseyde*." *Medievalia et Humanistica* 11 (1982): 211–27.
Cohen, Jeffrey Jerome. "Masoch/Lancelotism." *New Literary History* 28 (1997): 231–60.
Cohen, Jeffrey Jerome and Bonnie Wheeler, eds. *Becoming Male in the Middle Ages*. New York: Garland, 1997.
Coleman, Janet. *Medieval Readers and Writers*. New York: Columbia University Press, 1981.
The Complete Works of the Pearl-Poet. Trans. Casey Finch. Facing-Page Middle English Texts by Clifford Peterson, Malcolm Andrew and Ronald Waldron. Berkeley: University of California Press, 1993.
Conant, James. "Job: The Twofold Answer." *Dimensions of Job*. Ed. Nahum Glatzer. New York: Schocken, 1969.
Cook, Robert G. "The Play-Element in *Sir Gawain and the Green Knight*." *Tulane Studies in English* 13 (1963): 5–31.
Cooke, Thomas D. *The Old French and Chaucerian Fabliaux*. Columbia: University of Missouri Press, 1978.
Coon, Lynda. *Sacred Fictions: Holy Women and Hagiography in Late Antiquity*. Philadelphia: University of Pennsylvania Press, 1997.
Cooper, Helen. "The Supernatural." Brewer and Gibson. 277–91.
———. *Oxford Guides to Chaucer: The Canterbury Tales*. Oxford: Oxford University Press, 1989.
Cox, Catherine S. *Gender and Language in Chaucer*. Gainesville: University Press of Florida, 1997.
Cox, Philip. *Gender, Genre, and the Romantic Poets*. Manchester: Manchester University Press, 1996.

Crane, Susan. *Gender and Romance in Chaucer's <u>Canterbury Tales</u>*. Princeton, NJ: Princeton University Press, 1994.
Croce, Benedetto. *Aesthetic as Science of Expression and General Linguistic*. Trans. Douglas Ainslie. London: Macmillan, 1922.
Cross, F.L. *The Oxford Dictionary of the Christian Church*. 3rd ed. Ed. E.A. Livingstone. Oxford: Oxford University Press, 1997.
Curtius, Ernst Robert. *European Literature and the Latin Middle Ages*. Trans. Willard R. Trask. Princeton, NJ: Princeton University Press, 1953.
Damian, Peter. *Book of Gomorrah: An Eleventh-Century Treatise Against Clerical Homosexual Practices*. Trans. Pierre Payer. Waterloo, Ontario: Wilfrid Laurier University Press, 1982.
Dante Alighieri. *Convivio*. Ed. Franca Brambilla Ageno. Florence: Casa Editrice Le Lettere, 1995.
———. *The Convivio of Dante Alighieri*. Trans. Philip H. Wicksteed. London: Dent, 1903.
Davis, Natalie Zemon. *Society and Culture in Early Modern France*. Stanford, CA: Stanford University Press, 1975.
Deleuze, Gilles. *Sacher-Masoch: An Interpretation*. London: Faber and Faber, 1971.
Derrida, Jacques. *Acts of Literature*. Ed. Derek Attridge. London: Routledge, 1992.
Dinshaw, Carolyn. *Chaucer's Sexual Poetics*. Madison: University of Wisconsin Press, 1989.
———. *Getting Medieval: Sexualities and Communities, Pre- and Postmodern*. Durham, NC: Duke University Press, 1999.
———. "A Kiss Is Just a Kiss: Heterosexuality and Its Consolations in *Sir Gawain and the Green Knight*." *Diacritics* 24 (1994): 205–226.
———. "Reading Like a Man: The Critics, the Narrator, Troilus, and Pandarus." Shoaf (1992): 47–73.
Disbrow, Sarah. "The Wife of Bath's Old Wives' Tale." *Studies in the Age of Chaucer* 8 (1986): 59–71.
Dollimore, Jonathan. *Sexual Dissidence: Augustine to Wilde, Freud to Foucault*. Oxford: Clarendon, 1991.
Douay Rheims Bible. Rockford, IL: Tan, 1971.
Dover, K.J. *Greek Homosexuality*. New York: Random House, 1980.
Dronke, Peter. *The Medieval Lyric*. 3rd ed. Cambridge, UK: D.S. Brewer, 1996.
———. *Women Writers of the Middle Ages*. Cambridge: Cambridge University Press, 1984.
———. *Poetic Individuality in the Middle Ages: New Departures in Poetry, 1000–1150*. Oxford: Oxford University Press, 1970.
Dubrow, Heather. *Genre*. London: Methuen, 1982.
Dyer, Christopher. *Standards of Living in the Later Middle Ages: Social Change in England c. 1200–1520*. Cambridge: Cambridge University Press, 1989.
Eagleton, Mary. "Genre and Gender." *Re-Reading the Short Story*. Ed. Clare Hanson. Basingstoke: Macmillan, 1989. 56–68.
Edelman, Lee. "Queer Theory: Unstating Desire." *GLQ: A Journal of Lesbian and Gay Studies* 2:4 (1995): 343–46.

Eisner, Sigmund. *A Tale of Wonder: A Source Study of the "The Wife of Bath's Tale."* New York: Burt Franklin, 1957.

Elbow, Peter. *Oppositions in Chaucer.* Middletown, CT: Wesleyan University Press, 1973.

Emmerson, Richard K. and Ronald B. Herzman. *The Apocalyptic Imagination in Medieval Literature.* Philadelphia: University of Philadelphia Press, 1992.

Fantham, Elaine, Helene Peet Foley, Natalie Boymel Kampen, Sarah B. Pomeroy, and H.A. Shapiro. *Women in the Classical World: Image and Text.* New York: Oxford University Press, 1994.

Fehrenbacher, Richard W. " 'Al that which chargeth nought to seye': The Theme of Incest in *Troilus and Criseyde*." *Exemplaria* 9 (1997): 341–69.

Felber, Lynette. *Gender and Genre in Novels Without End: The British Roman-Fleuve.* Gainesville: University Press of Florida, 1995.

Ferrante, Joan. *To the Glory of Her Sex.* Bloomington: Indiana University Press, 1997.

Ferreiro, Alberto. "Job in the Sermons of Caesarius of Arles." *Recherches de thâeologie ancienne ete medievale* 54 (1987): 13–26.

Ferster, Judith. *Chaucer on Interpretation.* Cambridge: Cambridge University Press, 1985.

Finlayson, John. "The Wife of Bath's 'Prologue,' LL. 328–36, and Boccaccio's *Decameron*." *Neophilologus* 83 (1999): 313–16.

Fisher, Sheila. "Taken Men and Token Women in *Sir Gawain and the Green Knight*." *Seeking the Woman in Late Medieval and Renaissance Writings.* Ed. Sheila Fisher and Janet Halley. Knoxville: University of Tennessee Press, 1989. 71–105.

Foucault, Michel. *The History of Sexuality: Volume I: An Introduction.* Trans. Robert Hurley. New York: Vintage, 1978.

Fowler, Alastair. *Kinds of Literature: An Introduction to the Theory of Genres and Modes.* Oxford: Oxford University Press, 1982.

Fowles, John. *The Ebony Tower.* Boston, MA: Little, Brown, 1974.

———. *The Magus.* Rev. ed. London: Jonathan Cape, 1977.

Fradenburg, Louise. *Sacrifice Your Love: Psychoanalysis, Historicism, Chaucer.* Minneapolis: University of Minnesota Press, 2002.

———. "Sacrificial Desire in Chaucer's 'Knight's Tale.' " *Journal of Medieval and Early Modern Studies* 27:1 (1997): 47–75.

———. " 'Our owen wo to drynke': Loss, Gender, and Chivalry in *Troilus and Criseyde*." Shoaf (1992) 88–106.

———. "The Wife of Bath's Passing Fancy." *Studies in the Age of Chaucer* 8 (1986): 131–58.

Fradenburg, Louise and Carla Freccero, eds. *Premodern Sexualities.* New York: Routledge, 1996.

Frantzen, Allen J. *Before the Closet: Same-Sex Love from <u>Beowulf</u> to <u>Angels in America</u>.* Chicago: University of Chicago Press, 1998.

———. "Between the Lines: Queer Theory, the History of Homosexuality, and Anglo-Saxon Penitentials." *Journal of Medieval and Renaissance Studies* 26:2 (1996): 255–96.

Freiwald, Leah Rieber. " 'Swych Love of Frendes': Pandarus and Troilus." *Chaucer Review* 6 (1971): 120–129.

Freud, Sigmund. *Wit and Its Relation to the Unconscious.* 1922. London: Routledge, 1999.

———. "Medusa's Head." *The Standard Edition of the Complete Psychological Works of Sigmund Freud.* Ed. and trans. James Strachey. London: Hogarth, 1991. Vol. 18. 273–74.

Furrow, Melissa. "Middle English Fabliaux and Modern Myth." *English Literary History* 56 (1989): 1–18.

Fuss, Diana. *Identification Papers.* New York: Routledge, 1995.

Gaunt, Simon. "Romance and Other Genres." *Cambridge Companion to Medieval Romance.* Ed. Roberta Krueger. Cambridge: Cambridge University Press, 2000. 45–59.

———. "Straight Minds/'Queer' Wishes in Old French Hagiography: *La Vie de Sainte Euphrosine.*" Fradenburg and Freccero, 155–73.

———. *Gender and Genre in Medieval French Literature.* Cambridge: Cambridge University Press, 1995.

———. "The Significance of Silence." *Paragraph* 13 (1990): 202–16.

Gearhart, Suzanne. "Foucault's Response to Freud: Sado-Masochism and the Aestheticization of Power." *Style* 29 (1995): 389–403.

Gibbs, W. Wayt. "Gaining on Fat." *Scientific American* 275.2 (1996): 88–94.

Gittings, Christopher. "Zero Patience: Genre, Difference, and Ideology: Singing and Dancing Queer Nation." *Cinema Journal* 41:1 (2001): 28–39.

Given-Wilson, Chris. *The English Nobility in the Late Middle Ages: The Fourteenth-Century Political Community.* London: Routledge and Kegan Paul, 1987.

———. *The Royal Household and the King's Affinity: Service, Politics, and Finance in England, 1360–1413.* New Haven, CT: Yale University Press, 1986.

Glasser, Marc. " 'He nedes moste hire wedde': The Forced Marriage in 'The Wife of Bath's Tale' and Its Middle English Analogues." *Neuphilologische Mitteilungen* 85:2 (1984): 239–41.

Goddard, R.N.B. "Eugenius of Toledo and Marbod of Rennes in Marcabru's 'Pois la fuoilla revirola.' " *Medium Aevum* 57 (1988): 27–37.

Godfrey, Mary. "Only Words: Cursing and the Authority of Language in Chaucer's 'Friar's Tale.' " *Exemplaria* 10 (1998): 307–328.

Goodman, Jennifer. "Nature as Destiny in *Troilus and Criseyde.*" *Style* 31 (1997): 13–27.

Gottfried, Robert S. *The Black Death: Natural and Human Disaster in Medieval Europe.* New York: Free Press, 1983.

Gower, John. *The Complete Works of John Gower.* Ed. G.C. Macaulay. Oxford: Clarendon, 1899–1908. Grosse Point, MI: Scholarly Press, 1968.

Gravdal, Kathryn. "Poem Unlimited: Medieval Genre Theory and the Fabliau." *L'Esprit Créateur* 33:4 (1993): 10–17.

———. *Ravishing Maidens: Writing Rape in Medieval French Literature and Law.* Philadelphia: University of Pennsylvania Press, 1991.

Green, Richard F. "An Analogue to the 'Marital Dilemma' in 'The Wife of Bath's Tale.' " *English Language Notes* 28 (1991): 9–12.

———. "Troilus and the Game of Love." *Chaucer Review* 13 (1979): 201–220.

Grossman, Marshall, ed. *Aemilia Lanyer: Gender, Genre, and the Canon.* Lexington: University Press of Kentucky, 1998.

Grudin, Michaela Paasche. *Chaucer and the Politics of Discourse.* Columbia: University of South Carolina Press, 1996.

Gygax, Franziska. *Gender and Genre in Gertrude Stein*. Westport, CT: Greenwood, 1998.

Haines, Victor Yelverton. *The Fortunate Fall of Sir Gawain*. Washington, DC: University Press of America, 1982.

Halperin, David. "How To Do the History of Male Homosexuality." *GLQ* 6:1 (2000): 87–123.

———. *One Hundred Years of Homosexuality and Other Essays on Greek Love*. New York: Routledge, 1990.

Hamilton, J.S. *Piers Gaveston, Earl of Cornwall, 1307–1312: Politics and Patronage in the Reign of Edward II*. Detroit, MI: Wayne State University Press, 1988.

Hanna, Ralph, III and Traugott Lawler, eds. *Jankyn's Book of Wikked Wyves: The Primary Texts*. Athens: University of Georgia Press, 1997.

Hanning, R.W. "Roasting a Friar, Mis-Taking a Wife, and Other Acts of Textual Harassment in Chaucer's *Canterbury Tales*." *Studies in the Age of Chaucer* 7 (1985): 3–20.

———. "Sir Gawain and the Red Herring: The Perils of Interpretation." *Acts of Interpretation*. Ed. Mary Carruthers and Elizabeth Kirk. Norman, OK: Pilgrim, 1982. 5–23.

Hanrahan, Michael. "Seduction and Betrayal: Treason in the Prologue to the *Legend of Good Women*." *Chaucer Review* 30 (1996): 229–40.

Hansen, Elaine Tuttle. *Chaucer and the Fictions of Gender*. Berkeley: University of California Press, 1992.

Harris, Daniel. *The Rise and Fall of Gay Culture*. New York: Hyperion, 1997.

Harsanyi, John C. *Papers in Game Theory*. Dordrecht, Holland: Reidel, 1982.

Haruta, Setsuko. "Sir Gawain and the Grisly Game." *Medieval Heritage: Essays in Honour of Tadahiro Ikegami*. Ed. Masahiko Kanno, Hiroshi Yamashita, Matatoshi Kawasaki, Junko Asakawa, and Naoko Shirai. Tokyo: Yushodo Press, 1997. 283–96.

Harwood, Britton. "Chaucer on 'Speche': *House of Fame*, the 'Friar's Tale,' and the 'Summoner's Tale.'" *Chaucer Review* 26 (1992): 343–49.

Heffernan, Thomas. *Sacred Biography: Saints and Their Biographers in the Middle Ages*. New York: Oxford University Press, 1988.

Heller, Robert. "'The Knight's Tale' and the Epic Tradition." *Chaucer Review* 1 (1966–67): 67–84.

Heng, Geraldine. "A Woman Wants: The Lady, Gawain, and the Forms of Seduction." *Yale Journal of Criticism* 5 (1992): 101–134.

———. "Feminine Knots and the Other *Sir Gawain and the Green Knight*." *PMLA* 106 (1991): 500–514.

Henryson, Robert. "The Testament of Cresseid." *The Poems of Robert Henryson*. Ed. Denton Fox. Oxford: Clarendon, 1981. 111–31.

———. "The Testament of Cresseid." *The Poems and Fables of Robert Henryson*. Ed. H. Harvey Wood. Edinburgh: Oliver and Boyd, 1933. 103–126.

Hergemöller, Bernd-Ulrich. *Sodom and Gomorrah: On the Everday Reality and Persecution of Homosexuals in the Middle Ages*. Trans. John Phillips. London: Free Association, 2001.

Herlihy, David. *The Black Death and the Transformation of the West*. Cambridge, MA: Harvard University Press, 1997.

Hildebert of Lavardin. *Hildebert Cenomannenis Episcopi: Carmina Minora.* Ed. Brian Scott. Leipzig: Teubner, 1969.

———. *Les Mélanges poétiques d'Hildebert de Lavardin.* Ed. Barthélemy Hauréau. Paris: Pedone-Lauriel, 1882.

Hindman, Jane E. "Thoughts on Reading 'the Personal': Toward a Discursive Ethics of Professional Critical Literacy." *College English* 66:1 (2003): 9–20.

Hines, John. *The Fabliau in English.* London: Longman, 1993.

Hollis, Stephanie J. "The Pentangle Knight: *Sir Gawain and the Green Knight.*" *Chaucer Review* 15 (1981): 267–81.

Homer. *Iliad.* Trans. Richard Lattimore. Chicago: University of Chicago Press, 1962.

Horrox, Rosemary, ed. and trans. *The Black Death.* Manchester: Manchester University Press, 1994.

Howard, Donald and Christian Zacher, eds. *Critical Studies of Sir Gawain and the Green Knight.* South Bend, IN: University of Notre Dame Press, 1968.

Huizinga, Johan. *Homo Ludens: A Study of the Play-Element in Culture.* Boston: Beacon, 1950.

Ingarden, Roman. *The Literary Work of Art: An Investigation on the Borderlines of Ontology, Logic, and Theory of Literature.* Trans. George G. Grabowicz. Evanston, IL: Northwestern University Press, 1973.

Ingham, Patricia Clare. "Pastoral Histories: Utopia, Conquest, and 'The Wife of Bath's Tale.'" *Texas Studies in Literature and Language* 44 (2002): 34–46.

Iser, Wolfgang. *The Act of Reading: A Theory of Aesthetic Response.* Baltimore, MD: Johns Hopkins University Press, 1978.

Isidore of Seville. *Etimologías.* Ed. Luis Cortés y Góngora. Madrid: Biblioteca de Autores Cristianos, 1951.

Jaeger, C. Stephen. "Pessimism in the Twelfth-Century 'Renaissance.'" *Speculum* 78:4 (2003): 1151–83.

———. *Ennobling Love: In Search of a Lost Sensibility.* Philadelphia: University of Pennsylvania Press, 1999.

Jameson, Frederic. *The Political Unconscious: Narrative as a Socially Symbolic Act.* Ithaca, NY: Cornell University Press, 1981.

Jauss, Hans-Robert. "Littérature médiévale et théorie des genres." *Poetique* 1 (1970): 79–101.

Jensen, Emily. "Male Competition as a Unifying Motif in Fragment A of the *Canterbury Tales.*" *Chaucer Review* 24 (1990): 320–328.

Joachim of Fiore. *Il Libro delle figure dell'abate Gioachino da Fiore.* Ed. Leone Tondelli, Marjorie Reeves, and Beatrice Hirsch-Reich. 2nd ed. Turin: Società Editrice Internazionale, 1953.

Johnson, Glen. "Queering the Genre." *Harvard Gay and Lesbian Review* 2:2 (Spring 1995): 21–23.

Johnson, Lynn. *The Voice of the Gawain-Poet.* Madison: University of Wisconsin Press, 1984.

Jones, Edward Trostle. "The Sound of Laughter in *Sir Gawain and the Green Knight.*" *Mediaeval Studies* 31 (1969): 343–45.

Jordan, Mark. *The Invention of Sodomy in Christian Theology.* Chicago: University of Chicago Press, 1997.

Jordan, Tracey. "Fairy Tale and Fabliau: Chaucer's 'The Miller's Tale.' " *Studies in Short Fiction* 21 (1984): 87–93.
Jost, Jean. "Ambiguous Brotherhood in the 'Friar's Tale' and 'Summoner's Tale.' " Beidler 77–90.
Justman, Stewart. "Trade as Pudendum: Chaucer's Wife of Bath." *Chaucer Review* 28 (1994): 344–52.
Kaminsky, Alice. *Chaucer's Troilus and Criseyde and the Critics*. Athens: Ohio University Press, 1980.
Karlen, Arno. "The Homosexual Heresy." *Chaucer Review* 6 (1971): 44–63.
Kauffman, Linda S. *Discourses of Desire: Gender, Genre, and Epistolary Fictions*. Ithaca, NY: Cornell University Press, 1986.
Kay, Sarah. *Subjectivity in Troubadour Poetry*. Cambridge: Cambridge University Press, 1990.
Keiser, Elizabeth B. *Courtly Desire and Medieval Homophobia*. New Haven: Yale University Press, 1997.
Kelly, Henry. *Chaucerian Tragedy*. Suffolk, UK: D.S. Brewer, 1997.
———. "Shades of Incest and Cuckoldry: Pandarus and John of Gaunt." *Studies in the Age of Chaucer* 13 (1991): 121–40.
Kendrick, Laura. *Chaucerian Play: Comedy and Control in The Canterbury Tales*. Berkeley: University of California Press, 1988.
———. *The Game of Love: Troubadour Wordplay*. Berkeley: University of California Press, 1988.
Kimmelman, Burt. *The Poetics of Authorship in the Later Middle Ages*. New York: Peter Lang, 1996.
Kinney, Clare. *Strategies of Poetic Narrative: Chaucer, Spenser, Milton, Eliot*. Cambridge: Cambridge University Press, 1992.
Kitely, John F. " 'The Endless Knot': Magical Aspects of the Pentangle in *Sir Gawain and the Green Knight*." *Studies in the Literary Imagination* 4 (1971): 41–50.
Knapp, Peggy. *Chaucer and the Social Contest*. New York: Routledge, 1990.
———. "Alisoun of Bathe and the Reappropriation of Tradition." *Chaucer Review* 24 (1989): 45–52.
———. "*Gawain* and the Middle Ages: Teaching History, Teaching Genre." *Approaches to Teaching Sir Gawain and the Green Knight*. Ed. Miriam Youngerman Miller and Jane Chance. New York: MLA, 1986. 138–42.
Knight, Alan E. *Aspects of Genre in Late Medieval French Drama*. Manchester: Manchester University Press, 1983.
Knight, Rhonda. "Procreative Sodomy: Textuality and the Construction of Ethnicities in Gerald of Wales's *Descriptio Cambriae*." *Exemplaria* 14 (2002): 47–77.
Kolve, V.A. "Ganymede / *Son of Getron*: Medieval Monasticism and the Drama of Same-Sex Desire." *Speculum* 73 (1998): 1014–1067.
———. *Chaucer and Imagery of Narrative*. Stanford, CA: Stanford University Press, 1984.
Kruger, Steven F. "Claiming the Pardoner: Toward a Gay Reading of Chaucer's 'Pardoner's Tale.' " *Exemplaria* 6 (1994): 115–39.
Kuester, Martin. "Godgames in Paradise: Educational Strategies in Milton and Fowles." *Anglia: Zeitschrift für Englische Philologie* 115:1 (1997): 29–43.

Kuhn, Sherman M., ed. *Middle English Dictionary*. Ann Arbor, MI: University of Michigan Press, 1963.

Lacy, Norris, *Reading Fabliaux*. New York: Garland, 1993.

———. ed. *Text and Intertext in Medieval Arthurian Literature*. New York: Garland, 1996.

Ladner, Gerhart. "Terms and Ideas of Renewals." Benson and Constable 1–33.

Langland, William. *Piers Plowman: The C-Text*. Ed. Derek Pearsall. London: Arnold, 1978.

———. *Piers Plowman: The B-Text*. Ed. George Kane and E. Talbot Donaldson. London: Athlone, 1975.

———. *Piers Plowman: The A-Text*. Ed. George Kane. London: Athlone, 1960.

Laskaya, Anne. *Chaucer's Approach to Gender in the Canterbury Tales*. Cambridge: D.S. Brewer, 1995.

Leicester, H. Marshall, Jr. "New Currents in Psychoanalytic Criticism, and the Difference 'IT' Makes: Gender and Desire in 'The Miller's Tale.' " *ELH* 61 (1994): 473–99.

———. *The Disenchanted Self: Representing the Subject in the Canterbury Tales*. Berkeley: University of California Press, 1990.

Levine, Robert. "Pandarus as Davus." *Neuphilologische Mitteilungen* 92 (1991): 463–68.

Levy, B.J. *The Comic Text: Patterns and Images in the Old French Fabliaux*. Amsterdam: Rodopi, 2000.

Levy, Bernard. "The Wife of Bath's Queynte Fantasye." *Chaucer Review* 4 (1970): 106–122.

Lewes, Darby. *Dream Revisionaries: Gender and Genre in Women's Utopian Fiction, 1870–1920*. Tuscaloosa: University of Alabama Press, 1995.

Lewis, Robert. "The English Fabliau Tradition and Chaucer's 'Miller's Tale.' " *Modern Philology* 79 (1982): 241–55.

Leyerle, John. "The Game and Play of Hero." *Concepts of the Hero in the Middle Ages and the Renaissance*. Ed. Norman Burns and Christopher Reagan. Albany: State University of New York Press, 1975. 49–82.

Lindahl, Carl. *Earnest Games: Folkloric Patterns in the Canterbury Tales*. Bloomington: Indiana University Press, 1987.

Lindley, Arthur. " 'Ther he watz dispoyled, with spechez of myerthe': Carnival and the Undoing of Sir Gawain." *Exemplaria* 6 (1994): 67–86.

Lochrie, Karma. "Presidential Improprieties and Medieval Categories: The Absurdity of Heterosexuality." Burger and Kruger 87–96.

———. *Covert Operations: The Medieval Uses of Secrecy*. Philadelphia: University of Pennsylvania Press, 1999.

———. "Presumptive Sodomy and Its Exclusions." *Textual Practice* 13 (1999): 295–310.

———. "Women's 'Pryvetees' and Fabliau Politics in the 'Miller's Tale.' " *Exemplaria* 6 (1994): 287–304.

Lochrie, Karma, Peggy McCracken, and James A. Schultz, eds. *Constructing Medieval Sexuality*. Minneapolis: University of Minnesota Press, 1997.

Lomperis, Linda. "Bodies That Matter in the Court of Late Medieval England and in Chaucer's 'Miller's Tale.' " *Romanic Review* 86:2 (1995): 243–64.

Long, Walter. "The Wife as Moral Revolutionary." *Chaucer Review* 20 (1986): 273–84.
Longsworth, Robert. "Interpretive Laughter in *Sir Gawain and the Green Knight*." *Philological Quarterly* 70 (1991): 141–47.
Macherey, Pierre. *A Theory of Literary Production*. Trans. Geoffrey Wall. London: Routledge, 1978.
Maitzen, Rohan Amanda. *Gender, Genre, and Victorian Historical Writing*. New York: Garland, 1998.
Mann, Jill. *Feminizing Chaucer*. Cambridge: D.S. Brewer, 2002.
———. *Chaucer and Medieval Estates Satire: The Literature of Social Classes and the General Prologue to the Canterbury Tales*. Cambridge: Cambridge University Press, 1973.
Marbod of Rennes. In *Patrologia Latina*. Ed. J.-P. Migne. Paris, 1844–1904. Vol. 171, cols. 1458–1782.
Marie de France. *The Lais of Marie de France*. Ed. and trans. Robert Hanning and Joan Ferrante. Durham, NC: Labyrinth, 1978.
———. *Lais*. Ed. Alfred Ewert. Oxford: Blackwell, 1965.
Margherita, Gayle. "Criseyde's Remains: Romance and the Question of Justice." *Exemplaria* 12:2 (2000): 257–92.
———. *The Romance of Origins: Language and Sexual Difference in Middle English Literature*. Philadelphia: University of Pennsylvania Press, 1994.
Mate, Mavis. *Daughters, Wives, and Widows After the Black Death: Women in Sussex, 1350–1535*. Woodbridge, Suffolk: Boydell, 1998.
Matter, E. Ann. *The Voice of My Beloved: The Song of Songs in Western Medieval Christianity*. Philadelphia: University of Pennsylvania Press, 1990.
Matthews, William. "The Wife of Bath and All Her Sect." *Viator* 5 (1974): 413–43.
Maynadier, G.H. *"The Wife of Bath's Tale": Its Sources and Analogues*. London: D. Nutt, 1901.
McAlpine, Monica. *The Genre of Troilus and Criseyde*. Ithaca, NY: Cornell University Press, 1978.
McDaniel, Ellen. "Games and Godgames in *The Magus* and *The French Lieutenant's Woman*." *MFS: Modern Fiction Studies* 31:1 (1985): 31–42.
Mehtonen, Päivi. *Old Concepts and New Poetics: Historia, Argumentum, and Fabula in the Twelfth- and Early-Thirteenth-Century Latin Poetics of Fiction*. Helsinki, Finland: Societas Scientiarum Fennica, 1996.
Meyer, Robert. "Chaucer's Tandem Romances." *Chaucer Review* 18 (1984): 221–38.
Migne, J.-P., ed. *Patrologia Latina*. Paris, 1844–1904.
Mills, Robert. " 'Whatever you do is a delight to me!': Masculinity, Masochism, and Queer Play in Representations of Male Martyrdom." *Exemplaria* 13 (2001): 1–37.
Mohr, Richard. "The Thing of It Is: Some Problems with Models for the Social Construction of Homosexuality." *Gay Ideas: Outing and Other Controversies*. Boston: Beacon, 1992. 221–42.
Mooney, Catherine, ed. *Gendered Voices: Medieval Saints and Their Interpreters*. Philadelphia: University of Pennsylvania Press, 1999.

Morgan, Gerald. "The Significance of the Pentangle Symbolism in *Sir Gawain and the Green Knight.*" *Modern Language Review* 74 (1979): 769–90.

Morris, Colin. *The Discovery of the Individual, 1050–1200.* New York: Harper and Row, 1972.

Morrison, Susan Signe. "Don't Ask, Don't Tell: The Wife of Bath and Vernacular Translations." *Exemplaria* 8 (1996): 97–123.

Mulvey, Laura. "Visual Pleasure and Narrative Cinema." *A Critical and Cultural Studies Reader.* Ed. Antony Easthope and Kate McGowan. Toronto: University of Toronto Press 1994. 158–66.

Muscatine, Charles. *The Old French Fabliaux.* New Haven, CT: Yale University Press, 1986.

———. *Chaucer and the French Tradition.* Berkeley: University of California Press 1957.

Neuse, Richard. "'Alisoun Still Lives Here': Provocations, Politics, and Pedagogy in 'The Wife of Bath's Tale,' *Hamlet*, and *Paradise Lost*." *Exemplaria* 4 (1992): 469–80.

The New Oxford Annotated Bible with the Apocrypha. Rev. standard ed. Ed. Herbert May and Bruce Metzger. New York: Oxford University Press, 1977.

Norton, Rictor. *The Myth of the Modern Homosexual.* London: Cassell, 1997.

Nykrog, Per. *Les Fabliaux: étude d'histoire littéraire et de stylistique médiévale*, 1957. New ed. Genève: Librairie Drox, 1973.

Olson, Glending. "The Marital Dilemma in 'The Wife of Bath's Tale': An Unnoticed Analogue and Its Chaucerian Court Context." *English Language Notes* 33 (1995): 1–7.

———. "'The Reeve's Tale' as a Fabliau." *Modern Language Quarterly* 35 (1974): 219–30.

Olson, Paul. *The Canterbury Tales and the Good Society.* Princeton, NJ: Princeton University Press, 1986.

Paden, William D, ed. *Medieval Lyric: Genres in Historical Context.* Urbana: University of Illinois Press, 2000.

Papka, Claudia Rattazzi. "Transgression, The End of Troilus, and the Ending of Chaucer's *Troilus and Criseyde.*" *Chaucer Review* 32 (1998): 267–81.

Patterson, Lee. *Chaucer and the Subject of History.* Madison: University of Wisconsin Press, 1991.

Pearcy, Roy J. "The Genre of Chaucer's Fabliau-Tales." *Chaucer and the Craft of Fiction.* Ed. Leigh A. Arrathoon. Rochester, MI: Solaris, 1986. 329–84.

Pearl, Cleanness, Patience, Sir Gawain and the Green Knight. Ed. A.C. Cawley and J.J. Anderson. London: Dent, 1976.

Pearsall, Derek. "Courtesy and Chivalry in *Sir Gawain and the Green Knight*: The Order of Shame and the Invention of Embarrassment." Brewer and Gibson 351–62.

Potkay, Monica. "The Violence of Courtly Exegesis in *Sir Gawain and the Green Knight.*" *Representing Rape in Medieval and Early Modern Literature.* Ed. Elizabeth Robertson and Christine Rose. New York: Palgrave, 2001. 97–124.

Pratt, Robert A. "The Development of the Wife of Bath." *Studies in Medieval Literature in Honor of Professor Albert Croll Baugh.* Ed. MacEdward Leach. Philadelphia: University of Pennsylvania Press, 1961. 45–79.

Pugh, Tison. "Dialectical History, White Indians, and Queer Anxiety in Mark Twain's *A Connecticut Yankee in King Arthur's Court*." *Essays in Arts and Sciences* 31 (2002): 83–102.

———. "Boundless Hearts in a Nightmare World: Queer Sentimentalism and Southern Gothicism in Truman Capote's *Other Voices, Other Rooms*." *Mississippi Quarterly* 51:4 (1998): 663–82.

Puhvel, Martin. "The Wife of Bath's 'Remedies of Love.'" *Chaucer Review* 20 (1986): 307–312.

Putter, Ad. *An Introduction to the Gawain-Poet*. London: Longman, 1996.

Quintilian. *Institutio Oratoria*. Ed. H.E. Butler. Cambridge, MA: Loeb, 1958.

Raber, Karen. *Dramatic Difference: Gender, Class, and Genre in the Early Modern Closet Drama*. Newark: University of Delaware Press, 2001.

Raby, F.J.E. *A History of Christian-Latin Poetry*. 2nd ed. Oxford: Clarendon, 1953.

Rahner, Hugo. *Man at Play*. New York: Herder and Herder, 1972.

Ramey, Lynn Tarte. *Christian, Saracen and Genre in Medieval French Literature*. New York: Routledge, 2001.

Rapoport, Anatol. *Two-Person Game Theory*. Ann Arbor: University of Michigan Press, 1966.

Reale, Nancy. "'Bitwixen Game and Ernest': *Troilus and Criseyde* as a Post-Boccaccian Response to the *Commedia*." *Philological Quarterly* 71 (1992): 155–71.

Reid, David S. "Crocodilian Humor: A Discussion of Chaucer's Wife of Bath." *Chaucer Review* 4 (1970): 73–89.

Rendall, Thomas. "*Gawain* and the Game of Chess." *Chaucer Review* 27 (1992): 186–99.

Richardson, Janette. *"Blameth Nat Me": A Study of Imagery in Chaucer's Fabliaux*. The Hague: Mouton, 1970.

Ridley, Aaron. "Desire in the Experience of Fiction." *Philosophy and Literature* 16:2 (1992): 279–91.

Riese, Alexander. *Anthologia Latina*. Leipzig: Teubner, 1894–1921.

Robbe-Grillet, Alain. "For a Voluptuous Tomorrow." *Saturday Review* (May 20, 1972), 46.

Robbins, Rossell Hope. "The English Fabliau: Before and After Chaucer." *Moderna Sprak* 64 (1970): 231–44.

Roberts, Anna. "Queer Fisher King: Castration as a Site of Queer Representation (*Perceval, Stabat Mater, The City of God*)." *Arthuriana* 11:3 (2001): 49–88.

Root, Jerry. "'Space To Speke': The Wife of Bath and the Discourse of Confession." *Chaucer Review* 28 (1994): 252–74.

Rosmarin, Adena. *The Power of Genre*. Minneapolis: University of Minnesota Press, 1985.

Ross, Andrew. "Uses of Camp." Cleto 308–329.

Ross, Diane. "The Play of Genres in the *Book of the Duchess*." *Chaucer Review* 19 (1984): 1–13.

Roth, Norman. "'Deal Gently with the Young Man': Love of Boys in Medieval Hebrew Poetry of Spain." *Speculum* 57 (1982): 20–51.

Rowe, Donald W. *"O Love, O Charite!" Contraries Harmonized in Chaucer's Troilus*. Carbondale: Southern Illinois University Press, 1976.

Rowe, Kathleen. *The Unruly Woman: Gender and the Genres of Laughter.* Austin: University of Texas Press, 1995.
Rowland, Beryl. "What Chaucer Did to the Fabliau." *Studia Neophilologica* 51 (1979): 205–213.
———. "Pandarus and the Fate of Tantalus." *Orbis Litterarum* 24 (1969): 3–15.
Royle, Nicholas. "The Private Parts of Jesus Christ." *Writing the Bodies of Christ.* Ed. John Schad. Aldershot, England: Ashgate, 2001. 159–76.
Sacher-Masoch, Leopold. *Venus in Furs.* Trans. Jean McNeil. Deleuze 117–248.
Sands, Donald B. *Middle English Verse Romances.* Exeter: University of Exeter Press, 1986.
Saunders, Gill. *The Nude: A New Perspective.* London: Herbert Press, 1989.
Scala, Elizabeth. "The Wanting Words of *Sir Gawain and the Green Knight.*" *Exemplaria* 6 (1994): 305–338.
Scanlon, Larry. *Narrative, Authority, and Power: The Medieval Exemplum and the Chaucerian Tradition.* Cambridge: Cambridge University Press, 1994.
Schechner, Richard. "Playing." *Play and Culture* 1 (1988): 3–19.
Schehr, Lawrence. "A Queer Theory Approach: Gender and Genre in *Old Goriot.*" *Approaches to Teaching Balzac's* Old Goriot. Ed. Michal Peled Ginsburg. New York: MLA, 2000. 118–25.
Schenck, Mary Jane Stearns. *The Fabliaux: Tales of Wit and Deception.* Purdue University Monographs in Romance Languages 24. Amsterdam: Benjamins, 1987.
Schlauch, Margaret. "The Marital Dilemma in 'The Wife of Bath's Tale.'" *PMLA* 61 (1946): 416–30.
Schweickart, Patrocinio. "Reading Ourselves: Toward a Feminist Theory of Reading." *Gender and Reading: Essay on Readers, Texts, and Contexts.* Ed. Elizabeth Flynn and Patrocinio Schweickart. Baltimore, MD: Johns Hopkins University Press, 1986. 31–62.
Sedgwick, Eve. "The Beast in the Closet: James and the Writing of Homosexual Panic." *Sex, Politics, and Science in the Nineteenth-Century Novel.* Ed. Ruth Bernard Yeazell. Baltimore, MD: Johns Hopkins University Press, 1986. 148–86.
———. *Epistemology of the Closet.* Berkeley: University of California Press, 1990.
———. *Between Men: English Literature and Male Homosocial Desire.* New York: Columbia University Press, 1985.
Segre, Cesare. "What Bakhtin Left Unsaid: The Case of Medieval Romance." *Romance: Generic Transformation from Chrétien de Troyes to Cervantes.* Ed. Kevin Brownlee and Marina Brownlee. Hanover and London: University Press of New England, 1985. 23–46.
Semenza, Gregory M. Colón. "Historicizing 'Wrastlynge' in the 'Miller's Tale.'" *Chaucer Review* 38 (2003): 66–82.
Shoaf, R.A., ed. *Chaucer's* Troilus and Criseyde: *"Subgit to Alle Poesye"—Essays in Criticism.* Binghamton, NY: Center for Medieval and Early Renaissance Studies, 1992.
———. "The 'Syngne of Surfet' and the Surfeit of Signs in *Sir Gawain and the Green Knight.*" *The Passing of Arthur: New Essays in Arthurian Traditions.* Ed. Christopher Baswell and William Sharpe. New York: Garland, 1988. 152–69.
Shurtleff, Steven. "The Archpoet as Poet, Persona and Self: The Problem of Individuality in the Confession." *Philological Quarterly* 73 (1994): 373–84.

Sir Gawain and the Green Knight. Ed. J.R.R. Tolkien and E.V. Gordon. 2nd ed. Ed. Norman Davis. Oxford: Clarendon, 1967.

Sir Gawain and the Green Knight. Ed. Israel Gollancz. Introductory essays by Mabel Day and Mary Serjeantson. London: Early English Text Society, 1940.

Smith, Paul. *Discerning the Subject*. Minneapolis: University of Minnesota Press, 1988.

Smith, Warren. "The Wife of Bath Debates Jerome." *Chaucer Review* 32 (1997): 129–45.

Spear, Thomas, ed. "Autobiographical Que(e)ries." *Auto/biography Studies* 15:1 (2000): 1–165.

Spearing, A.C. *The Gawain-Poet*. Cambridge: Cambridge University Press, 1970.

Spitzer, Leo. "Note on the Poetic and the Empirical 'I' in Medieval Authors." *Traditio* 4 (1946): 414–22.

Stanbury, Sarah. *Seeing the Gawain-Poet*. Philadelphia: University of Pennsylvania Press, 1991.

———. "The Voyeur and the Private Life in *Troilus and Criseyde*." *Studies in the Age of Chaucer* 13 (1991): 141–58.

Stehling, Thomas, trans. *Medieval Poems of Male Love and Friendship*. New York: Garland, 1984.

———. "To Love a Medieval Boy." *Journal of Homosexuality* 8 (1983): 151–70.

Stein, Edward, ed. *Forms of Desire: Sexual Orientation and the Social Constructionist Controversy*. New York: Routledge, 1992.

Steinberg, Diane Vanner. "'We do usen here no wommen for to selle: Embodiment of Social Practices in *Troilus and Criseyde*." *Chaucer Review* 29 (1995): 259–73.

Stevens, Martin. "The Performing Self in Twelfth-Century Culture." *Viator* 9 (1978): 193–212.

———. "Laughter and Game in *Sir Gawain and the Green Knight*." *Speculum* 47 (1972): 65–78.

Sticca, Sandro. *Saints: Studies in Hagiography*. Binghamton, NY: Medieval and Renaissance Texts and Studies, 1996.

Stock, Brian. *The Implications of Literacy: Written Language and Models of Interpretation in the Eleventh and Twelfth Centuries*. Princeton, NJ: Princeton University Press, 1983.

Stockton, Kathryn Bond. "Christ's Queer Wound, or Divine Humiliation Among the Unchurched." *Writing the Bodies of Christ*. Ed. John Schad. Aldershot, England: Ashgate, 2001. 127–44.

Stone, Brad Lowell. "The Self and the Play-Element in Culture." *Play and Culture* 2 (1989): 64–79.

Straus, Barrie Ruth. "The Subversive Discourse of the Wife of Bath." *English Literary History* 55 (1988): 527–54.

Strite, Sheri Ann. "*Sir Gawain and the Green Knight*: To Behead or Not To Behead— That *Is* a Question." *Philological Quarterly* 70 (1991): 1–12.

Strohm, Paul. *Social Chaucer*. Cambridge, MA: Harvard University Press, 1989.

———. "Storie, Spelle, Geste, Romaunce, Tragedie: Generic Distinctions in the Middle English Troy Narratives." *Speculum* 46 (1971): 348–59.

Sturges, Robert S. *Chaucer's Pardoner and Gender Theory: Bodies of Discourse*. New York: St. Martin's, 2000.

———. *Medieval Interpretation: Models of Reading in Literary Narrative, 1100–1500*. Carbondale: Southern Illinois University Press, 1991.

Sturm-Maddox, Sara and Donald Maddox, eds. "Intergenres: Intergeneric Perspectives on Medieval French Literature." *L'Esprit Créateur* 33:4 (1993): 1–100.

Suchomski, Joachim. *Delectatio und Utilitas*. Bern: Francke, 1975.

Suits, Bernard. *The Grasshopper: Games, Life, and Utopia*. Toronto: University of Toronto Press, 1978.

Summers, Claude. "Homosexuality and Renaissance Literature, or the Anxieties of Anachronism." *South Central Review* 9:1 (1992): 2–23.

Szarmach, Paul, ed. *Holy Men and Holy Women: Old English Prose Saints' Lives and Their Contexts*. Albany: State University of New York Press, 1996.

Szittya, Penn R. *The Anti-Fraternal Tradition in Medieval Literature*. Princeton, NJ: Princeton University Press, 1986.

Todorov, Tzvetan. *Genres in Discourse*. Trans. Catherine Porter. Cambridge: Cambridge University Press, 1990.

The Towneley Plays. Ed. Martin Stevens and A.C. Cawley. Oxford: Early English Text Society, 1994.

Troyan, Scott D. "True Tokens: Of Signs and Words and Other Things Bespeaking Truth in *Sir Gawain and the Green Knight*." *The Arthurian Yearbook III*. Ed. Keith Busby. New York: Garland, 1993. 141–70.

Ullman, Walter. *The Individual and Society in the Middle Ages*. Baltimore: Johns Hopkins University Press, 1966.

Van, Thomas. "False Texts and Disappearing Women in the Wife of Bath's Prologue and Tale." *Chaucer Review* 29 (1994): 179–93.

Vance, Eugene. "Augustine's *Confessions* and the Grammar of Selfhood." *Genre* 6:1 (1973): 1–28.

Vaszily, Scott. "Fabliau Plotting Against Romance in Chaucer's 'Knight's Tale.' " *Style* 31 (1997): 523–42.

Vries, Hent de. *Philosophy and the Turn to Religion*. Baltimore, MD: Johns Hopkins University Press, 1999.

Wallace, David. *Chaucerian Polity: Absolutist Lineages and Associational Forms in England and Italty*. Stanford, CA: Stanford University Press, 1997.

Wallace, David L. "Out in the Academy: Heterosexism, Invisibility, and Double Consciousness." *College English* 65:1 (2002): 53–66.

Weed, Elizabeth and Naomi Schor, eds. *Feminism Meets Queer Theory*. Bloomington: Indiana University Press, 1997.

Weisl, Angela Jane. *Conquering the Reign of Femeny: Gender and Genre in Chaucer's Romance*. Suffolk, UK: D.S. Brewer, 1995.

Weiss, Victoria. "The Playworld and the Real World: Chivalry in *Sir Gawain and the Green Knight*." *Philological Quarterly* 72 (1993): 403–418.

Werner, J., ed. *Beiträge zur Kunde der lateinischen Literatur des Mittelalters*. Hildesheim: Georg Olms, 1979.

Whiting, B.J. and H.W. Whiting. *Proverbs, Sentences and Proverbial Phrases*. Cambridge, MA: Harvard University Press, 1968.

Williams, Linda. *Hard Core: Power, Pleasure, and the "Frenzy of the Visible."* Berkeley: University of California Press, 1989.

Williman, Daniel, ed. *The Black Death: The Impact of the Fourteenth-Century Plague.* Binghampton, NY: Medieval and Renaissance Texts and Studies, 1982.

Wilson, Robert Rawdon. "Rules/Conventions: Three Paradoxes in the Game/Text Analogy." *South Central Review* 3 (1986): 15–27.

———. "Godgames and Labyrinths." *Mosaic* 15:4 (1982): 1–22.

Windeatt, Barry. *Oxford Guides to Chaucer: Troilus and Criseyde.* Oxford: Oxford University Press, 1992.

Winny, James, ed. *The Wife of Bath's Prologue and Tale.* Cambridge: Cambridge University Press, 1965.

Wogan-Browne, Jocelyn. *Saints' Lives and Women's Literary Culture, c. 1150–1300: Virginity and Its Authorizations.* New York: Oxford University Press, 2001.

Yamamoto, Dorothy. " 'Noon Oother Incubus But He': Lines 878–81 in the 'Wife of Bath's Tale.' " *Chaucer Review* 28 (1994): 275–78.

Zeikowitz, Richard. *Homoeroticism and Chivalry: Discourses of Male Same-Sex Desire in the Fourteenth Century.* New York: Palgrave, 2003.

———. "Befriending the Medieval Queer: A Pedagogy for Literature Classes." *College English* 65:1 (2002): 67–80.

INDEX

abandon   143, 147–9
Adam of Usk   84
Aelred of Rievaulx   26
agency   160 n.9
Alain de Lille   11, 12
Allen, Judson Boyce   42
Andreas Capellanus   186 n.17
Aquinas, Thomas   111, 112
Arthur, Ross   49
Astell, Ann   129, 137
Athleticus Dei   132
Auerbach, Eric   14

Bakhtin, Mikhail   133, 169 n.16
Barney, Stephen   186 n.20
Barron, W.R.J.   197 n.53
Baudri of Bourgueil   15–16, 17, 18, 21–7, 30–3, 35, 37–8, 40, 41, 43, 151, 152, 153, 154, 165 n.51
Bawarshi, Anis   155
Bédier, Joseph   174 n.3
Beebee, Thomas   14
Bernard of Clairvaux   25, 40
Bloomfield, Morton   113
Bond, Gerald   26, 31
Boswell, John   24, 186 n.26
Bowers, R.H.   197 n.55
Boyd, David Lorenzo   142, 203 n.102
Brams, Steven   192 n.12
Brewer, D.S.   49, 78, 174 n.3
Burger, Glenn   19–20, 48, 52–3
Burrow, J.A.   114
Busby, Keith   180 n.46
Butler, Judith   8, 10
Bynum, Caroline Walker   26

Caesarius of Arles   132
camp   159 n.6
Carruthers, Mary   67
Carton, Evan   186 n.20

Cary, Meredith   179 n.36
Case, Sue-Ellen   8
Chaucer, Geoffrey
    Works:
    "The Canon Yeoman's Tale"   57
    The Canterbury Tales   45–79, 96, 151, 152, 153
    "The Clerk's Tale"   61
    "The Cook's Tale"   16, 45–9, 51, 59–63
    "The Friar's Tale"   16, 45–57, 49–51, 56–9, 62, 78, 132–3
    "The Knight's Tale"   50–3, 68, 70
    The Legend of Good Women   57
    "The Man of Law's Tale"   68
    "The Merchant's Tale"   16, 45–9, 51, 59–63, 66, 72, 77, 78
    "The Miller's Tale"   16, 45–56, 58, 60, 61, 62, 66, 68, 73, 74, 78, 94
    "The Monk's Tale"   97
    "The Nun's Priest's Tale"   79
    "The Pardoner's Tale"   95
    "The Parson's Tale"   192 n.16
    "The Physician's Tale"   57
    "The Reeve's Tale"   16, 45–7, 49–56, 58, 60, 61, 62, 66, 68, 69, 73, 74, 78
    "The Shipman's Tale"   16, 45–9, 51, 59–63, 64, 65, 66, 77, 78
    "The Squire's Tale"   79
    "The Summoner's Tale"   16, 45–51, 56–9, 62, 78
    "The Tale of Sir Thopas"   57, 79
    "To Rosemounde"   57
    Troilus and Criseyde   16–18, 58, 81–106, 151, 153
    "The Wife of Bath's Prologue" and "Tale"   16, 45, 49, 51, 57, 60 63, 66, 67–79
Christmas, Peter   144
Cicero   14
circumcision   135–37, 145, 199 n.76
Clark, Roy Peter   53

INDEX

Clayton, John 149
Clough, Andrea 98–9
comedy 98–106
Conant, James 203 n.101
concupiscence 12
Cooke, Thomas 180 n.39
Cooper, Helen 64, 182 n.56, 200 n.81
Cox, Catherine 67
Crane, Susan 7, 77
Croce, Benedetto 2
Cross, F.L. 199 n.76
cuckoldry 52, 72
Curtius, Ernst 14, 24

"daliance" 57–8
Damian, Peter 11, 12, 173 n.50
Dante 111
Deleuze, Gilles 130, 198 n.71
Derrida, Jacques 2, 200 n.79
De Vries, Hent 145
Dinshaw, Carolyn 83, 139, 142, 196 n.47
Disbrow, Sarah 78–9
Dollimore, Jonathan 13
Dronke, Peter 21
Dubrow, Heather 20
Dyer, Christopher 176 n.16

Edelman, Lee 9
Edward II 187 n.26
eschatology 36, 172 n.40
exemplum 17, 107, 108, 114–29

fabliau 2, 16–17, 45–79, 173 n.1
  in relation to romance, 64–7, 77–9
"fag-bashing" 6
Ferrante, Joan 170 n.19
Ferreiro, Alberto 132
Foucault, Michel 1, 4
Fowles, John 110
Fradenburg, Louise 75, 90–1, 130, 134, 180 n.43
Francis of Assisi 26
Frantzen, Allen 5
Freiwald, Leah 95
Freud, Sigmund 48, 199 n.77
Furrow, Melissa 65
Fuss, Diana 194 n.31

games and godgames 17, 107–29, 192 n.12
Gaunt, Simon 7, 155, 196 n.45

Gaveston, Piers 187 n.26
Gawain-Poet 11–12, 17–19, 153
  Cleanness 11, 155, 202 n.97
  St. Erkenwald 200 n.80
  Sir Gawain and the Green Knight 17–19, 107–49
gaze 93–4
Gearhart, Suzanne 143–4
gender
  performance of 10
  sexuality, as distinct from 8
genre
  classical genres 14, 165 n.44
  conservatism of 2, 13–14, 20
  definition of 1–2
  feminist critique of 7–8, 163 n.24
  "genre contracts" 13–14
  heteronormativity of 2
  historical mode 1, 3
  performance of 10–11
  play of 13–14, 20
  queer vs. queering genres 2
  queering genres 2–15, 157–8
  relationship to gender 6–10, 162 n.20
  social nature of 155–6
Gerald of Wales 154–5
Glasser, Marc 74
Goddard, R.N.B. 168 n.6
Godfrey, Mary 56
Goodman, Jennifer 104–5
Gravdal, Kathryn 14, 148
Green, Richard 88
Grudin, Michaela 189 n.45
Guibert de Nogent 42

hagiography—*see* saints' lives
Halperin, David 134, 164 n.37
Hamilton, J.S. 187 n.26
Hanning, R.W. 77, 144, 182 n.61
Hanrahan, Michael 83–4
Hansen, Elaine Tuttle 92, 101
"The Harrowing of Hell" 112
Harsanyi, John 195 n.32
Harwood, Britton 179 n.32
Heffernan, Thomas 190 n.4
Heng, Geraldine 201 n.88
Hergemöller, Bernd-Ulrich 161 n.11
heteronormativity and heterosexuality 2–6, 12–13
Hindman, Jane 204 n.7

Hines, John 174 n.3
Hilderbert of Lavardin 15, 16, 17, 18,
    21–7, 33–7, 40–3, 151–4, 165 n.51
Hollis, Stephanie 118–19
homosexuality 1
    essentialism vs. social constructionism
        12–13, 161 n.16
    fear of (homophobia) 3, 11
    homosexuality vs. queerness 4–5
    inversion, as sign of 35–40
    possibility of anachronism 4, 12, 161 n.16
    potential normativity of 4
    see also: queer
Huizinga, Johan 109, 191 n.9

Iliad 5
imitatio 24
Ingarden, Roman 86
Ingham, Patricia Clare 183 n.65
inversion 35–40, 169 n.16, 172 n.40
Iser, Wolfgang 186 n.16

Jaeger, Stephen 25, 84
Jameson, Frederick 13
Jensen, Emily 50
Jesus 26, 33, 135, 138
Joachim of Fiore 172 n.40
Job 132, 133, 137, 146, 203 n.101
Johnson, Glen 2, 160 n.7
Johnson, Lynn 126
Jones, Edward 144
Jordan, Mark 173 n.50
Jordan, Tracey 53
Jost, Jean 178 n.29

Karlen, Arlo 24
Keiser, Elizabeth 11
Kelly, Henry 97, 188 n.34
Kendrick, Laura 64–5
Kimmelman, Burt 22
Kinney, Clare 102
Kitely, John 197 n.48
Knapp, Peggy 76, 107
Knight, Alan 156
Knight, Rhonda 154–5
Kolve, V.A. 23, 33
Kruger, Steven 95

Lacy, Norris 66
Ladner, Gerhard 171 n.36

Levine, Robert 85
Lewis, Robert 174 n.3
Leyerle, John 120
Lindley, Arthur 139
Lochrie, Karma 4, 52, 60, 162 n.17
Lomperis, Linda 178 n.24
lyric 15, 16, 17, 18, 21–43
    lyric "I" 22, 42–3
    lyric personae/performance 22, 25–7,
        40–3
Lysistrata 5

Macherey, Pierre 86
Mann, Jill 179 n.35
Marbod of Rennes 15, 16, 17, 18, 21–30,
    35, 38–41, 43, 151–4, 165 n.51
Margherita, Gayle 98
Marie de France 3
McAlpine, Monica 99, 104
Mehtonen, Päivi 14
Meyers, Robert 77
Mills, Robert 130, 135
Morgan, Gerald 128
Mulvey, Laura 133
Muscatine, Charles 49

Olson, Glending 49
Olson, Paul 56
Other 1, 11, 153–5

Papka, Claudia 103
Pearcy, Roy 176 n.15
Pearsall, Derek 124
pedagogy 157–8
play 108–13
    in relation to seriousness 48, 60, 72, 77–8
Poincaré Henri 148
Potkay, Monica 145
Puhvel, Martin 182 n.64
Putter, Ad 124–5

queer
    anxiety 47–8
    Christianity, relationship to 15, 151–5
    feminism, relationship to 7–10
    homosexuality, relation to 4–5, 173 n.2,
        179 n.33
    salvation 35, 39–40
    see also: homosexuality; genres, queering
Quintilian 165 n.44

Raby, F.J.E.   41
rape   74, 75, 179 n.35
Rapoport, Anatol   192 n.12
readers and reading   2, 9, 17, 20, 43, 81, 87, 106, 117, 128, 129, 144–9, 155–8, 160 n.8, 170 n.19, 194 n.31
Reale, Nancy   102
Reid, David   181 n.51
Richard II   83–4, 185 n.7
Ridley, Aaron   149
Robbins, Rossell   176 n.15
Roberts, Anna   158
romance   2, 17, 45, 73–9, 107–49, 190 n.2
"romance tragedy"   99
Rosmarin, Adena   156
Ross, Andrew   159 n.6
Roth, Norman   28
Rowland, Beryl   83, 174 n.3
Royle, Nicholas   135–6
Ruiz, Juan (Archpriest of Hita)   42

Sacher-Masoch, Leopold von   130
sado-masochism   17, 130–49
saints' lives   17, 107, 129, 130–47, 190 n.4
Saunders, Gill   138
Scala, Elizabeth   197 n.49
Scanlon, Larry   190 n.2
Schechner, Richard   131
Sedgwick, Eve   6, 8, 47, 92, 175 n.6
semiotics   17, 144–9, 203 n.102
sexuality
   see heteronormativity and heterosexuality; homosexuality; queer
Shurtleff, Steven   40–1
silence   81–2, 86, 88, 90
Smith, Paul   160 n.9

Song of Songs   29, 33
Spearing, A.C.   128
Spitzer, Leo   42
Stanbury, Sarah   93, 100
Stehling, Thomas   24
Stevens, Martin   42
Stockton, Kathryn Bond   147
Stone, Brad   109
Straus, Barrie Ruth   66
Strohm, Paul   185 n.7, 185 n.9
Sturges, Robert   183 n.71, 204 n.5
subjectivity   160 n.9, 166 n.54, 168 n.4
Suits, Bernard   108
Summers, Claude   13

teleology   102–6
Todorov, Tzvetan   1
The Towneley Plays
   see "The Harrowing of Hell"
tragedy   2–3, 16, 96–106
Trevet, Nicholas   188 n.34

Vance, Eugene   42
Vere, Robert de   83–4, 185 n.7
La Vie de Sainte Euphrosine   155

Wallace, David   49
Wallace, David L.   157
Walsingham, Thomas   83–4
Weisl, Angela   66
Weiss, Victoria   119
Williams, Linda   133, 199 n.75
Wilson, Robert   108, 109, 110, 131
Winny, James   67

Zeikowitz, Richard   5–6, 19–20